The Monk Who Howled Like a Wolf

Also by the Author:

Iskut Ridge (fiction)

The Monk Who Howled Like a Wolf

The Mystic's Path of Kriya Yoga

Norman Anton Sollie

Iola Publishing
Healy, Alaska

Iola Publishing
Healy, Alaska USA
iolapublishing.com

Copyright © 2018 by Norman Anton Sollie

All rights reserved. This book may not be reproduced in whole, or in part, or transmitted in any form without written permission from the publisher, except by a reviewer who may quote brief passages in a review; nor may any part of this book be reproduced, stored in a retrieval system, or transmitted in any form, or by any means electronic, mechanical, photocopying, recording, or other, without written permission from the publisher.

Cover design by Alexander Sollie
alexander.sollie@gmail.com

Editing by Erica Watson ericawatson.wordpress.com

Printed by Ingram Spark

ISBN: 978-1-948189-01-9 (paperback edition)

DEDICATION

Remembering James Ramsey and Mary Rihanek

ACKNOWLEDGEMENTS

Many thanks and much appreciation to those who encouraged my interest in the unseen world and in writing about the mystical, among them Michael Adcock, Jean Balay, Leatrice Big Crow, Andrea Blakesley, Susan Braun, Barbara Brease, Cheryl Brush, Dianna Dodson, Brenda Fleming, Jeff Forsythe, Bob King, Tina King, Ivan Kolpacoff, Kriyananda, Heidi Lindemann, Mike Perry, Alexander Sollie, Elizabeth Sollie, Sage Sollie, Stephanie Stosek, Whitley Streiber, the Teacher, Shelley Trimmer, Erika Watson (my patient and skilled editor), Alan Wartes, Nunpa White Plume, Beau Yonkee, and...

The Kriya Yoga lineage.

CONTENTS

1—The Monk Who Howled Like a Wolf 1

2—The Lineage 5

3—The Center 13

4—The Sweat Lodge 19

5—Kriya Yoga 25

6—What's the Catch? 33

7—Guarding the Gate 39

8—Tending the Fire 47

9—The Four Pillars 53

10—Practices & Techniques 61

11—Gurus & Disciples 67

12—The Thornapple Tree 75

13—The Woman at the River 81

14—Is That So? 87

15—Watch Your Adverbs! 93

16—Dust Rising 101

17—*Tawapaha Olowan* 107

18—Reunited 111

19—*Brahmacharya* 119

20—Echoes of the Past	123
21—Give Them Cigarettes & Booze	127
22—Making the Call	131
23—The Soul Picks the Mother	137
24—Who Are We?	141
25—The Student & the Demon	149
26—The Rabbit & the Cobra	157
27—What Are You Doing & Why Are You Doing It?	163
28—*Iwa* Awareness	169
29—Awareness Exercise	175
30—Awareness & Death	181
31—Happiness Unshakeable as a Shadow	187
32—*Ananda*	193
33—Meditate, Meditate, Meditate	197
34—The Four Pillars of Meditation	205
35—Sit Down & Think About That	215
36—Sufficient Unto One Life	223
37—To Love & To Learn	227
38—Consciousness Entombed	233
39—What Haven't You Done?	239
40—Prepare for Death	243

41—The Third Way 249

42—The Programming of Karma 257

43—Nothing is Good Nor Bad Lest We Make It So 263

44—The Yogi, the Stag, & the Hunter................................... 267

45—The General & the Monk 273

46—Inaction Within Action... 281

47—Loving Kindness 287

48—The Work of the Indwelling Sun................................... 293

49—The Dreams of Others 301

50—Path Opens.. 309

51—Twenty Tools of Manifestation 317

52—Hang Onto the Paddle & Pull the Red Cord................... 327

53—Acceptance 333

54—Letting Go 337

55—Surrender 343

56—Samadhi.. 347

57—The Nature of Enlightenment... 351

58—Techniques for Enlightenment 363

59—We Are Here For One Reason.. 371

Conclusion—Putting the Practice Into Practice 375

APPENDIX A—The Traditional Schools of Yoga................. 382

APPENDIX B—The Limbs of the Eight-Fold Path of Yoga..383

APPENDIX C—The Four Pillars for the Spiritual Aspirant...384

—The *Sadhana Chatushtaya*

APPENDIX D—Encouraging Mental Discipline (*Shama*).....385

APPENDIX E—Encouraging Body & Sense Control.............386

(*Dama*)

APPENDIX F—Maintaining *Samadhi* (*Samadhana*) 387

APPENDIX G—Practices of the Kriya Yogi 388

APPENDIX H—The Inner & Outer Practices.........................389

for Attracting Healthy Relationships

APPENDIX I—Neutralizing Action Karma............................390

APPENDIX J—The Twenty Tools of Manifestation 391

APPENDIX K— The Seventh House..392

as the Form of Enlightenment

Sanskrit Glossary 395

Index 409

ONE

The Monk Who Howled Like a Wolf

Mist concealed the far shore. One gnarled hand gathered russet brown robes above wrinkled knees. Another gripped the bobbing gunwale of an old rowboat. With a gentle push away from the rocky beach, the man sprang in and found his seat on a damp plank stretched across the center of the narrow hull. He arranged his robes and set the oars in their locks. Lean arms familiar with the dip and pull of paddles in green water, his breathing soon paced the pattern of creaking oars and hull. Moisture from the fog beaded his short-cropped greying hair.

With glances over his shoulder, he rowed the boat towards a vague darkness that resolved into the tree-lined shore of an island. The man scanned the passing bank and turned the boat to enter a sheltered cove with a sandy beach. He rowed hard onto the shore, anchoring the keel into the dark sand, and paused, gazing into the woods. From the bow he gathered a bag of rice and other provisions.

He stepped into the tangled green of the island, chanting under his breath. One hand fingered the wooden beads of his necklace. He smiled slightly, but walked stiffly at first,

The Monk Who Howled Like a Wolf

complaint in his knees.

Before the man had gone far his brow furrowed and he released his beads to rub the point between his brows. A primal and disturbing wail, like that of a wild animal, pierced the trees.

"Ooooowwww-woooh!"

He quickened his pace, sandals slapping the muddy path, and swept into an opening in the green, dripping woods. He set down the provisions and studied a young man at the far end of the clearing seated cross-legged on a bamboo mat with eyes closed. His soft brown face was unlined and peaceful. The youth's jet-black hair was starting to grow back on a shaved scalp and he looked healthy and well fed beneath the folds of his orange robe.

The older man's frown shifted into surprise as the young man broke into a smile, eyes still closed.

"Master, you are here!" The young man's eyes flew open and he jumped to his feet and ran to the older man like a big clumsy dog. The resemblance was magnified by the peculiar accident of birth that gave the young man one disconcerting pale blue eye along with one of the customary brown—like the rough guard dogs of the mountains.

The rower waved the younger man back with a fluttering of one hand and a turning aside of his head.

"I appreciate your enthusiasm, but remember: Though you are still an initiate, you are a monk of our venerable Order. Some dignity, please."

"Yes, Master. My apologies, sir." He bowed from his waist, a delighted smile brilliant white.

The Master sighed inwardly, picking up the supplies before he spoke again.

"As I landed at the beach, there was a noise…"

"Well, that must have been me, Master. Oh! I see by your face that I have it wrong *again*! I am so thick in the head—I cannot remember the proper chant for five minutes. Please, one more time, Master!"

The old monk burst out, "You were howling like a dog! I thought I was going to find wolves eating you." He smiled, softening. "Such a waste of good rice…"

The Monk Who Howled Like a Wolf

The Master caught himself shifting the focus of his gaze from the young man's brown eye to his blue eye, then back again. He sighed and straightened his back. "All right then, one more time. The chant is, '*aum*.' All sounds come from *aum* and *aum* resonates with the Cosmic Self. *Aum* is everything. Speech and breath find union in *aum*. When chanting the sacred *aum* in meditation, begin with a drawn out 'ahh' sound, then slide into "ooh" then "mmm" last of all. Try to spend equal amounts of time intoning each of the three sounds. Like this: aaaahhhhoooooooommmmm..." The old monk's gravelly baritone filled the air with susurrous vibration.

"There is a fourth and final sound not pronounced, yet immanent throughout: *amatrah*, the no-letter of pure existence. Make room for it in your breathing and in your awareness.

"Practice this chant to prepare yourself for deeper meditation. *Aum* is the mother sound of all creation and the most important of all chants. *Aum* will take you beyond fear, to infinite peace. When you have mastered this sacred *mantra* I will give you another to practice."

"Thank you, thank you, most kind Keeper of the Wisdom! I do not deserve your patience. You have again set me on the correct path and now I may correctly chant this most holy of *mantras*. May I someday have half your knowledge of the Teachings!"

The Master's mood softened. He could not deny the young man's sincerity and earnest desire to advance on the path.

"I know that this trial here on the island is difficult for you, son."

The young man looked down at the ground bashfully and drew a circle in the mud with his big toe.

The Master continued, "Being alone here with nothing to do but meditate in silence day after day is hard for an initiate like you—so full of the life force and delighting in your senses. However, you must apply yourself to this ancient path in order to advance ever so slowly towards the goal of expanded awareness. With the utmost earnestness and focus on the old traditions you too may see yourself someday progress like the older monks, and experience the bliss of meditative absorption

The Monk Who Howled Like a Wolf

in *samadhi*. If you are very, very lucky and very, very studious you may eventually be released from the bondage of *karma* and rebirth on this world."

"Oh, Master, I wish that it may be so."

Satisfied that the initiate had learned what he could at his present level of spiritual growth, the monk made his leave-takings and returned down the trail to his boat.

Rowing smoothly through the dense fog, the teacher was halfway back to the far shore of the lake when he heard a splashing, growing louder and closer from the direction of the island. Peering anxiously into the mist, the monk was stunned to see the young man catching up to the boat, jogging across the water. The difficult student skidded to a halt, his sky blue eye unnaturally bright in the gloomy morning light.

The initiate blurted, "Master! I am *so* foolish! Already I have forgotten the sacred sound. Please, Master, remind me of the sacred chant one more time." The younger monk's feet were steady on the green, deep water.

The older man hesitated for just a moment before he tipped his head far back and answered with a wail, "Ooooowwww-woooh!"

CHAPTER TWO

The Lineage

I squinted up the dim and narrow stairwell of the walk-up flat in North Chicago and wondered what the evening had in store. For a couple of years Roxanne had been sharing stories about this group that studied Kriya Yoga, but this was my first visit to see her and what her parents called a cult. Though I was open to sampling different spiritual traditions, I wasn't looking for a cult, but that night my friend introduced me to a world that continues to hold my attention years later.

Past the top of the stairs, a couple dozen people were crowded into a tasteful and tidy two-bedroom apartment. The welcoming smells of curry and fresh bread filled the flat. Guests efficiently unloaded plates and dishes onto two tables pushed together and covered with a large cloth. Seeing my interest in the assortment, Roxanne warned me that we wouldn't be eating until the talk was over.

"Let's find a place to sit while there's still space up front," she said, and steered me into the living room, already filling up with expectant students. The chairs were filled, but it felt right to sit on the floor, cushioned by one of the small blankets Roxanne handed to me from a pile in a corner.

The center of attention was a slim man in his mid to late fifties. Thick silver hair below his shoulders and a full beard ringed a bald pate. He too settled on the floor, covering his legs with a fringed prayer shawl. In the dozen times that I was to see David Lipschutz sitting this way (tailor fashion, half lotus, or full lotus I can't say because of the prayer shawl) I never saw him break or shift his pose for the duration of these one to two hour events.

Having no idea what to expect, I followed Roxanne's lead and sat quietly, studying the carpet in front of me as David began to speak about awareness, service, *karma*, reincarnation, and Kriya Yoga. Except for Kriya Yoga, these were subjects I was familiar with, but tonight I was in a room filled with people that shared my interest. The unrehearsed lecture was not earth shattering in the details, but what I was hearing resonated inside of me—it all felt *right* and as if I had found a home of sorts. This was a place where I was not an oddball, but just another student at the feet of a teacher. I listened carefully to every word of his talk and the question and answer period that ended it.

Afterwards, David was ringed with enthusiastic listeners, mostly in their 20's and 30's, peppering him with more questions and comments. Roxanne and I joined the line trailing away from the food tables.

She turned her dark eyes towards me and asked, "So, Norman—what do you think?"

"That was *amazing*. I see why you like these people so much."

She bobbed her head slightly in satisfaction, lips pressed together, but smiling. "I am *so* lucky to have this group right here where I live."

"Yeah," I said wistfully. "You are lucky."

We loaded up on good food. We ate and chatted with some of the others. Everyone was friendly and approachable and no one tried to recruit me into a cult. They were just like people anywhere at a dinner party.

As the crowd around him thinned, I maneuvered over to David. I corralled him into a corner where I gushed my appreciation for his eloquent words and shared my disappointment that I could not learn more in my own town about this Kriya Yoga philosophy and way of life.

The Lineage

He asked me where I lived.

"Denver."

David furrowed his eyebrows for just the slightest moment. I gathered that I had missed something important.

"What part of Denver do you live in?"

"The northwest."

"You're in luck then. There's a Kriya Yoga Center in northwest Denver. A man who was here in Chicago for years runs it."

Roxanne explained to me later that both David and the Denver teacher were disciples of an older man, the founder of the Chicago Temple of Kriya Yoga, Kriyananda. (The Kriyananda of Chicago and France. There is another Kriyananda, a direct disciple of Paramahansa Yogananda, based in California.) She always spoke of Kriyananda with a deep respect for his wisdom, intelligence, and humor.

Before the end of that trip I went with Roxanne to the Chicago Temple, the physical center of this "cult." We filed into a large basement room crowded with two hundred disciples and students, facing a carved wooden chair on a low stage. There was a sound system and even a videographer. Precisely at noon, a robed Kriyananda, long grey hair swept back over his head and a thick beard covering his chest, walked down the center aisle and took his place on the stage behind a microphone. All two hundred of us sat enthralled as this twinkling man in his late seventies spoke for an hour with great intelligence and love for his students. He gave the impression of caring deeply for each of us, while encouraging us to become better people.

In that hour I was inspired to believe that spiritual growth was not just for the few, but within my reach through the mysticism of Kriya Yoga. I determined to learn more about this path.

*

I walked to the Denver Kriya Yoga Center. It was only a mile and half from my house and there was almost no snow or ice on the sidewalks this December. I was prepared with a blank notebook and a pen and had left myself plenty of time.

A few days earlier, freshly back from Chicago, I had swung by the Kriya Yoga Center of Denver (on Tennyson then) to look in the windows and find a schedule. The glass storefront was closed and dark. I squinted through the glass at a church pew, a bulletin board, and plant-topped shelves. The interior was gloomy, receding back into the unlit building, and I wondered if someone was in there looking out at me. I left quickly and returned home.

But on this bright winter day I rounded a corner to see three people chatting on the sidewalk, standing close to the curb where they could enjoy the late morning sunshine out from under the shade of the low building. I slipped quietly through the doorway behind another early bird.

Within seconds a barrel chested man with tightly curled salt and pepper hair approached me.

He greeted me with a smooth deep voice and shook my hand. The teacher looked to be in his mid-fifties and strong (after years of Hatha yoga, bicycling, skiing, and hiking). His hair and beard were neatly trimmed and he was dressed casually.

He encouraged me to sit at the pew to take off my shoes. "Why don't you get a yoga blanket or two from the prop room and find a place for yourself?"

I saw that the regulars favored the long south wall opposite the altar where they could lean back in relative comfort. I found a place in the center of the floor not too close and not too far from the teacher and would claim that spot for the rest of my time at the Center. Remembering David Lipschutz and his unchanging seated pose, I began a long (and pointless) campaign to sit through one of this teacher's hour long Sunday morning *satsangs* without shifting my legs from a half lotus position.

Six photo portraits hung on the wall next to the altar in a single vertical framed mat. In the bottom photo I recognized a beaming Kriyananda. Second from the bottom was another older white man, nearly bald, his beard billowing enormous and silver around his neck. The third picture was the same as the cover of a book Roxanne had shown me when I visited her and her boyfriend years before on the Pine Ridge Reservation in South Dakota. This was Paramahansa Yogananda, the yogi who had sparked a storm of curiosity in North America's lecture halls and churches starting in 1920. His *Autobiography of a Yogi*, first published in 1946, has been read by millions in 34 languages, and is still in print. He is the subject of the popular 2014 documentary, *Awake: The Life of Yogananda*. For many in the Western world *Autobiography of a Yogi* is the first and perhaps only mention of Kriya Yoga that they will ever hear.

As I waited for my Denver teacher-to-be to begin whatever it was that he did every Sunday, the significance of the photos began to dawn on me: This was the family tree of this Center—from *guru* to *guru*, right down to this teacher's own *guru* (Kriyananda). I vaguely understood then that a *guru* was some sort of a spiritual teacher to his students. The lineage of this Center was on the lath and plaster wall in front of me. Yogananda was the *guru* of the Denver Teacher's own *guru's guru*. It would be some months before I would learn the names of all of the men under mat and glass. *Mahavatar* Babaji at the very top was represented with a rough drawing of a longhaired young man. *Mahavatar* means "great avatar," a divine being descended to earth. Below Babaji was *Lahiri Mahasaya*, then Sri Yukteswar, then Paramahansa Yogananda, then Shelley Trimmer, and finally Kriyananda. The Denver mystic who taught then in my own neighborhood is seven steps removed from *Mahavatar* Babaji in the Kriya Yoga *guru* to disciple lineage.

Some hint that Babaji is an incarnation of Krishna, a Hindu deity and historical figure dated to 3,200 BCE, re-born into a physical body hundreds of years ago. His birthday is arbitrarily celebrated on April 21st. Some believe that a divine Babaji, forever youthful, is with us still, appearing occasionally to those who need him. There are also accounts of his equally enlightened and radiantly beautiful sister, Mataji, said to inhabit a marvelous cave in the Himalayan foothills.

And here was Babaji, at the head of the family tree of the Denver Kriya Yoga Center.

In 1861, thirty-three year old Lahiri Mahasaya took a late afternoon break from his accountancy work in military engineering. He took a walk in the rugged hills above Ranikhet in the northern Indian state of Uttarakand 100 miles from the border with Nepal. He was startled to hear his name called from the slopes of Drongiri Mountain above him. Though worried that he would be overtaken by darkness, he followed the impulse to climb upwards, seeking the source of the mysterious voice.

In a clearing surrounded by caves, a smiling young man with beautiful long copper hair greeted Lahiri by name. The man invited Lahiri to rest for a while in one of the cool caves dotting the steep mountainside. Inside, Lahiri found a few folded woolen blankets and begging bowls.

Sitting down across from him, the mysterious young man encouraged Lahiri to delay his return to Ranikhet and asked if Lahiri did not remember this cave and the blankets. Then the young man stepped forward and lightly tapped Lahiri on the forehead. This nudge brought memories of a past life flooding back. Overwhelmed by emotion, Lahiri fell at the feet of this mysterious man.

"I remember! You are my guru, the avatar Babaji, who has been with me always!" Lahiri cried out, sobbing with joy.

Babaji then told Lahiri that he had been waiting for Lahiri for over three decades since Lahiri's death in his last body. He had arranged Lahiri's transfer to Ranikhet so that they might meet again. This very cave had been Lahiri's home for years when he had been an ascetic in the high hills.

Babaji manifested a purifying liquid in Lahiri's bowl from this recent lifetime of devotion and urged Lahiri to drink it. He told Lahiri to lie in the growing darkness at the edge of the nearby creek while the draught did its work. After a time, Lahiri was collected by a disciple of the avatar and brought to a golden palace glittering with precious gems. The disciple admitted to the astounded Lahiri that Babaji had materialized the entire royal abode with the creative power of his expanded consciousness solely for Lahiri's amusement.

Inside, Lahiri found Babaji seated in the lotus position on a golden throne in a vast hall.

Babaji greeted Lahiri and explained that he had created the palace to quench Lahiri's earthly desires. Lahiri was to be initiated back into Kriya Yoga this very night. Babaji created a bonfire altar surrounded by fruits and flowers and instructed

The Lineage

Lahiri in ancient Kriya Yoga techniques designed to encourage his enlightenment.

Babaji dematerialized the palace after Lahiri had a chance to explore its precious art works, fine tapestries, and jewel-studded furnishings.

Returning to the humble cave in the company of Babaji and a small group of his devoted disciples, Lahiri was treated to a meal of his favorite foods out of his old begging bowl. He could never eat his way to the bottom of the inexhaustible vessel. When Lahiri was full and wished for a drink, the bowl immediately filled with clear water.

Retiring to his old meditation blanket, Lahiri fell into a seven-day state of blissful samadhi *(deep meditation)*.

Upon awakening Lahiri, Babaji explained that the accountant must go back to the everyday world to be an example for common householders searching for meaning in their lives.

Lahiri pleaded to remain with Babaji, but Babaji explained, "You have been chosen to bring spiritual solace through Kriya Yoga to numerous earnest seekers. The millions who are encumbered by family ties and worldly duties will take new heart from you, a householder like themselves. You must guide them to see that the highest yogic attainments are not just for celibates, but also for those with families. Even in the world, the yogi who faithfully discharges his responsibilities without personal motive or attachment treads the sure path of enlightenment. No necessity compels you to leave the world now, Lahiri, for inwardly you have already sundered its every karmic tie. Though you are no longer of this world, you must yet be in it. Many years still remain during which you must conscientiously fulfill your family, business, civic, and spiritual duties. From witnessing your balanced life, a sweet new breath of divine hope will penetrate the arid hearts of worldly men. They will understand that liberation is dependent on inner, rather than outer, renunciations."

Lahiri reluctantly agreed to return to his life in the world below. Babaji gave Lahiri instructions on the transmission of yoga teachings from guru to disciple. Lahiri got permission to loosen the demanding prerequisites required of new initiates to *receive the secret Kriya Yoga techniques.*

At last Lahiri returned to Ranikhet and the co-workers who had given him up for dead. Soon he was transferred back to his original job in Danapur (this too was said to have been done by Babaji). Lahiri began his life's work of initiating thousands of disciples into the ancient and now reborn order of Kriya Yoga.

CHAPTER THREE

The Center

I became a regular of the Denver Teacher's Sunday morning gatherings on Tennyson (timed at 11:00 AM Mountain Time to coincide with Kriyananda's noon talks in Chicago). The Teacher's warm charisma and my affinity for the rituals and the Teachings made these events the high point of my week—a break from my job managing construction projects at a nearby university.

Although Kriya Yoga is a path of individual mystical experience, the support of other Kriyabans (students of Kriya Yoga) reinforces this quest for union with the spiritual big "S" Self (as opposed to the little "s" ego self) through the power of action, *kriya shakti*, and focused life force, *prana*.

The events the Teacher holds on Sunday mornings are called *satsangs*, similar to the services of organized religion. It is a gathering of those seeking to learn more about the Teachings, and is generally led by a *guru* or other advanced student of Kriya Yoga. The *sangha* is the community of Kriyabans who attend *satsangs*. *Satsangs* gather all over the world with elements common to my teacher's *satsangs*.

The Kriya Yoga Center of Denver on Tennyson was tasteful, tidy, and clean. No furniture cluttered the carpeted floor, which also served as a yoga studio. The Denver Teacher had painted each plane of the walls and ceiling distinct pastel colors and dyed cotton cloths of *mandalas* and Hindu deities hung about the room. There was a quiet water fountain for soothing background noise during meditation.

The lineage photos and an identical tall and narrow frame containing traditional depictions of the seven *chakras* (energy centers near the spine of the human body that serve as a link between the physical and the spiritual) flanked a simple altar on the north wall—a white bookshelf, four feet high, inset into the space between the wall studs. The shelves of the altar supported another picture of Kriyananda in its own free-standing frame, one or two brass Hindu icons, small votive candles, and a hinged wooden box containing an inch of fine white sand in which the Teacher burned sandalwood or rosewood incense during *satsangs*.

A considerate Kriyaban (a florist) often brought fresh flowers for the altar—sometimes orchids, but always long-lived blooms. The flowers, incense, and candles were a modern echo of Babaji's bonfire altar.

Behind and to the left of the altar, was a small prop room containing yoga blankets, blocks, and straps, and folding chairs for those who wanted or needed them.

Opposite the shielded entrance area on the west wall was a short hall on the east leading to two doors. The door on the right led into a small bathroom (cleaned with precision and care by the Teacher every Sunday morning before *satsang*) and another door on the left led into the Teacher's cramped office where he sometimes gave astrological readings surrounded by folding tables, water urns, and a small file cabinet.

The Denver Teacher reserved a spot for himself with the altar on his right, within reach of the candles and incense. Between *satsangs* and classes he kept his own mat and cushion in the office, separate from the studio props. Sometimes a notebook or other teaching materials sat on the floor beside him. Occasionally one of the Kriyabans would leave a question on a scrap of paper next to his cushion.

I arrived as early as seemed polite for our Sunday gatherings

The Center

and especially enjoyed the days when I could chat with my teacher for a minute or two. Then I would stake my spot on the floor with my notebook and pen and head for the prop room for a yoga blanket and a block.

Typically, as others entered alone and in pairs, I sat down on my blanket cushioned block and exchanged news of the week with the other regular Kriyabans I was beginning to know. The Denver Teacher greeted each of us in turn, checked the thermostat, made sure the CD in the stereo was properly queued, and arranged the remote and his water bottle next to his cushion.

Kriya Yoga is not just for monks on an island retreat, but it is also for regular people, with regular jobs and families ("householders"). Our group included married couples with families and commitments and single women and men, like myself, with careers and busy schedules. Our motivations ranged from a desire for a quiet Sunday morning ritual that wasn't church, to serious study of the Kriya path. For four years this place would support my spiritual growth.

Even on its own, Kriya Yoga offers much for self-awareness, contentment, and life improvement, but its study requires work and dedication. The Denver Teacher's *guru*, Kriyananda says, "Kriya Yoga is the school of no praise and no blame. This is not a pat-on-your-back system. The teaching is bigger than us and will outlast us."

Each of us had our own reasons for being in that room, but to the Teacher there was only one purpose, "In Kriya, the only *dharma* is to seek your enlightenment... *period*." (*Dharma* is similar to the Western concepts of a "calling" or "life's work.")

Kriya Yoga goes to great lengths to instruct us on how to seek our transcendence, but in the words of this teacher from the south side of Chicago, "It is not a one-size-fits-all path. Everybody has their own path." Everyone's circumstances require a unique approach to spiritual growth. Some may need celibate seclusion and chanting on an island with occasional guidance from an older monk, but for most of us this journey will have all the everyday concerns of paying the bills and juggling schedules. No matter how chaotic and distracting, this life *is* the spiritual life.

Self-awareness, service, relationships, non-attachment, mystical experience, and many more topics are subjects of the Teacher's *satsangs*, classes, and retreats. In those hours on the floor behind a glass storefront on busy Tennyson Street, my Teacher (nicknamed South Side Yogi) invited us to take a spiritual journey in which our progress was measured in sincerity and self-discipline.

Despite the talk of transcendence from the physical world, the Denver Teacher is an accessible instructor and knows many people. Acquaintances light up when they see him even if they aren't aware of his deep connection to a mystical past. The Teacher knows and greets by name the restaurant owner where he buys the occasional meal out and the teenager who shoots baskets at the park around the corner. He has a confidence, focus, and compassion that others find compelling. He brings his yogi awareness with him into the world, radiating appeal and competence far beyond the circle of friends, disciples, and students that understand his place in the Kriya Yoga lineage.

Similarly, the West is generally not aware of how Kriya Yoga has impacted our culture and history. We find the early Kriya Yoga lineage—Babaji, Lahiri, Sri Yukteswar, and Yogananda—peeking back at us from the cover of the Beatles' *Sergeant Pepper* album cover. Kriya Yoga has been taught in North America since Paramahansa Yogananda first arrived in 1920. Yogananda himself accepted thousands of disciples and many of them in turn took on their own disciples. Clara Clemens, daughter of the author Samuel Clemens (Mark Twain) was herself a student of Yogananda. And Mahatma Gandhi was perhaps the most famous initiate to Kriya Yoga, in turn influencing many social movements around the world with his insistence on non-violent protest.

As the clock approached 11:00 AM, the Teacher wrapped up his meet-and-greet duties and settled onto his cushion and closed his eyes. We took this as the signal to stop chatting, get comfortable for the hour or more ahead, and close our own eyes. The conversation hushed and then stopped altogether while the Teacher waited for an unseen signal to begin, pausing, I thought, until the assembly was focused on the spiritual. I used this time

The Center

to concentrate on my breath and meditate.

Finally, the Denver Teacher broke the silence by saying, "Let's say the three *aums*, shall we?"

Keeping my eyes closed, I listened for his inhalation and tried to begin the first *aum* at the exact moment that he did.

"Aaahhhhuuuuuummmm..."

Long and drawn out just like the monk instructed the initiate.

A pause while we listened for our teacher's inhalation and then another round.

"Aaahhhhuuuuuummmm..."

One more time.

"Aaahhhhuuuuuummmm...

"*Shanti* everybody."

We opened our eyes and returned his greeting, pressing the palms of our hands together, fingers tips pointing straight up, the sides of the thumbs lightly touching the upper chest.

With the three *aums* behind us, the Teacher aimed his remote at the stereo and we sang along to a *mantra* (*mantras* are a phrase or verse, usually Sanskrit, put to music), individual voices drowned out by the volume of the stereo. Our teacher favored the deep voice of Krishna Das and the silky notes of Deva Premal in those days, with such *mantras* as *Om Nama Shivaya*, *Govinda Hare*, the *Gayatri Mantra*, *Teyata*, and my personal favorite, Deva Premal and Miten's version of *Lokah Samasta*. I closed my eyes again during the music to suppress my bashfulness at singing in front of others and joined in.

At the end of the *mantra*, the Teacher turned off the stereo. We sat serenely for a few moments, savoring the mellow feeling in the wake of the music. Then the Teacher began to speak and invite questions on spiritual matters and Kriya Yoga for the next forty-five minutes. He quoted as needed from the Bible, Zen Buddhism, African folklore, Osho, or Rumi and used any source helpful to illustrate his topics.

At the end of the hour the Denver Teacher brought the *satsang* to an end by bowing.

"*Namaste*, everybody."

The Monk Who Howled Like a Wolf

CHAPTER FOUR

The Sweat Lodge

"The Native Americans have the truest form of spirituality on this continent."

—Kriyananda

As we bent low to cross the threshold, we each cried in turn, "*Ho! Mitakuye oyasin!*" and scuttled clockwise inside the darkened dome to claim our spots. Outside, in the relative brightness of early evening, the Fire Keeper picked the sacred stones one by one out of the glowing coals with a pitchfork, carefully brushed the faintly glowing surfaces free of ashes, and delivered each grapefruit-sized rock into the central pit of the lodge.

At first the rocks were welcome in the lodge amongst this gathering of European blooded students of this First Nations spiritual ceremony. The glowing stones began to warm the chill autumn air that had filled the *inipi* ("sweat lodge" in the North American Lakota language), but with each new stone it grew warmer and warmer inside and I no longer regretted that I had entered this womb of *Maka Ina* ("Mother Earth") with only swim trunks and a towel between me and the elements. This crowded *inipi* was hot even before the flap was closed for the first "endurance." The canvas-covered back wall was still cool, but the heat off of the shallow rock-filled pit in front of us was strengthening. I pulled my feet away from the stones, shrinking back on the blankets and scattered sage fronds covering the earthen floor.

Choking smoke rose from a scattering of overlooked ashes on the hot rocks. Holding my towel over mouth and nose, I edged back further from the rock pit and grazed shoulders with the woman on my right—up till now a clothed friend from the rest of my world in the Colorado Rockies. I wondered what traditional Native Americans would think of us whites (the *washichu*—the fat eaters) playing at Indian, some even entering the sacred lodge of the Great Spirit naked as my friend instead of clothed in simple cotton *inipi* dresses or shorts—the reverential tradition. Although I was excited to take part in a traditional ceremony with Lakota songs, presided over by a white lodge keeper that had been taught by an *Oglala* Lakota medicine woman, I knew of the legitimate concern and anger that some First Nations traditionalists felt about Europeans "borrowing" native spiritual traditions. I wondered if it was true that this was just one more example of us *washichu* stealing the best "fat."

In the dim light coming through the open doorway, I examined the underside of the willow branch frame of the lodge in the half-light. Wands, ends anchored in Mother Earth like fence posts, arched across the lodge above our heads, lashed together with orange nylon bailing twine where they overlapped. Someone had hung a string of prayer ties from the willow, a chain of little red ghosts of fabric squares, heads containing a pinch of tobacco.

I stared into the stones in front of me. The volcanic rock glowed with mysterious suggestive patterns on the rough surfaces just beyond my ability to interpret them. Soon I would feel the full heat of the stones. I reached up unconsciously and found my towel still draped over a bare shoulder.

We braced ourselves for the first endurance as the water

The Sweat Lodge

bucket, dipper, a drum, and a deer antler were passed in to the Lodge Keeper at her place to the left of the doorway. She set down each item within easy reach so that she could find them in the coming darkness. Fresh cedar was sprinkled on the hot stones, the aroma instantly filling the lodge. The Lodge Keeper recited a short prayer in Lakota and then it was time to close the door flap and begin the first endurance.

The Lodge Keeper had us rearrange the tarps as needed to blot out any light of the fading day. All went dark except the dull red glow of the stones in front of us. Having left all metal behind as instructed, I had no glasses on, but the fiery rocks were the only things to see and they were so close that my poor vision was no issue.

The heat began to build as soon as the door was closed. I arranged my towel over both shoulders so that I could close the cloth across my chest from the inside with one hand.

The Lodge Keeper began a Lakota *inipi* song, maintaining a steady beat on her drum. Those who knew the words joined in. I went inward instead, building a mental wall between my body's complaints and my inner Self. At this point in another sweat lodge I had heard someone call out, "*Ho, mitakuye oyasin!*" the magic words to ask for the flap to be thrown back. The claustrophobic man crawled out haltingly then, weaving around and over all the people between him and the door. Not being claustrophobic, I felt now that it might be a better option to collapse of heat stroke than to leave in the middle of this lodge.

I heard the drum put back in its place, a shifting of weight and a quiet splashing of water. The lodge was silent when the hiss of steam came from the central pit. The Lodge Keeper was pouring a dipper of clear cold water onto the rocks. There was an immediate change in the air of the tight space as I felt the roiling vapor reach down from the ceiling, the layer growing thicker and deeper, settling onto my thinning scalp with a scalding heat that made me duck instinctively. I pulled the towel up over my head and gripped it tightly closed in front of me as the steam layer crept lower and lower.

There were both gasps of shock at the heat and also macho calls of appreciation for the steam and I could feel another wave of people shifting in their places and trying to slump towards the earth. I knew a few of the regulars and the Lodge Keeper would remain sitting straight upright, but, anonymous in the dark, I tipped sideways as close to the cool ground as I could get.

The Lodge Keeper poured another dipper. And a third, and a fourth—cooling the glowing rocks until just one or two faint patches of deep red remained. The calls of appreciation for the heat died out. The rocks did not radiate as much now, but their fire had been transferred to the thick air around us. Each breath was a trial for me, though I was careful to breathe slowly through my nose to cool the air as much as possible before it got to my lungs.

Wanting only to shelter in a walled off place in my mind, I was pulled out of my stupor by a round of prayers, each person in turning having a chance to beseech *Wakan Tanka* (the Great Spirit) for guidance for themselves or loved ones, out loud, or silently. When it was my turn I kept my prayers to myself until I yielded to the person on my left. Then I was able to focus on the sweat running off my forehead and down my chest and the heat pressing in on all sides.

Following her own mystical timepiece after five minutes, or twenty—I couldn't tell—the Lodge Keeper called out, "*Ho, mitakuye oyasin!*" and the helper on the right side of the door flung back the door flap. Within a second or two the cool night air flooded in and I began to revive, using my towel to blot up the cooling sweat on my face and bare torso. A dipper was passed around and even the most germ-squeamish amongst us accepted seconds of the quenching water. Then the Lodge Keeper called out to the Fire Keeper for more stones to be brought in, hot from the fire.

One endurance down, three more to go.

At the end of the fourth and final endurance, the Fire Keeper threw open the door flap, letting in a little light from the dying fire outside. I came limply through the last endurance of this sweat lodge and out of a timeless trance, my self-defense to ward off the steam. In later lodges I would sometimes imagine a disembodied presence, moving darkly across my awareness, and once heard a male voice, singing in Lakota, that no one could

The Sweat Lodge

account for. But on this night I had no hint of the mystical experience that I craved.

To the right, my friend's slim torso was silhouetted by the glow as she turned towards me.

"What happened to you in the third round?"

"Umm... What do you mean?"

"Where did you go? I didn't see you leave, but you weren't in here and now you're back again."

"I didn't go anywhere." Drained people were on their hands and knees behind me waiting to crawl out of the lodge and change back into their street clothes by the fire so the conversation had to end.

Inching for the door, she said over her shoulder, "Look, Norman, you were practically sitting in my lap and then you were *gone* in the third round."

The Monk Who Howled Like a Wolf

CHAPTER FIVE

Kriya Yoga

tapaḥ svādhyāy-eśvarapraṇidhānāni kriyā-yogaḥ
samādhi-bhāvana-arthaḥ kleśa tanū-karaṇa-arthaś-ca
avidyā-asmitā-rāga-dveṣa-abhiniveśaḥ kleśāḥ

Kriya Yoga, the path of action,
includes self-discipline, study,
and dedication to the supreme being,
to weaken the obstacles of
ignorance, ego, attachments, aversions, and clinging to life,
for the purpose of attaining *samadhi*.

—*The Yoga Sutras of Patanjali*; Book 2, Verses 1-3

Kriya Yoga is one of several philosophical systems or schools of yoga. Yoga means to "join" or "unite." The common aim of all the schools of Yoga is union with the higher transcendental or spiritual Self.

Although Kriya Yoga got a shot in the arm from Babaji as recently 1861, the Kriyaban may explore this ancient wisdom in much older foundation texts. Patanjali's *Yoga Sutras* are one of the best resources. This work dates from no more recent a period than the fifth century. Some scholars believe the *Yoga Sutras* began as memorized oral tradition, finally transcribed at about the time of Christ. Originally in Sanskrit, the 196 spare verses or *sutras* are an information-packed how-to guide for the budding mystic. *The Yoga Sutras* convey as much material as possible with maximum brevity. It reads as an outline of a larger document.

The sage Patanjali (believed to be an actual flesh and blood author) included no stories or parables. Some say the pages describe how to know God. At the very least the *Sutras* detail very specific steps towards enlightenment. Students of Kriya Yoga will find a good translation with commentary fascinating. Reading three or four verses a day gives me plenty to think about. One could spend a lifetime studying this work and putting its directions into personal practice.

Kriya Yoga and *Raja Yoga* are the only forms of yoga specifically mentioned in the *Yoga Sutras*. Kriya Yoga follows a path of self-discipline, study, service, and non-attachment to one's actions while *Raja Yoga* focuses on self-awareness through meditation. Swami Nityananda Giri describes Kriya Yoga as "the practice part of yoga." Kriya favors action, while *Raja* takes a more cerebral and introspective approach. The teachings I experienced at the Temple of Kriya Yoga in Chicago and the Kriya Yoga Center of Denver draw on both of these traditions and much more.

Besides Kriya and *Raja*, there are four more traditional schools of yoga recognized in the ancient Hindu scriptures. Each school has since spawned offshoots, reformed movements, and splinter schools that survive to this day.

Bhakti Yoga is a path of selfless devotion to God and renunciation of attachments. The Hare Krishnas practice *Bhakti Yoga* with the Hindu deity, Krishna, as their focus of devotion. When I had enthusiastic stories to tell of a trip to the Hare Krishnas' New Vrindaban center in West Virginia, my Teacher warned me in hushed tones, "You know the Hare Krishnas are a cult, don't you?" I hid a smile, knowing that is exactly how some people see the Kriyabans.

With a stress in the West on *asana* (yogic postures), *Hatha*

Kriya Yoga

Yoga traditionally also employs body cleansings and various techniques for the conscious manipulation of spiritual energy with a goal of *samadhi* (absorption in meditation).

Jhana Yoga is known as the yoga of knowledge, coupling the intellectual pursuit of metaphysics and philosophy with meditation on the breath and posing the profound question, "Who am I?" Any reader of metaphysical books has some characteristics of a *Jhana* yogi.

The yoga of service to others dedicated to a sacred concept or higher power is known as *Karma Yoga*. Acts of service naturally dissolve the bondage of *karma* (the spiritual effects of an individual's conscious and unconscious actions during past and present lives) and bring the practitioner closer to *samadhi* and union with the Divine.

While *The Yoga Sutras* are spare, specific, and brief, the *Bhagavad Gita* ("Song of the Beloved Lord") is full of poetic metaphor and has a more conventional plot line. Ironically, these verses are superficially all about combat, as it follows the moral struggles of General Arjuna on the battlefield. This "mighty armed" archer is faced with the inevitability of a civil war in which he finds himself pitted against his own relatives and teachers. Arjuna is in luck however, as it turns out that his charioteer and friend happens to be none other than Krishna, a divine incarnation with unfathomable power and wisdom. During the course of the dialog between Krishna and Arjuna they discuss such esoteric topics as *karma*, enlightenment, meditation, reincarnation, the soul, and spiritual reality. When Arjuna considers refusing to fight on conscientious grounds, Krishna points out the inevitability of action in this world and the need to live one's own *dharma*, even if that *dharma* requires Arjuna to be a warrior in a bloody battle against people he loves.

The *Bhagavad Gita* is said to hold the same importance in Hinduism as the Bible does for Christian traditions. Based on events thought to have occurred in the third millennium BCE, the *Gita* has over 700 short verses in the original Sanskrit. The *Gita* is chapters 23 through 40 in the larger Book of *Bhishma*, which is itself the sixth of the 18 books of the enormous epic *Mahabharata*. The *Mahabharata a*ppeared in its final form sometime between 500 BCE and 200 CE.

The *Bhagavad Gita* covers much more ground than the drama of a vacillating leader before battle. Traditional and modern commentaries suggest that the *Gita* uses war as a metaphor for the conflicting needs and motivations within the human psyche—a battle for control between the soul and the ego. Whether the battlefield setting was intended literally or not, the *Gita* tackles many subjects of great interest to the spiritual seeker.

I spent months chewing on the words from verse 31 in Chapter 2: "There is nothing more fitting than a warrior battling in accord with his *dharma*." What does this mean? Does it mean that war and battle are acceptable fates? Those words made me reconsider my preconceptions of war. I used to think of being a soldier as contrary to our nature as spiritual beings, but this passage suggested to me that the world has reasons for being the way that it is. The *Gita* is saying that war may be the natural expression of a spiritual being and prodded me to consider my own *dharma*. What "battles" are in accordance with my *dharma*?

These sacred texts are not just stories to entertain us through a rainy afternoon. Generations of wise people have focused their attention on these concepts and left esoteric signposts behind. People who have established a relationship with their inner voice (attaining Self-realization) have conveyed these Teachings through generations.

In addition to *The Yoga Sutras* and *The Gita* there are other traditional South Asian texts that the serious Kriyaban may consider studying, most importantly perhaps the *Brahma Sutras* and the *Upanishads*. "Upanishads" translates literally as, "sitting at the feet of," referring to students listening to a master, as I listened to my teacher. There are over 200 short writings up to 2,700 years old classified as *Upanishads*. The *Brahma Sutras* are a summary of the concepts of the *Upanishads*, particularly as related to knowledge of *Brahman*. In more modern writings, *The Spiritual Science of Kriya Yoga* by Sri Kriyananda stands out as an excellent resource, particularly for those interested in learning more about astrology, meditation, *mantra* and the purpose and effect of various *asana*.

These writings are engaging stories and history lessons from the distant past, but no reader or student would be out of line to ask what Kriya Yoga has for us in the here and now.

A Teacher says, "Kriya Yoga is the art of balanced being. It is a system designed to release the individual from pain and suffering. Kriya releases us from the swings of good and bad feeling..." In his seminal book, *Kriya-yoga: The Science of Life Force,* Swami Nityananda Giri defines the goal of Kriya Yoga as, "spiritual evolution ending with unity of the individual self with the Transcendental Self." The "Transcendental Self" is similar to what the western world thinks of as the soul. Kriya Yoga seeks to achieve union with the soul through two fronts. The first approach is seeking unbroken equanimity or self-control and the second front is through an active practice of various yogic techniques.

Kriya's call for mental equanimity includes cultivating wisdom, control of mind and ego, faith in the divine, confidence in one's teachers, and trust in the lessons of traditional yogic texts. Mental equanimity is also sought by removing the influence of attraction and aversion, neutralizing the effects of ego, uncoupling self-identification from body and mind, acceptance that the physical world is illusory, and surrendering all of one's actions to the divine.

Traditional Kriya Yoga practices include self-study, development of the intellect, reducing the pull of sensual pleasure, practice of *asana* to still mind and body, cultivation of spiritual vigor (*virya*) through breath techniques, meditation, and *samadhi* (an altered meditative state devoid of ego awareness). Ultimately, Kriyabans seek the Self-realization that Yogananda and Swami Nityananda Giri speak of—unity of the individual self with the Transcendental Self.

Kriya teaches us to seek contentment, allowing us to see what is truly important about our time here on earth. It teaches us to find a balance between our inner and outer lives, and to access our own wisdom. Kriya Yoga helps us to accept ourselves, as we are, where we are.

As the Teacher says, "There should be something that you are devoted to; something that will outlast you; something that will open your heart." The Kriya Yoga Teachings *can* soften the heart and mind and bring contentment to a harried life. With this softening comes compassion, first for the individual, then expanding compassion for the larger world.

One of the goals of Kriya Yoga is a simplification of our lives. It is said that happiness is the focused mind. Yoga trains us to focus on one thing at a time, whether it is our breath, an *asana*, a career, a relationship, a home, or our *dharma*. Kriya prods us to give up our tendency to scatter ourselves in thoughts, possessions, and pastimes, and to instead look for the handful of things that bring us true happiness and to focus and excel at them. In our world of instant gratification and endless entertainment, Kriya Yoga is a tool to help us put down the cell phone or turn off the Blu-Ray player, focusing instead on the family or the redecorating project. By narrowing our focus in life, we magnify our effectiveness on what we truly value.

With the changes that Kriya may inspire comes a heightened ability to make good decisions. Kriya Yoga studies and philosophy offer greater competence and self-reliance. Its practice enhances the perception of both opportunities and potential pitfalls before they arrive on the scene. It also gives insights into our natures that allow us to make better choices than we have made in the past.

I've mentioned finding our calling or *dharma*. *Dharma* is one's natural state of being and should be sought, acknowledged, and surrendered to. In our natural state of being we feel most alive and satisfied. Our *dharma* may have us on the battlefield or mortaring bricks together, fathering a daughter or living in a cave. Kriya Yoga helps us to make decisions without attachment to old ways that no longer serve our needs.

One of the most important goals of transcendence in Kriya Yoga is to melt the boundaries between you and the outer world. Kriya teaches that distinctions between the two are arbitrary. Kriyabans are taught to transcend the concept of the individual ego and to realize that anyone's joy is our own joy and anyone's pain is our own pain. There is no male or female, yin or yang when it comes to spirit. There is no plant or animal or mineral.

Kriya Yoga

There is only a consciousness that we all share. Like the connection between a mother and her child, other beings become a part of us and we move through the world with a new courtesy and respect because we no longer are at odds with our neighbors, but in communion with all these far-flung aspects of ourselves.

Kriya means both "action" and "to act" in Sanskrit. Kriya Yoga is distinct from other types of yoga in that the Kriyaban consciously acts to lift out of this world and out of her own ego. Of central concern in Kriya Yoga are the actions we commit that produce a consequential re-action of events or circumstance, either in this life or a future life. This cause and effect dynamic is known as *karma*. Avoiding *karma* takes more than having a positive attitude and thinking good thoughts. It is all the actions of thought, word, and deed that create *karma* so Kriya Yoga teaches us to be thoughtful in our acts in order to avoid accumulating binding new *karma*.

Kriya Yoga shows that by shedding *karma* we are shedding outer layers that are concealing the true essence of our being underneath. The best Kriya removes that which we are not, revealing the radiant source. In effective meditation we listen to the counsel of this source—the sacred guidance within all of us.

This is our job as Kriyabans: To find the one Self that dwells within, drawing us to the final goal and promise of Kriya Yoga—release from this troubled world in perfect harmony with the divine.

The Monk Who Howled Like a Wolf

CHAPTER SIX

What's the Catch?

Raised tail swaying back and forth, a scorpion scuttled to the edge of the stream and squinted across the wide water at the far bank and a wading crane. The scorpion's unblinking eyes noticed a green frog in the reeds nearby.

"Frog, you're a good swimmer. Will you carry me on your back across this water? I sink like a stone."

The frog hopped further back into the reeds and eyed the scorpion warily.

"But you are a scorpion and I am a frog. You will sting me and I will die of your poison. Besides, I have been waiting here for hours so that I can cross without being eaten! There is one of those wading birds on the other side waiting to spear me for a meal."

"Oh, frog, you are not thinking clearly. If I sting you then you won't be able to swim and I will fall into the water and drown. If I am on your back that old bird won't dare bother you for fear of my deadly sting! Together we can both cross the water safely."

"I have been waiting here for so long... You promise you won't sting me?"

"Of course I will not sting you! That would mean my own death as well as yours. I trust you not to drown me, so you can *trust me not to sting you. Come, let's cross this stream together."*

Hesitantly, the frog hopped out of the reeds and down to the edge of the water where he waited for the scorpion to climb onto his back.

"Remember your promise, Scorpion."

"Enough talk. Swim!"

So the frog began to paddle and kick, being careful not to lose his passenger. In the center of the stream, with the end of the ferry ride just a minute away, the frog felt a searing in his neck and immediately began growing numb. Shocked, the frog looked up at the scorpion clutching onto his green back.

"But now I will die and you will drown! Why would you sting me?"

The scorpion shrugged. "You knew what I was."

My teacher once suggested the need for someone to write a book called *How Yoga Ruined My Life: I Will Never Be Unconscious Again.* Yoga isn't really going to ruin anything of true value in your life, but sometimes I mourn for the days when I didn't have to think about the consequences of *everything* I do, second guess the motivations for my actions, or puzzle over the true nature of reality.

So there are catches and we are right to be cautious in choosing whom we ask for a ride across this stream of reality. There are scorpions and there are cults and there are many ways for the seeker to waste time and money. Kriya Yoga has catches even if we don't wander off the path or tumble from an existential cliff. Sometimes the path is exhausting and forces us to see what we would rather not.

Yes, it is true that we have a body of knowledge, the Kriya Yoga Teachings, to keep us moving across the stream. But the Teachings drift with each telling. This East Indian approach to spirituality has suffered from linguistic and cultural misinterpretations in the knowledge transplant to Europe and the Americas. In this transmission, the original form and intent of Kriya Yoga—and yoga in general—has experienced a dilution of meaning and context, much to the dismay of purists like my

What's the Catch?

teacher.

Care must be exercised with every source of information and every teacher we face. Even translations of ancient works are suspect. Just as Anglos may be guilty of well meaning, but unfortunate modifications when they perform Native American ceremonies, translators may take what was meant to be a literal truth and describe it as metaphorical or make literal what was metaphorical. To avoid doctrinal traps don't lean on any one source.

Eastern traditions, like the sweat lodge ceremony in white America, have been co-opted and transformed by western culture with its focus on appearance and money. The Denver Teacher laments that yoga in the United States confuses physical techniques with spiritual growth. The drift of the Teachings often conceals the spiritual message beneath a superficial focus on strength and flexibility. Is it important if someone can stay in handstand for three minutes and has great abs? What have they accomplished? Doing *asana* or perhaps a little breath work (*pranayama*) is not taking advantage of the greater body of yoga wisdom. The yoga of the Western world promises much, but often delivers little more than "core strength" without any real change for the better in people's lives.

We have been taught to believe that if we work hard at something we will get a prize or other tangible benefit. That is not necessarily the case with Kriya Yoga. The spiritual world has priorities far beyond and far different from that which we normally hold near and dear to us on planet Earth. It is difficult to imagine, but from a spiritual perspective the greatest benefit to our souls may come from the agonizing loss of a love or in experiencing gnawing hunger. We do not necessarily get wealthier, more beautiful, or find the perfect sexual partner when we embark on the path. As the Teacher says, "*Why* are you on the path? You can't do it to get more." This path offers us the possibility of contentment in the face of the discord in our lives.

Part of the goal of self-awareness is to become in touch with elements of our being that we may otherwise ignore for a lifetime. Kriya Yoga is not for those uncomfortable with self-examination. "*Yoga*" means to join or to integrate—to *yoke*. Part of the joining referred to in the word "yoga" is a joining of disparate parts of us that normally operate independently. But there is also a higher union sought in Kriya Yoga—union with our own divine spirit.

Another challenging concept in Kriya culture is that desire for everything of this physical world must someday be left behind. This includes everything that we may now find near and dear: Ice cream, sunsets, crying toddlers, and aging uncles. These pleasant sense objects are the velvet bonds that keep us stuck on earth. All must someday be transcended before we are able to move on to the next stage.

Our monoculture is not friendly to the person committed to a non-denominational spiritual lifestyle. We are a culture of groups and organizations. Kriya is a solitary mystical Path better suited to loners, cave dwellers, and outcasts. Our society does not respect or recognize the importance of these non-social outliers. To this day in India there are those called "sky-clad." These are naked ascetics or *sadhus* (those who pursue a *sadhana*, or spiritual practice) sometimes clothed only with the sky, who eschew possessions, live from offerings, and spend their time studying sacred texts, meditating, and in *asana*. Their focused goal is the shedding of *karma* (along with their clothes) and attaining enlightenment. Never mind that most of the "developed" world is too cold for such a sky-clad way of life—what reception, respect, or cooperation would the sky-clad receive in the West?

The Kriyaban lives in the developed world below the radar of their own culture: Dressing and talking like the rest of us, marrying, having families, and all the while attempting to incorporate as many of their Kriya beliefs as possible into their lives without offending those around them.

Obviously, the Kriya Path is not easy. The Teachings themselves have a perspective alien and unsettling to the Western mind. As my teacher admits, "I'm giving you the yogic teaching and usually it's not palatable." Kriya Yoga requires a commitment. Holding ourselves responsible for our thoughts, words, and deeds does not come overnight. Accepting that we

What's the Catch?

have earned every trial and travail in our lives is not a comforting, feel good philosophy.

"The Teaching never lets you get away with anything," my teacher says, because *everything* is of our own doing.

Kriya's structure and demands of our time and attention require self-discipline. In many areas there are few Kriyabans to provide support or a spiritual *sangha*. By and large, we must be strong enough to walk alone. When we get into trouble or hit a sticky patch, advice may not be nearby. But the sooner we start down the path, the sooner we reach the destination. We *can* make progress and be better people for our efforts. This world is *the* place, *the* ground, *the* sacred environment in which to seek our enlightenment.

This path requires direct, individual mystical experience. Each path is different; no one can initiate this trip for another. Kriya Yoga is challenging because we must think for ourselves. the Denver Teacher says, "If you subscribe to the philosophies without thinking, you're in big trouble." It's not enough to soak in the words of a teacher or an interesting book. "Yoga's not about being good. It's about being wise."

Meanwhile, every thought, every word spoken, every action taken is influenced by the *thousands* of lives we have already experienced. The imprinting and prejudices we carry with us from past events are staggering. *Karma* is weed seeds germinating in the fertile soil of a new life. We have to pull the weeds as they gather strength reaching for the light. Without uncommon awareness, we are unconscious of the state of our gardens.

Kriya Yoga also requires us to let go of the familiar and to strike off into new territory. We must do our practice with commitment and regularity, letting go of all expectations, particularly of the expectation of reward. Sometimes we have to try less hard, because trying hard is a striving that can stand between us and surrender. Striving for enlightenment is the last obstacle. Enlightenment is gained only when it is not sought, but simply lived.

We are encouraged these days to get in touch with our emotions, but Kriya teaches us that emotionality is a barrier to success. *Karma* floats to the surface when we are emotional. The true Kriyaban learns to witness and accept emotion, yet immediately releases the feelings and their attendant *karma*.

Even our relationships may be affected by a study of Kriya Yoga. In Kriya Yoga we do not externalize blame. Troubles with a boss or a romantic partner are *our* problems. If our partner is insufferably timid or a tedious perfectionist, most likely these are qualities we share as well. Can we love our boss in spite of her bouts of unreasonable anger? Can we love this quality in ourselves? We see what is *relative* to us. If we did not understand or know it, we would not perceive it external to ourselves. We come to know the outside world through the precedence of internal experience.

The Kriyaban also understands that we become like the people we associate with. As our awareness grows and priorities shift, we may decide to cultivate new associations with people who better represent our ideals. In the process, we may let go of current friendships. Old social ties may even dissolve spontaneously as our priorities change. These changes should be made with love, however, if for no other reason than to avoid the pain of causing pain to others.

Yes, the study of Kriya Yoga may have a catch. But the catch is not a hit to the wallet or a time commitment. The catch is that life may be transformed as we abandon the old ways that did not serve spirit and instead chart a new course to adventure and mystery.

CHAPTER SEVEN

Guarding the Gate

"Let me in! I want to see my father. He runs this sun dance!"
I blocked the opening in the fence, my mind racing. I wanted to stand back and let him in—would anyone blame me? I was intimidated by this young Lakota man. This was Porcupine District—where many of Crazy Horse's people settled when they were finally forced onto the Rez. They aren't known for giving up easily.

"Come on. Smudge me and let me in." He took a step closer, raising his arms above his sides.

I was on gatekeeper duty with a large plastic bag of sage on the ground beside me (picked that morning on the dry hillside to the east of the dance grounds) and a coffee can of glowing coals from the sacred fire on the other side of the gate. When a dancer or dance supporter had to enter the restricted area of tipis and sweat lodges behind me I would drop some of the sage into the can, sending up clouds of sweet smelling smoke that made my Denver Teacher's altar incense look like the minor leagues. Then I would swing the coffee can around by the improvised bailing wire handle and fan the haze of incense over the entrant's arms, front, back, legs, and even the soles of their feet. Sage was used to dispel negative influences long before images of Catholic masses reached the Plains Indians.

"Oh, your father is the sun dance leader? What a great man. He's not here, though. The dance is over for the day. I think he's back at the house."

Everything that I said was the truth, but it felt like I was giving him the run around.

"He's not in there?"

"Not now. He headed out a while ago. Some of the dancers are sleeping. We probably shouldn't bother them. Can you check the house first?"

"Oh, dancers are sleeping? Man, I've danced two times." He reached for his upper chest and felt for something through the flannel of his shirt—probably the old scars where the skewers had ripped out. "It's tough, sleeping on the ground with no water. But we do it for *Tunkashila*, right, man?"

"Right!" I said brightly, though I've never sun danced.

He looked at me as if seeing me for the first time. "He's up at the house?"

"Yeah. Hey, take care."

He walked off and I began to relax, hoping I had done the proper thing in turning away the son of the patriarch of the family that owned this parcel of land. I had accepted an invitation from my friend (known on Pine Ridge as Gunnison Mike) to help out with the annual sun dance he attended, but I thought that I was going to be tending the fire, not working crowd control. As a scrawny middle-aged white guy, I was taken by surprise when I heard the patriarch sun dance leader call me "Security" earlier in the day. The promotion from helping out to Security on a reservation of 30,000 Lakota took me by surprise, but I accepted this as one more plot twist among many on Pine Ridge.

The sun dance is the revered intersection of many mystical elements of traditional Lakota spirituality. It represents all that the Lakota hold *wakan* (sacred). To dance is the biggest sacrifice a Lakota man can make for his people and, after childbirth, the second most important sacrifice a Lakota woman can offer.

Guarding the Gate

While the Lakota have their sun dances, *inipis*, sage burning, creation stories, holy people, and *Wakan Tanka*, the Kriyabans have fasting, *pujas*, the modern creation story with Babaji and Lahiri, meditation, teaching stories, techniques, *gurus*, *avatars*, and *Ishvara* (the divine being). One of the core belief systems of the schools of Yoga is the "Eight Limbs of *Ashtanga*," often shortened to the "Eight Limbs." The earliest written reference to the Eight Limbs is in the *Yoga Sutras of Patanjali*. As in his (or her!) usual approach, Patanjali gives a bare bones presentation of the Eight Limbs, stressing that these are an essential part of the effort to attain expanded consciousness (*samadhi*) and eventual liberation (*kaivalya* or *moksha*).

The *Eight Limbs* are not exclusively practiced by Kriyabans. Several branches of yoga specifically espouse the qualities and goals of the *Eight Limbs*. From a historical perspective, it is difficult to defend any serious discipline defining itself as yoga, in the traditional sense, that does not give a nod of respect to the *Eight Limbs of Ashtanga*.

The first five of the Eight Limbs are *external* practices (*bahiranga sadhana*—*sadhana* meaning "practice"). These five practices involve the outside world and one's interactions with that world. The last three of the Eight Limbs are called *internal* aids to Yoga (*antaranga sadhana*). These are primarily internal adjustments or mental practices.

The Eight Limbs kick off with the Laws of *Yama*, the "Abstentions."

Practice of the *Yamas* prevents the dissipation of the spiritual energy of *prana*, keeping our spiritual health fed, toned, and limber. The spiritually adept can harness this energy on the path towards liberation.

The Denver Teacher says, "Those five *Yamas* are critical. They free you in the long run because you are no longer generating new *karma*."

This avoidance of *karma* starts off with the first of the *Yamas*: *Ahimsa*—abstaining from violence. *Ahimsa* is defined as doing no harm to others and may be broadened in scope to include all sentient beings. A practice of *ahimsa* even asks us to abstain from violence to ourselves.

The second of the *Yamas* is *satya*—abstaining from deceit. my teacher takes this *Yama* very seriously. "One of the deadliest things in Kriya Yoga is to say one thing and to do something else," he teaches.

Cultivating individual awareness is critically important in a soul's evolution, but the practice of deceit can be so ingrained as to blind the deceiver himself to the truth. I have heard Kriyananda tell a story in which he was trying to defend a questionable course of action to his *guru*, Shelley. Shelliji (a respectful form of "Shelley") patiently listened to Kriyananda's earnest rationalizations before growling sternly, "Kriyanandy, you can lie to me. You can even lie to God. But do not ever, *ever* lie to yourself."

The third *Yama* is *asteya*—abstaining from stealing. I was particularly struck and challenged by my Teacher's observation that so much as stealing someone's peace of mind violates the Kriyaban's prohibition on stealing.

Here comes a tough one in the fourth position: *Brahmacharya*—variously and diplomatically translated as sense control, monogamy, constraint of the genital organs, or even literal celibacy. (There's a "catch" for you—I'm sorry I didn't mention it earlier.) I've looked at the original *Sanskrit* and the word does seem to intend "sexual chastity" in this context, although I am miles away from being a *Sanskrit* scholar.

Before we presume that Kriya demands celibacy of us, remember that the supposed origin of Kriya Yoga in modern times came about with Babaji's revelations and teachings to Lahiri Mahasaya, a married and presumably non-celibate man.

The fifth and final Law of *Yama* is *aparigraha*—abstaining from greed or possessiveness, particularly as applied to sense objects. These sense objects do not have to be tangible physical objects. One can be greedy about sex.

And one probably is.

Aparigraha is a more subtle practice than I once assumed. Where does greed come from? My Teacher thinks of greed as a derivative of fear—the fear of being deprived—of sex, money, food, housing, or even entertainment. A visceral fear of basic needs not being met generates attachment to those needs. The

Guarding the Gate

Denver Teacher asks, "Think about when you are emotional about something—isn't it a form of greed?"

One of the Buddha's most important teachings, that desire creates suffering, is repeated in the *Yoga Sutras* (YS 2.15). With desire eliminated, piece of mind grows. My Teacher quotes an old saying, "Who is poor? Those who want more." It doesn't matter how much stuff, food, square feet, cars, or sexual partners that we have. If we feel we don't have enough, we feel poor.

My Teacher also said:

> Non-greed equals the key to controlling life energy. Greed can devastate your energy. If greed can be removed on all three levels (thought, word, and deed) then the other four *Yamas* should be fine.

From a spiritual point of view, a greedy life is a failure. How can we develop compassion or a sense of unity with other beings if we are focused on getting more for ourselves?

The Masters tell us that the effectiveness of any spiritual discipline hinges on the effort we put into it. At the sun dance I worked as fire and gatekeeper, security, and *inipi* doorkeeper. Sometimes I held all the duties at the same time, stoking the fire, with an eye on the back gate. Or smudging down people coming in through the gate and racing back now and then to feed the fire and grab some more coals for the smudge pot. The work under the intense August South Dakota sun was challenging, yet also extremely fulfilling, with its focus on the spirit world.

Both years I did this I worked an eight-hour shift each of the four consecutive days of the dance. The second year I volunteered for night fire keeper, as the fire had to be kept burning throughout the dance. Those night shifts were a challenge: Staying awake sitting on an upended log round, staring into the mesmerizing bonfire. Sometimes a dancer emerged from a teepee and sat for a while to tell me their story. Dancers usually dance for someone: A sick relative, a friend in prison, or to fight drug and alcohol addiction in themselves or in the *oyate* ("the people").

Early in the evening an *inipi* leader might tell me to get some rocks ready. I didn't always have much warning, but they didn't want the rocks very hot. The dancers were exhausted by the end of the long day out in the sun—the last thing they needed was to get hotter. The dancers looked forward to the sweats because the no-water rule didn't apply inside the lodges. Between endurances they had a chance to drink from the dipper.

Gunnison Mike let me know that I shouldn't bring water or food into the dancer area so I usually went without during my shifts or sometimes I hid a water bottle in the woodpile outside of the fence. My thirst was nothing compared to that of the dancers. I could drink all that I wanted the other sixteen hours of the day.

The men were usually pierced through the skin of the upper chest while lying on the ground at the base of the cottonwood sun dance tree. On any one of the four days of the sun dance a male dancer will lie down on a buffalo skin at the base of the tree while two or three others squat at his side (they usually include a holy man and the sun dance leader). One of the men pinches the dancer's flesh and stretches it away from the dancer's body before carefully pushing a scalpel blade through. The scalpel removed, a short wooden peg is pushed through the wound until both ends are exposed. They connect the two ends of the wooden peg together with a rawhide tie and that loop is then connected to a long rope previously anchored in the upper branches of the tree. Each dancer gets two or more piercings. Immediately after getting pierced, the dancer is helped to his feet and he dances towards and away from the tree (to the drumming and chanting from the singers in the shade of a pine-covered arbor). During the first three trips backwards the dancer keeps the ropes slack, but the fourth time he will back-pedal quickly until the ropes tighten suddenly, ripping the wooden pegs loose.

When I have seen dancers pierce there has been surprisingly little blood, perhaps because dances happen at the height of summer and the participants are dehydrated.

There are other ways to pierce. I watched Gunnison Mike get pierced four times through his upper back and then he dragged a heavy buffalo skull, bouncing behind him, until the last peg pulled out. It took a long time.

Guarding the Gate

As I mentioned, Lakota women also sun dance. Childbirth is considered even more of a sacrifice than dancing, but even so, mothers will dance. Women pierce on their upper arms. The women I saw getting pierced didn't even sit down.

One year the daughter of the sun dance organizer danced. I was at my post at the back gate when she came towards me from the dance grounds with paper towels and bottled water. Together we cleaned up the dried blood trailing down her brown arms. While we blotted and daubed we chatted about the meal she had to help prepare back at her father's house.

At the end of that sun dance Gunnison Mike and I gave her a ride back to her home in Fort Collins. She and Mike talked until their exhaustion took over and they dozed while I drove through darkness across the gentle hills and plains of northeast Colorado and replayed the experiences of the last four days. I was now a very small part of the mystical Lakota world that I had thought about for so many years, but my own spiritual journey was just beginning.

The Monk Who Howled Like a Wolf

CHAPTER EIGHT

Tending the Fire

The five Laws of *Niyama* (Observances) of the Eight Limbs begin with *shaucha*. Translations of the word suggest cleanliness (physical, along with spiritual). While the Kriyaban isn't asked to endure physical hardship or austerities for the sake of their spiritual growth, the process of fasting and sweating through days of heat and *inipis* that the sun dancer goes through is a highly effective purification process for body and soul. The Kriyaban's less challenging practice of *shaucha* includes attention to bodily hygiene and grooming along with a healthy and nourishing diet and occasional fasting. My teacher and Kriyananda stress clean drinking water as a way to cleanse the body of toxins.

The purification process may involve *material* fasting as well: Shedding possessions that are not used or useful. Excess or disorganized possessions can reveal imbalanced spiritual *shaucha*.

Shaucha includes nurturing healthy thoughts and words. Though physical purity is important, spiritual cleanliness becomes increasingly the focus as the physical world loses relevance to the Seeker. The Laws of *Yama* (abstaining from violence, deceit, theft, sensual indulgence, and greed) may be practiced internally as an internal expression of purity.

The second of these five *Niyamas* is *santosha*—contentment. Contentment comes when we harmonize our inner and outer worlds. My Teacher says, "Contentment is the lack of expectations. If you are content you don't need anything. That's why it's the most exalted of the *Niyamas*."

The next *Niyama* is that of mental self-discipline, or *tapas*. *Tapas* is stressed in Kriya Yoga because any significant accomplishment requires self-discipline. The Denver yogi teaches that *tapas* should not be forced. "It should be joyful," he says. Being inspired to fuel our bodies with healthy foods is self-discipline.

Kriyananda told his students at one of his Retreats, "What do you want out of life? Whatever it is, you have to apply self-discipline to attain it."

The mental self-discipline of *tapas* may appear to be an austere approach to life. The yogi is self-controlled, quiet, focused, careful in diet, and consistent in her sleep patterns. *Tapas* may be practiced even in speech. My Teacher suggests pre-screening our words with the litmus test: "Is it kind? Is it true? Is it necessary?" A good yogi chooses words thoughtfully, and avoids insult, cliché, rumor, and negativity.

The fourth *Niyama*, *svadhyaya*, translates as "self-study." This study focuses on the traditional texts of importance in Kriya Yoga, like the *Bhagavad Gita* and *The Yoga Sutras of Patanjali*, as well as engaging in a literal self study.

My Teacher says, "Through self-study you are bestowing an ever growing enlightenment upon yourself."

Svadhyaya may be journaling or dream interpretation or we may take a lesson from the *Jhana* yogis and repeatedly ask ourselves the question, "Who am I?" Through this meditation, we uncover successively deeper layers of self, confronting what we had concealed, and revealing more and more of the divinity that dwells at our center.

Finally, *Ishvara pranidhana* is the last of the five Observances. You may think of *Ishvara pranidhana* in many ways: As submission to God or the *Brahman* of Hinduism ("the source of life, beyond time and space," *Shvetashvatara*

Tending the Fire

Upanishad I.7), surrender to the life force, identification with the creator, union with the divine; attuning to "the indwelling reality" as my Teacher sometimes suggests; or even dedication to the Great Spirit of the Lakota. This *Niyama* asks us to place our trust in something more meaningful and noble than our physical reality. *Ishvara pranidhana* is surrender to divinity and spiritual guidance. Kriyananda encourages his students to "Try to set down the dream of humankind and pick up the dream of God."

These first two of the Eight Limbs, the five *Yamas* and five *Niyamas*, may be practiced wherever we are. They don't require spiritual mastery or expanded consciousness. However, a personal practice of the *Yamas* and *Niyamas* is crucial to maximizing the flow of *prana*—the spiritual energy or life force pervasive within our world. It is this *prana* that the Kriyaban enhances and directs to connect to higher consciousness and eventual enlightenment.

Third of this multi-legged beast *of Ashtanga* is *asana*—the physical postures that have become confused with yoga in western culture. While the postures are useful to quiet the body and ego and thus free the mind to plunge deep into meditation, the *asanas* are a tool rather than the end that we often make of them. I have come out of yoga studios with a mellow high and sometimes confuse that high with what my body has just been through. The elation and bliss is a mental state—not a physical one. We can experience that peace without *asana*. Just like the yoga block is a prop to help the yogi into some poses, the *asana* is a prop to help the yogi achieve levels of *samadhi*.

Shelliji admitted that he had once considered taking up *asana*, but he lay down until the urge passed.

If your life is filled with exertion and flexion through work or play, it may not be necessary to do any specific *asanas* (though it is indisputably of value for body and spirit). As long as we are able to quiet the mind and body when we sit in meditation we have fulfilled the general purpose of *asana*. During any exercise in our daily lives, we can focus on the breath and encourage awareness of *prana*.

Mystics from many traditions link the breath with the spirit.

Kriya Yoga actively exploits this link to magnify spiritual energy. The fourth Limb, *pranayama*, or breath control, is another way to keep the body and ego occupied so that we can hear the voice of our inner Self. Breath-work is considered central to Kriya Yoga since breath is a manifestation of life force. In *The Yoga Sutras*, the word *pranayama* is sometimes used synonymously with spiritual energy—or shortened to *prana*. *Kundalini* is another word that you might have heard used to describe manifestations of spiritual energy in the body. In a link to the Lakota sun dance, some Eastern mystical thought also perceives our sun as the source of life force and *prana*.

Breath-work is a way to channel and strengthen *prana* and is thought to hasten spiritual evolution. There are many types of *pranayama*. Swami Nityananda says, "Since everyone is breathing, everyone is a potential yogi." But it does help to have a healthy body, free of pain and discomfort. Some Kriya *pranayamas* are widely known and accessible, but some advanced techniques should only be used with the help of a master or *guru*.

Fifth among the Eight Limbs is *Pratyahara*, usually described as "sense withdrawal," but *pratyahara* has a subtlety of meaning that goes beyond this translation. *Pratyahara* is a decoupling of our identity from the outer world. Rather than requiring of us to not like the taste of chocolate, *pratyahara* asks that we not tie chocolate, or anything else in the physical world, to our mental condition.

*

Over twenty years ago, during my first stint of living in Alaska (where I eventually settled and still reside) and before I ever sat in a sweat lodge or went to Pine Ridge, I completed a twenty-four hour vision quest on the tundra a few miles from my cabin. In those pre-Internet days I was driven by an intense interest in everything Lakota, and went so far as to learn some of that beautiful language.

I cut four willow sticks in preparation for my quest, each about twenty inches long and as thick as my forefinger. I carefully scraped off all the bark then tied one square flag of fabric to each stick. Black for the west, white for the north, red for the east, and yellow for the south. I packed these and some offering tobacco and hitched a late morning ride a few miles out the same Stampede Road soon to achieve fame through mention in Jon Krakauer's book, *Into the Wild*, about Christopher McCandless' own quest to test his resources in the wilderness twenty miles further west.

From the side of this lonely gravel road I saw a low rise clear of brush half a mile to the south in the broad valley between ridges. I knew that the rocky mound would be drier than the surrounding tundra. A light rain fell as I left the road and crossed the grassy tussocks, picking my way around low patches of wet dwarf birch. I was glad for the olive-brown army surplus poncho draped over me.

The hillock was perfect for my vision quest. It was only a couple of hundred feet across, but elevated above the tundra so I could see in all directions. I put my trust in *Wakan Tanka* for the day, but I felt better knowing I might have time to react to any grizzly bears headed my way.

Further south yet, at the base of the nearby ridge, stood a cluster of three granite erratics, or tors, rising out of the moss and Labrador tea. Geology describes these monuments as boulders left behind by retreating glacial ice, but native Athabascan tradition says that tors are particularly accomplished shamans that have turned their bodies to stone. During my night on the tundra I felt the watchful presence of this trio of shamans on their own ancient vision quest.

Settled on my mound, I propped up each willow flag with a pile of stones at the cardinal directions of a fifty-foot wide imaginary circle—this was to be the boundary of my world until the same time the next day.

I had learned a Lakota prayer to the four directions from cassette tapes and recited it now as a way to mark the beginning of my quest. In the Alaskan gloom and drizzle of late summer, I began praying and meditating, surrendering my fate to what was to be an uneventful night.

*

Now we move to the three internal aids to *samadhi* (the *antaranga sadhana*). The first of these three is *dharana*, known simply as "concentration," or "harmony with one's thoughts." The *Yoga Sutras* identify *dharana* as the necessary starting point of the meditative process (YS3.04).

The seventh Limb is *dhyana*, or meditation. Meditation is one of the most important practices for a seeker of expanded consciousness.

The eighth and final Limb of the Eight Limbs of Ashtanga is *samadhi*. I have briefly defined *samadhi* as "meditative absorption" and "expanded consciousness." As we climb further up this mountain of self-discovery, the English language begins to fail us in our attempts to describe the sights we can see from the trail. *Samadhi* is both a profound mystery and so common that we tend to overlook it when it comes our way spontaneously. We experience *samadhi* when we start out on an errand and suddenly find ourselves at our destination with no recollection of time passed, what we saw along the route, how fast we walked, or what we were thinking about—arriving safely with no conscious attention to the task. Finding stillness in the beauty of a sunset is also a level of *samadhi*. *Samadhi* happens to all of us at some point.

In *samadhi* we are not *thinking* in the way we normally define thought. The *Yoga Sutras* describe *samadhi* as the moment when meditation becomes the thought and the mind empties of its own nature (YS3.03). It is the continual immersion of consciousness on one point of attention (YS3.11 & 12). The *Yoga Sutras* refer to nine layers of *samadhi*. In the upper levels the ego has melted away and we are pure, unchanging consciousness without the need or impulse to do anything. The "I" that we think of when we think of "I" is gone. We have something to brag about when we can live in this bliss throughout our daily life.

Of course, we won't feel the need then to talk at all.

I didn't find *samadhi* or a vision as I sat cross-legged inside my army surplus poncho in the damp of interior Alaska. The flags of the four directions fluttered in the light breeze of that long murky night, restless as my thoughts.

CHAPTER NINE

The Four Pillars

My first six months of focused daily meditation were difficult. I mucked about in my own head and discovered some skeletons. Meditation reveals the dark thoughts hidden in our psyches. It is said that we are never as dishonest as when looking in a mirror, but the mirror of meditation doesn't allow us to strike a flattering pose, suck in our gut, and thrust out our chest. This mirror reveals our mediocre profile, the excess baggage, and the sagging principles.

It's good that meditation allows us to see ourselves as we are. The ego is the insincere sycophant, filtering reality, shielding us from the unpleasant, and encouraging self-righteousness, pride, selfishness, and indignation. For the Kriyaban seeking truth, meditation is less expensive than therapy.

We aren't necessarily born meditators and we must work through various levels of facility in meditation once we have begun the practice. Hindu traditions describe four stages to life, starting with *brahmacharya* (student life), moving into *garhasthya* (family life), then *vanaprastha*, the forest life, and finally, *yativrata*, the renunciate life. The forest life is the natural home of the meditator first becoming serious about the practice.

The seeker may already have filled their head with book knowledge (formerly instruction at the feet of a master in a wooded *ashram*), but has little first hand experience of the altered states of consciousness that they seek through meditation. This is the stage of indirect knowledge (no matter how well-informed), but the beginnings of serious practice.

Yogic tradition describes the essential qualities of a seeker. Coming to us from the early days of advanced human culture (even before the *Yoga Sutras of Patanjali*) are the Four Pillars of the Spiritual Aspirant. These are preparations for expanded consciousness—the *Sadhana Chatushtaya* in Sanskrit. These pillars are the foundational attributes that anyone seeking enlightenment must establish before moving forward.

The first of these Four Pillars is *viveka*: Awareness of the genuine and enduring. Someone with this awareness perceives the physical world (being temporary and illusory) as less tangible than the spiritual world (being real and permanent).

Viveka doesn't excuse us from the laws of the physical world. As Kriyananda cautions, "You think that this world is an illusion? Just step out into traffic and see how an illusion feels." However, there is value in this perspective of *viveka*. A practice of *viveka* helps us to remember that there are imperatives and a reality more relevant to the immortal soul than jobs, families, and sense gratification. The mystic or *sadhu* sees this physical plane as a rest stop on the journey to union with the Self. We should not become comfortable here.

The second pillar, *vairagya*, is non-attachment to glittering physical sense objects. Yogis see attachment as literal bondage to the difficult physical planes. Non-attachment is non-gluttony. We may still eat at the table and enjoy the meal, but without overindulging.

Rather than being oppressive and dull, *vairagya* promises freedom from fears and dissatisfaction. When we have no attachment to the pretty, the comfortable, the luxurious, or the rewarding, then we aren't disappointed when things don't go our way. In fact, since we have no preconceived "way" we are hardly aware of lack. When we do not expect, we do not feel loss. Once desire is banished, the soul has an easier time

The Four Pillars

concentrating on the work of expanded consciousness.

The third pillar is a bundle of six personal qualities that encourage liberation (yet another term for enlightenment). This bundle is described by various Sanskrit names but I will be using *shat sanpatis* (six routes) as the name of the third pillar.

This first of the *shat sanpatis* is *shraddha*, faith in the effectiveness of the ancient yogic path. Traditionally, *shraddha* has focused on three areas of faith or belief: Faith in one's self, faith in the traditional scriptures, and faith in *guru*.

The Denver Teacher says, "Confidence is the realization that you are a divine spirit. Confidence is never surrendering, never giving up." For the Western student of Kriya Yoga, faith in oneself also means having confidence that we do not have to be an Eastern yogi to achieve enlightenment. Enlightenment is a potential for every sentient being. We *can* do this.

How do we develop faith in the traditional texts—words written by people far away and long ago? Consider this: These texts are drawn from accumulated knowledge of millennia of inquiry by thousands of very wise people in cultures that were supportive of attaining personal spiritual growth. A great beginning for the study of traditional works is the *Bhagavad Gita*. If the *Gita* resonates with you then you are off to a good start.

Now, tackling the subject of faith in *guru*.

Kriya Yoga doesn't ask for blind obedience. Faith in ourselves and faith in the ancient texts come first. However, a *guru*—a sincere, selfless, inspired instructor in these ancient arts—is a powerful ally for those on the Path. When we get lost on a trip we stop and ask directions from people along the way. The *guru* is the local resident who knows the conditions of the road up ahead because she has been there before. The right *guru* wants us to succeed, just as a mature parent wants nothing more than to see the child journey on independently one day.

Maybe as I did, you will find your *guru* in a Kriya Center within walking distance of your home. You too may have overlooked someone waiting for you. Or your teacher may be the "crazy" old guy that lives by himself in a small house on the edge of town. Or your perfect teacher may be the foster child that needs a home. Or the *guru* may even be a book handed to you by an acquaintance.

Gurus are everywhere. Remember, the *guru* needs the student as much as the student needs the *guru*. The *guru* looks for you.

> *"If you are on the Path there is basically nothing in your life that should upset you."*
>
> —*The Denver Teacher*

The next of the six aptitudes of the *shat sanpatis* is *titiksha*. *Titiksha* means endurance, forbearance, or patience. *Titiksha* is balance despite the ups and downs of life; serenity in the face of heat or cold, hunger or feast, pain or comfort; non-attachment to the good and to the bad; not letting events or sensations unseat equanimity.

A person in a constant state of *titiksha* does not experience anxiety, irritation, or self-pity. They accept what life brings to them. This forbearance is not passive. Mental state is not defined in *reaction* to the exterior environment. The yogi may still be proactive in making her life more comfortable and less stressful, but mishaps and discomfort do not derail her from focus on the spiritual path. She sees challenging circumstances as opportunities to address her karmic debt. She realizes that she is not that which feels too hot or hungry or sad or angry. She is an immortal soul with a body that feels these temporary sensations.

An aware person naturally moves towards longer and more stable periods of *titiksha* because he knows that emotional reactions to outside events are what cause the *karma* that binds us to the physical body and to the earth. Further, the aware being understands that we are the result of our accumulated *karma* and that nothing is being done to us. Instead, we orchestrate the events of our lives on a mystical level.

Titiksha is an enormously important and challenging state to attain for any period of time. We all experience *titiksha* in odd moments: When we wake in a warm bed and realize that it's the weekend; while sitting on the floor playing blocks with a child;

while soaking in a hot bath; or as we jog effortlessly on a warm spring day. But then the dog jumps on the bed or the bath water gets cold or the child calls us fat or we catch a whiff of diesel exhaust from the bus roaring by and *titiksha* is gone.

It might seem like anyone that could stay in this composed and serene state would have it made, but *titiksha* is not the end of the journey.

The next of the necessary six aptitudes of the aspirant is *shama*. *Shama* is the work of maintaining the more passive *titiksha*. *Shama* is the proactive mind-control necessary to sustain the normally fleeting mental serenity and tranquility of *titiksha*.

Shama frees us to focus on the ultimate goal of expanded consciousness. If we can train the mind, we are at the controls of our life. Unfortunately, the practice of mind control for tranquility is difficult. Jack Kornfield relates in his excellent book, *After the Ecstasy, the Laundry: How the Heart Grows Wise on the Spiritual Path* a wonderful story of how a man, after returning from a Buddhist retreat, maintained an exemplary, peaceful state of loving enlightenment for six glorious months... until his mother came to visit.

There went the *titiksha*.

Anytime we are overcome by a desire, thought, or emotion (like the Buddhist thrown off center by old patterns with his mother), our mind is no longer under control. We have to eat, but we must control the desire for food, rather than the desire controlling us. If the desire controls us we have lost autonomy over own thoughts and mental energies. The everyday mystic needs disciplined mental energies to move forward on the path; that is why *shama* is so important on the list of aptitudes for the spiritual aspirant.

Dama is the fourth of the six aptitudes. *Dama* is the conscious mental and physical control of the senses. *Dama* is a natural extension of the mind control of *shama*. Once we have control of the mind we can then exert control over the mental and physical effects of the sensory input coming into the mind.

We constantly perform conscious rational control of the effects of our senses in our daily activities. We resist sneezing while someone is speaking. We do not scratch our groins in front of others. We skip second helpings of the rhubarb pie. We don't drink to drunkenness. *Dama* is important for the Seeker because giving ourselves over to the allure of the senses drops us into a consciousness tied to the temporary illusions of the physical world.

Some ways in which we may use *shama* to instill the sense control of *dama*:

- ॐ Be aware in the moment of the effect our senses might be having.
- ॐ Indulge our senses to satisfy needs rather than desires. Have sex to cement and deepen a loving and respectful relationship, not to fulfill a craving for an orgasm. Eat to keep the body healthy and strong, not for the feeling of fullness in the belly or the tastes of fat and sugar on the tongue.
- ॐ Satisfy the senses through uplifting stimuli such as feasting our eyes on great art or on a beautiful sunrise, preparing delicious and nutritious meals for ourselves or loved ones, or by drinking in the fragrance of the flowers in the garden while we tend the soil.
- ॐ Keep the senses actively engaged in non-harmful pursuits so we may continue our work. Use *asana* to occupy the body while clearing the mind. Burn incense, chant *mantra*, or focus on the breath during meditation.
- ॐ Consciously direct our senses to serve a higher purpose, such as watching uplifting movies that move us closer to illumination.
- ॐ Limit our activities to those that contribute to bringing merit to the world and that propel us further on the path of *dharma* (calling).

We shouldn't suppress our physical needs and desires to meet some borrowed notion of "holiness." My Teacher points out that suppression does not make human drives go away. We are physical beings that need to eat, sleep, and have the company of our own kind. The trick is to satisfy our needs without moving

The Four Pillars

into excess and senseless indulgence.

The fifth of the aptitudes of the *shat sanpatis* is *uparati*, performing, in a constant state of contentment, only those actions required by necessity or those actions intended to foster spiritual growth.

A friend recently returned from a visit to a place she had been gone from for years. She saw many old friends in their homes. She shared an observation that has stuck with me: "The people were the same, except they had a lot more *stuff*."

When we fill our lives searching for pleasure and *stuff*, we divert our energies away from the spiritual path. *Uparati* asks us to examine our own spiritual growth.

Uparati means not being led by our noses to seek the source of sweet smells; or by our tongues for the next taste treat; or by our eyes staring hypnotically at the latest big screen television. *Uparati* means leaving distracting desires behind in favor of building a gracious home for your soul. *Uparati* means dropping the use of *things* to define us and instead focusing, through all of our actions, on the polishing of our spirits. *Uparati* means living with joy in the present moment, not wanting more in the vain hope of gaining some sense of security. Have *enough* nice clothes, enough food, enough friends, and a big enough home. But we should not strive to acquire *more* than enough.

> "*Samadhana*—the development of one-pointed concentration which is continually directed towards the person's life goal."
>
> —A Teacher

An end goal of sorts, *samadhana*, the sixth aptitude, is focused peaceful concentration or, literally, "dispelling disturbance." *Samadhana* is an active, ongoing practice. It is fine to rest in peaceful concentration or meditation in a cave or on the island of the mystic monk, but can the aspirant remain centered and calm on a London subway or while caught up in a riot?

Samadhana and *samadhi*, the Eighth Limb of Yoga, are both variations of the same *Sanskrit* root word. *Samadhana* is the active maintenance of the blissful state of mind, *samadhi*.

The Monk Who Howled Like a Wolf

In Chapter 2, verse 54 of the *Gita*, Arjuna asks Krishna what someone established in perfect meditation looks like. Krishna responds in verses 55-59 with a list of the attributes of someone practicing *samadhana* to attain *samadhi*: Undisturbed by discomfort; free from desire; free from extreme emotions such as passion, fear, and hate; thoughtful; without sentimentality; without gloating, mourning, or hatred; and non-attached to worldly objects and pleasures.

S*amadhana* rests upon the mastered qualities of the other five aptitudes of the third pillar: *Shraddha* (faith in your yogic journey); *titiksha* (non-attachment to the good or the bad); *shama* (control of your mind to remain peaceful even in adversity); *dama* (control of the effects of the senses on your awareness); and *uparati* (peaceful focus only on actions of necessity or to further spiritual growth).

The last of the four essential pillars of the *Sadhana Chatushtaya* for the spiritual seeker is *mumukshutva*: An intense desire to gain enlightenment. *Mumukshutva* is the drive behind all of this inner work. Without the desire to transcend *karma*, gain enlightenment, and move past physical existence, the Four Pillars are meaningless. Why cultivate the non-attachment of *vairagya* if we are anxious to linger on the physical plane as long as possible? However, if we yearn for the expanded consciousness that is the core subject of this book, the rest of the three pillars are logical extensions and manifestations of that goal.

CHAPTER TEN

Practices & Techniques

A young couple, Jerry and Sybil, were attentive new students of the Denver Satsang. They were actively involved in my Teacher's classes, learning all they could about Kriya Yoga, and among the first of many from Denver to sign up for the annual autumn Retreat with Kriyananda in Illinois just outside of Woodstock. I went too, trying to outlast David Lipschutz's perpetual lotus pose or whatever was going on under the prayer shawl... and also attending Kriyananda's talks.

The Denver contingent took their meals together at one of the large round tables in the cafeteria. One afternoon Jerry and Sybil caught me alone at the table. They were anxious to talk to me about something, but took a few minutes to broach the subject.

Jerry started out carefully.

"Norman, what did Kriyananda mean when he said that we shouldn't talk to each other about the yoga cities?"

"Yoga *cities*?"

"Yeah, that's what he said!" Sybil burst in. " He said that he knew some of us were telling others about the yoga cities and that we should stop."

It took me a moment or two to understand. "Oh! I get it.

'Yoga *siddhis*,' not 'cities.' *Siddhis*." I couldn't help smiling. "Yoga *siddhis* are spiritual abilities that people on the path sometimes develop or have happen to them spontaneously. You know, like telepathy, out of body experiences, levitation and such. He doesn't want anyone bragging about *siddhis* and making others feel inadequate. He wasn't talking about a place where all the yogis go to live."

"Oh, *siddhis*," Sybil broke in. "That makes more sense. See, I had that funny vibration thing happen while I was meditating, remember we told you about it at breakfast? And he said that talking about our yoga *siddhis* might cause hard feelings. Oh, that makes a lot more sense than cities."

Jerry continued, "And our Teacher said yesterday that he thought Kriyananda sometimes astral travels during Retreats to check on his disciples. So when Kriyananda said he knew that some of us had been bragging we wondered if he'd been checking up on us."

Sybil said, "I never should have talked about that vibration thing. Now I feel like we're in trouble with Kriyananda. He *had* to be talking about me."

"Hey," I tried to be soothing, "Kriyananda knows that if two hundred yogis get together that someone out there is talking about yoga *siddhis*. He doesn't have to astral travel to get that prediction right. Anyhow, if he stopped in to check on you I bet he could tell that your hearts are in the right place."

"Really?"

"I wouldn't worry about it."

I liked the idea of the yoga cities though. Sandalwood incense wafting on the warm breeze; a constant Deva Premal *mantra* soundtrack whispering through the trees; Babaji materializing palaces right and left. I'd like to retire to the yoga cities when I am ready to hang up my blanket.

> "The whole purpose of any spiritual path is to get in touch with what you really are: *Atman*. We are immortal."
>
> —A Teacher

Practices & Techniques

Remember the novice monk that howled like a wolf during meditation and yet walked on water? That story demonstrates that the mystic must discover her own techniques in the end, but a Kriyaban's development is reinforced with the regularity of a daily practice that is simple, satisfying, and repeatable.

There are basic Kriya practices to get the mystic started. First, mind and attitude must be prepared to create a fertile ground for spiritual growth. The *yamas* and *niyamas* of the Eight Limbs are an important part of this mental preparation. They encourage the moral framework that allows the aspirant to focus on spiritual development. Some serious initiates also practice food, speech, and even sleep fasts to train the mind to do the spirit's bidding.

Meditation is the essential centerpiece of the Kriyaban's practice, but first the physical body must be convinced to cooperate. Yoga poses are a good route for some to gain mastery over a restless body. Kriya teachers tend towards *Hatha* yoga for teaching *asanas*, but each student must seek the discipline that works for them. Jogging for two miles, a walk, or doing your morning crunches may be all the preparation your body needs before going to the meditation mat.

Other elements of a practice may include *tarka*, a review of how your day went from a spiritual perspective, or the chanting or singing of *mantras* may be useful and enjoyable parts of a daily practice. In Hindu cosmology, sound is the primal energy of creation and the sounds of *mantra* focus the energy for our individual creative acts. Besides "*aum*," the most important *mantra* in Kriya Yoga is the "twelve-lettered" *Vasudeva mantra* (which doubles as *pranayama*). This is the *mantra* usually given to new initiates (*jyotis* or "auspicious lights") to Kriya Yoga.

Prana-focusing *mudras* may be part of a practice. Mudras are usually finger and hand arrangements, though they can involve some or all of the rest of the body.

Pranayama is breath control or breath exercises intended to strengthen and direct *prana* (spiritual energy). *Kundalini* energy is one manifestation of *prana*. Abundant and harnessed *kundalini* energy is thought to have the ability to quicken the pace of spiritual development. The quiet *hamsa* breath practice (in which long inhalations through the nose are internally heard as "sah" and exhalations as "ham") is considered part of basic training for the Kriyaban. My Teacher suspects that a second hidden purpose of many *mantras* is to provide *pranayama* as the structured melodies guide our breath patterns.

Included in a practice may be the study of traditional texts (such as *The Yoga Sutras of Patanjali*, the *Bhagavad Gita*, the *Upanishads*, and the *Brahma Sūtras*). But don't spend all of your time reading. My teacher points out: "All the knowledge does you no good until you put it into practice."

The Kriyaban is encouraged to consider a more vegetarian diet. Kriya Yoga teaches that we are to avoid harm to *any* sentient being. Food as ingested cells is also thought to carry with it impressions of its life (and death). Relatively evolved animal cells have the potential to carry more negative imprints with them than do plant cells. These ingested imprints (such as experiences of violence, pain, gluttony, attachments and aversions) may hamper the goals of the mystic.

The Denver Teacher stresses the need for the Kriyaban to perform selfless, considered acts of service. "*Karma* yoga—probably the easiest way for most westerners to burn off *karma*," he says. "That is doing service consciously on behalf of all beings. Service without imposing—focused from wisdom and love."

My Teacher also cautions that the Kriya Yogi needs to set past misdeeds right. "Once you realize you should have done something there has to be some movement, some action, some *kriya*. It's only balanced if something is done."

Eventually, as our practice begins to bear fruit, we may find ourselves moving past the basic Kriya practices into esoteric and mystical territory (with yoga cities?). Within this mystical territory lie obscure "*kriyas*"—actions or advanced techniques to seeking enlightenment that may be transmitted directly by a traditional *Kriya guru*. Dedicated application of these *kriyas* helps to accelerate progress along the path. Along the way, we may also stumble upon *yoga siddhis*.

"To be exposed to the Teachings is a great blessing. The Teachings are always alive,

> but they come and go just like us.
> And the fact that you are here probably means that you have something to do with the lineage."
>
> —A Teacher

When we resonate with Kriya Yoga we notice changes as we realign with our new internal environment. A meditation practice may deepen creative abilities or spark insight into issues that once seemed unresolvable. As we explore the inner worlds, we may experience disembodied touch, knowing the unknowable, hearing voices, or visits from the dead. Unbidden mystical experience may come as a practice deepens. We may even feel that we can encourage and gain some control over abilities beyond the norm.

It is easy to convince oneself that natural events are somehow magical. There is a reason that the words "mad" and "mystic" are often linked together. My Teacher once had a chuckle over my "visions" of lights dancing in the air in front of me. He reminded me that I had suffered a concussion just a few weeks before and that my "visions" were a natural symptom of brain trauma.

Even without concussions, the everyday mystic may at some point experience one or more of the *siddhis*—these may be unusual abilities or manifestations sparked by unconscious expressions of rising *kundalini* energy. My Teacher explains, "*Siddhis* are givers of insight, wisdom, and prophecy... changing size and weight; manifesting, obtaining, controlling, and the ability to transform elements."

It's important not to take these *siddhis* personally or to get sidetracked by a pursuit of glitzy spiritual trophies. The *siddhis* are the spark of electric discharge as we walk across the carpet. The spark is interesting and startling, but we have more important things to do with electricity than shocking the tip of our friend's nose. The energy behind the *siddhis* can be channeled into making an elegant and enduring home for the soul. The *siddhis* themselves are not a parlor trick to entertain friends. Attachment to spiritual tricks is still attachment and as such can deepen our karmic debt.

The Denver Teacher says, "Ultimately, the yogi sought no breath and thus no mind." Meditators sometimes report becoming aware of the unforced stilling of their breath (*kevala kumbhaka*) and the feeling that their ego consciousness has been absorbed into Observer consciousness (the internal equivalent of the time my friend insisted that I had been gone from the sweat lodge). Instead of being frightening, this stilling of the breath and departure of the ego is often a peaceful and soothing experience. The masters teach that this is a state of pure *prana*.

Another milestone in the life of the everyday mystic is when they begin to understand the supremely powerful role that *karma* has had and continues to have in their life. As my Teacher says, "You realize that what you do in this life will have a profound impact on the next life."

The *sadhu* perceives *karma* as palpable—an almost physical force, like the current of a stream on a swimmer. The experienced swimmer in *karma* develops strategies for staying out of the most destructive currents so that they might survive the flood and reach the far shore.

CHAPTER ELEVEN

Gurus & Disciples

>"Gurus are different.
>They don't think like we do."
>
>—A Teacher

The word "*guru*" does not have a single clearly accepted English definition. Sometimes a *guru* in the western world is simply a coach or advisor. But for East Indians, *guru* may have more symbolic meaning such as "*dispeller of darkness*" or illuminator of the path.

When considering *gurus* we might also think of the archetypal heroic *guru* of Hinduism. The *avatar* is an advanced soul that takes a body on earth during times of darkness or ignorance in order to shed spiritual light for those who need it most. Babaji was an exceptional *mahavatar*, coming to earth in 1861 on a spiritual undertaking to resurrect a neglected Kriya Yoga tradition.

Unfortunately, the *Mahavatars* aren't offering seminars or collecting "likes" on Facebook. We need a definition for the kind of *guru* we are likely to encounter on the mortal plane in our journey of spiritual discovery.

The Monk Who Howled Like a Wolf

Sanskrit dictionaries have over a dozen entries under the word *"guru."* The definitions cluster around the large (either in the physical sense or in the sense of large achievements or extensive education) or around instruction or teaching (particularly in spiritual matters). Blending these definitions I get:

A large, loud, challenging, important, educated and respected spiritual instructor existing somewhere between mortals and the Gods.

And that's about right.

We can't talk about *gurus* in Kriya Yoga without also considering disciples. A disciple is traditionally referred to as a *shala* or *jyoti*, often translated as "initiate." A Kriya Yoga *guru* initiates the *shala* with a transfer of specific techniques for spiritual growth. In other words, the *shala* is initiated by learning one or more Kriya practices. This initiation is normally followed by months or decades of mentoring and monitoring of the student's progress, with additional Kriya techniques introduced as the student advances.

Finding a *guru* or "master" is considered by traditional teachers and texts to be one of the best ways to move forward on the path. A master in this sense (and the sense in which I use the word throughout this book) is a master of his or her craft, not a master over other people. Sometimes this *guru* or master is someone we seek and sometimes they come unbidden to us when we're ready.

What a student *thinks* they need in a *guru* and what they *really* need may be two different things. It's tempting to look for kindness, compassion, and endless patience. But what may really help is a drill sergeant to instill discipline. Knowledge comes through many forms.

A Kriya *guru* plays three roles—teacher, student, and servant. As a teacher, a *guru* may see us more clearly than we see ourselves. They can see our level of spiritual development, and can advise practices or approaches. The Denver Teacher says, "My job is to be able to attune to what *you* need."

Not surprisingly, the teacher is also the student: "To teach is to learn... I teach to gain greater understanding and to serve." The *guru* reinforces his knowledge by seeing the effects and transformations of the Teachings on disciples.

My Teacher again: "He sees the divine nature in you and is your servant." Though a guru's attention may at times seem harsh or critical, he should always be motivated by seeking a path for his students to grow in love and learning. A worthy instructor will echo my Teacher when he tells us, "I wish for you that which you seek. I will strive my best to not hold you down."

Our *guru* holds up a mirror. As with all our experiences of the external world, our impressions of the *guru* reflect aspects of our own nature. We are forced towards self-examination through our reactions to the still surface of the master. If something upsets us about the master, it is an opportunity to come to terms with that quality in ourselves. Equally, our appreciation for certain qualities in our *guru* means that we also contain those qualities, finding them personally identifiable and relevant.

In the words of my teacher, "The age old battle for *gurus*: Do we try to give them what they need? Or what they want? You end up upsetting them if you give them what they need and they don't hear you anyways and you get bad *karma*." This is the *guru's* uncomfortable choice: Practicing kindness versus firmly guiding the *shala* to the knowledge and growth that they need. The loving and courageous *guru* will do what they need to do to get us on track, even if that means taking on *karma* for any pain they trigger.

A *guru* may speak bluntly about what we are doing right and what we are doing wrong. A *guru* may tell us great stories or insist on silence. A *guru* may be flattering and thoughtful or may strip away our emotional clothing, leaving us metaphorically naked and vulnerable. And a *guru* may consider our needs more important than their own.

The Denver Teacher says, "Even if a *guru* says to call on him, there's a roaming charge." As with anything of value, the services of a *guru* come with a cost. Our *guru* sees the karmic ruts in our spiritual being. The process of restructuring our psyche may feel like open-heart surgery and even take us down the occasional dead end.

Kriyananda tells the story of asking his *guru*, Shelley, if he should devote his career to making a success of himself in the corporate world. Shelley encouraged him to do just that and for years Kriyananda labored successfully as a white-collar worker. Yet even though the promotions and high salary came easily enough, he did not feel that he was following his *dharma*. After twelve years he went back to Shelley.

Shelley replied, "Well, I guess that's the last time you ask *me* for advice!"

Did Shelley send Kriyananda down a dead end? Or was this a deliberate lesson in developing self-confidence? I don't know, but Kriyananda went on to become a Hindu priest and a *guru*, initiating thousand of disciples, most of whom in turn ask *him* for advice.

We should not follow the *guru's* every instruction without hesitation. We would be extraordinarily fortunate to find an incorruptible, fully divine, and omniscient being as our *guru*. Kriya Yoga is the mystic's path: No one can lead another to enlightenment. There are instructors that call themselves Kriya Yoga masters that perhaps are not so masterful. We must do our homework before investing ourselves emotionally or monetarily in any role model.

"Disciple," "discernment," and "discipline" all derive from the common Latin root, *discere*, "to learn." Our job in this mentoring relationship is to learn as much as possible and to make the most of our *guru's* teachings. As students, my Teacher says, "It is our job to attune to the teacher. We don't stop breathing and complain that there is no oxygen." Give the *guru* a chance to win your confidence. As in any relationship, we must jump into this fire and trust that we will come out the other side without burns.

There are limits to the knowledge and power of the *guru* although I have heard tales of *gurus* having out-of-body experiences, reaching through solid matter, conveying messages through telepathy, giving insightful past life readings, or achieving bi-location, and levitation. But even these tales revolve around teachers who need to eat and drink, will occasionally be sick or irritable, who need to sleep, and like a glass of wine now and then.

Sananda Lal Ghosh, one of Yogananda's brothers, produced an interesting and loving book about Yogananda entitled *Mejda: The Family and the Early Life of Paramahansa Yogananda*. Mejda is a nickname meaning second oldest brother—that was his placement in a family of four brothers and four sisters. Sananda Lal Ghosh was the last surviving sibling of Yogananda, dying October 10, 1979. Ghosh tells how Yogananda cajoled his well-to-do father into buying him a motorcycle with sidecar in 1911. In the book, Sananda Lal Ghosh describes how he acted as chauffer for Yogananda while barely a teenager. Ghosh writes:

> ...sometimes I drove Mejda to Sri Yukteswar's ashram; and at other times Mejda and I would ride on the motorcycle, with Sri Yukteswar in the sidecar. Everyone on both sides of the street turned to look at us!

Our *guru* may be like an older brother or a professor. While we expect a professor to be at a different level of knowledge (or awakening), we may still share conversations and jokes, and occasionally catch them in a misstep. The Denver Teacher admits, "Just because I'm here doesn't mean I don't have a lot to learn. *Gurus* don't always know what is going on."

Gurus may be slow to accept the sincerity of the seeker or may rebuff or ignore requests for assistance or guidance. My Teacher points out, "You have to ask Kriyananda three times before he will give you advice." *Gurus* find that most students like the idea of a teacher, but resist putting the teacher's advice into practice. As students we must be willing to give up control and recognize the need to change deeply entrenched patterns of behavior.

The *gurus* that I am writing about usually need payment for the services they render. This exchange may come in the form of a tithe, payment for classes, cash offerings in a bowl at the entrance to the meeting hall, or service useful to the *guru* such as preparing for Satsangs, transcribing recorded lectures, keeping the altar stocked with flowers, or organizing potlucks.

In the traditional *guru/shala* structure the disciple may leave the relationship behind at any time, but the *guru* has made a commitment to persevere with the student until that disciple achieves enlightenment. The Kriya *guru* must honor her commitment to her student for as many *lifetimes* as it takes. A wise *guru* is, of course, hesitant to accept disciples. This is a far, far greater commitment than that of marriage. It is beyond, "till death do us part" for the *guru*. In turn, the disciple should honor the etiquette and responsibilities of this relationship.

Some disciples find that they eventually no longer need the help of a *guru*. They may feel that they are ready to go out into the world alone or they may find themselves in doctrinal or mystical conflict with their teacher. "Many disciples struggle with loyalty to their *guru*," My Teacher says. "I think most people tend to go lockstep listening to a teacher. You have to find your own way. Find your own path."

> "If I could teach you this one thing,
> I would consider myself successful:
> Be fearless!"
>
> —Kriyananda

One late summer day in mountainous Denali National Park a co-worker and I rounded a corner in our work truck to see two grizzly bears a hundred feet apart foraging for berries on a tundra-clad hill above us. Seeing two bears together caught our attention because—except sows with young or pairs that come together for a couple weeks to mate—grizzlies are loners. But this was the wrong time of year for mating and both bears seemed full grown.

The darker colored bear, furthest up the slope, abruptly pulled her head out of the bushes and surged down the open hillside directly towards the lower, blonde bear. The blonde bear immediately wheeled away from the attacker and an epic chase ensued. The bruins barreled down the open hillside until the lead bear pushed through low brush onto the gravel road behind us. It made an abrupt course change and began running straight down the road toward our truck. It was beautiful and awe-inspiring to look in the rear view mirror and see two massive grizzlies, in thick fall coats, galloping full bore down the road, the bear in front seemingly fleeing for his life.

We sat still in the safety of the large truck as the bears passed down the middle of the road like a hairy, rippling storm front. Averaging over twenty miles per hour for a quarter mile (we followed from a discrete distance), the lead bear veered off into flat tundra as the pursuing bear closed the gap. Despite the blonde's last zigzag effort, the muscled dark bear caught up and a brief scuffle ended with the dark bear holding the light bear's neck between her teeth. She held this pose for a few seconds while the blonde bear crouched motionless. Then the dark bear released her grip and walked stiffly away.

I was relieved to see a harmless end to the fracas. Grizzlies will kill other grizzlies, but it was obvious now that we had seen a sow getting assertive with her nearly full-grown cub. It was time for Blondie to leave the nest, but he didn't feel ready for the break from momma.

Sometimes our grizzly has to let us know it's time to leave and sometimes we figure it out on our own.

The Monk Who Howled Like a Wolf

CHAPTER TWELVE

The Thornapple Tree

A robed yogi walked through the forest, her short reddish brown hair shining in the occasional patch of sunlight. She paused briefly when she heard a wailing cry for help through the dense trees and brush, then hurried toward the dreadful commotion.

The yogi soon came upon a man hugging a Thornapple tree, the sharp thorns piercing his bleeding flesh. Even his face, twisted in anguish, was pressed against the spines.

"Can you help me? I am in such pain!"

The yogi said, "I will help you and we can relieve your pain, but you must listen carefully, and do everything that I say. Can you do that?"

"Yes! Yes! I can do that, I promise you. Just tell me what to do!"

"Okay," said the yogi, "the first thing you must do is to stretch your right arm out to the side like this."

And the woman demonstrated, lifting her arm away from her body until it was stretched straight away from her side.

The man obeyed, crying with pain as the thorns pulled loose from his flesh, but it was obvious that he'd shed some of his burden.

"Oh, that is so much better, kind guru. Thank you for freeing my arm, but surely there is more that you can do for me now? I am still in such agony."

"Yes, I can do more for you. Next, you must do the exact same thing with your other arm. Like this..."

The yogi then showed the man how to pull his left arm from the tree.

Once again the relief was immediate, but the man, his cheek and body still pressed into the sharp thorns, said, "So much better, wise guru, but surely there is more yet you can do to release me from the endless suffering I have endured? Will you not take all this pain away?"

"I shall do my best to serve you, sir, but you must do exactly as I say. All right?"

"Yes, yes, Master! I shall do as you say. You are so much wiser than I, how could I doubt your words?"

"Very good. Now then, take three steps backwards and I am certain you will feel better immediately." The yogi demonstrated this last movement towards freedom. Moments later the man had backed away from the tree and its cruel thorns.

Grateful, the man cried out, *"Oh, no more pain! I feel so much better! You must be very wise, oh, magnificent guru."*

But then the man's expression turned from joy to suspicion, and he lunged again to the Thornapple tree, clinging to it even more tightly than before.

He snarled at the yogi, *"You just wanted my Thornapple tree for yourself!"* And he began to cry again with renewed pain.

The yogi shook her head sadly and walked back into the peaceful green forest, leaving the man alone with his tree.

Sukha-anuśayī rāgaḥ
Attachments develop from the experience of pleasure.

—*The Yoga Sutras of Patanjali*; Book 2, Verse 7

The Thornapple Tree illustrates a dynamic between *gurus* and disciples and how we often cling to actions or people that hurt us. The *yogi* in the story has the impersonal perspective of a *guru* who can see the damage done by attachments. Disciples may still insist they know better than the *guru* and they often cling to their attachments harder than ever. Attachments are not only painful, but can pull our attention away from what truly matters on our spiritual journeys.

In the traditional texts, *"ragah"* is frequently used for attachment (BG 2.64, 3.34, and 18.51 and YS 1.37, 2.03, 2.07). *Ragah* is an intense desire, passion, or craving for pleasure based on past experiences of pleasure.

Even attachment to the "good" things in life, such as our loved ones, is bad if our goal is peace of mind. My Teacher says, "All is change. All the people in your life will leave at some point or you will leave them." The *Gita* points out that pleasures born of sense contact, like our relationships, are sources of suffering since they have a beginning and an end (BG5.22). Everything around us is temporary. Our *bodies* are temporary. Everything that we count on here will pass away and leave us dissatisfied, but our dissatisfaction is not the fault of the things and people that we have grown to count on; the letdown is the fault of our attitude towards these things.

Living in Alaska, where the sun is hidden behind the mountain ridge to the south of here for several weeks starting in early December, I can't afford to be attached to the leaves of summer when autumn comes. Winter and its implacable chill will come. I cannot set my hopes on having a year round tan or wearing sandals every day. Clinging to the transitory, whether it is a season or a lover, is one of many unhealthy attachments.

When we desire, we pull ourselves from the present moment. If we are sitting warm and comfortable on our meditation cushion, supposedly clearing our mind, but we are actually thinking about the dreaded presentation we need to do at work tomorrow, or rehearsing an uncomfortable confrontation we expect with the next door neighbor, we are not listening to the still, quiet voice of Self.

Want may advance aggressively into the attachment of greed with caustic effect on relationships. Any dependency on other human beings for our happiness will eventually result in disappointment. No one dedicates herself or himself wholly to another's happiness.

Someone jumps into the sea, clutching an anchor.

I love this *koan*. Haven't we all clutched an anchor and jumped into a sea, refusing to let go as we drown?

The Buddha taught that all desire equals suffering. *All* desire. All is temporary in the physical world. We want events to go the way that we imagine them, but find ourselves in pain because almost nothing works out as expected.

Attachment can also obscure reality—we fixate on illusions while under the hold of greed and fear. We judge without truly knowing, and form prejudices based on our judgments. We blind ourselves to the spiritual reality behind the illusions of this physical world. Attachments clamor at us for attention, fill us with the stress and striving to grasp ever more, convince us that this physical world is all there is, nudge us towards a fear-based perspective, and turn us from a spiritual point-of-view. We strive to attain and hang on to things, only to find out, sooner or later, that these things have not prepared us for what comes *after*.

Attachments may ensnare even the yogi. My Teacher says, "Many people have been lost pursuing the powers." There is a danger of losing our moral compass in pursuit of the power in yoga *siddhis*. If yoga *siddhis* come, we shouldn't hang onto them or get caught up in how clever and powerful they make us feel. The *siddhis* are merely a side effect of something much more splendid and grand.

Attachment/*ragah* comes down to two core motivations familiar to us all—attraction and aversion. These two seemingly opposing motivating principles are well known and discussed in both the ancient texts and by advertising firms—this is how we are manipulated and induced to make poor decisions, both with our wallets and with our souls.

The Denver Teacher says, "Attraction and aversion are the great obstacles in yoga—you go back and forth between those two like a ping pong ball."

Attraction comes in many forms, of course: The greed for more; compulsive gratification of the senses or emotions; the

The Thornapple Tree

idea that something new will make us happy; even a desire for self improvement attracts us like moths to a flame.

Aversions (*dvesha*) are based on sensory input (such as pain) and powerful illusions and misperceptions maintained by the ego. These illusions include the perception of the universe as hostile and meaningless, the sense that there is never enough for individual survival, and the deadly illusion of death.

Think of attraction and aversion as two dogs on leashes, one held in your left hand, one in your right. You are walking along a narrow trail. On one side are thick and thorny brambles; on the other side is a pond, covered with thin ice. One dog sniffs something interesting in the brambles and keeps tugging at its leash—and you—desperate to investigate. The other dog, also smelling some creature in the brambles, fears the worst and tries to rush away, out onto the thin ice. Either one of these dogs can pull you into disaster at any moment. You can hardly make a step forward on the trail with all the tugging and pulling in every direction. You need to leave the dog of attraction and the dog of aversion at home while walking on this path!

Attachment to spiritual growth itself is the "last nightmare" that I have mentioned before. Grasping at enlightenment is like grasping at water. Change comes when we no longer seek it, when the mind is soft and non-resisting.

Unattached.

CHAPTER THIRTEEN

The Woman at the River

> "You are already the sun.
> You are already the universe.
> What is there to get?
> It's about getting rid of things."
>
> —A Teacher

A well-known master from a monastery high in the mountains was on a long journey with one of his students. They had traveled far, stopping at centers for ascetics and isolated villages along the way. Everywhere they went people crowded into tapestry-lined halls to hear what the master had to say about the rules of his Order and about enlightenment.

On this day, the two pilgrims descended into a steep-sided valley of potato and barley fields divided by piled rock walls. They needed to cross a cold stream in order to make their way to an abbey high on the slopes beyond. At the edge of the pebbled bank they found a beautiful young woman standing by the ford, hesitating at the high water. Remembering his vows not to consort with women, the young student kept his gaze averted from this terrible temptation.

The Monk Who Howled Like a Wolf

His master, however, stopped at the woman's side. To the astonishment of the student, this revered and famous teacher bent to take the woman in his arms, gesturing with a nod of his head for the flabbergasted student to carry her things across the river. With the smell of mysterious perfumes from her clothing bag making his eyes water, the student grudgingly followed his master through the cold stream.

He watched as the young woman stole a quick glance up into the Master's face, an involuntary "Ah!" escaping her lips as she saw the one blue eye and realized that this was the famous mystic monk showing her such kindness. After setting the grateful woman down safely on the far bank, the master went striding on again, up the trail.

Puzzled by the unseemly behavior of his unorthodox instructor, the student lagged behind and pondered these events as if chewing on a koan. How could his Master have taken the beautiful woman into his arms back at the stream? She had been so young and so desirable. How could the howling monk break the rules of the Order and embrace a woman?

After many miles the student was unable to remain silent and hurried to the side of the older man.

He asked, "Master, how could you of all people—you, the one that so many students on the path look up to—how could you have held that young woman in your arms and carry her across the stream?"

The master stopped to face his student with a gentle smile.

"She was *beautiful, wasn't she? But I put that woman down miles ago. I think you carry her still."*

The Woman at the River is a teaching story about attachment and non-attachment. The master shows us that non-attachment is defined not so much by what we do in the outer world as by what we do in our inner world.

I use the compound word, "non-attachment" rather than "detachment." Detachment makes me picture emotionless androids, insensitive to the suffering of others. Detachment is a lack of feeling. Non-attachment is the negation of attachment—a lack of desire. When we say we don't want to be hot, we aren't saying that we want to be cold. What we want to be is non-hot—somewhere in the middle. Attachment and detachment are opposites on a scale of possibilities. Somewhere in the middle is non-attachment: Not clinging to things.

There is a similar Sanskrit term used in the *Narada Bhakti Sutras* (a text of the *Bhakti* school of devotional yoga), *sangatyagah*, which means renunciation of attachment.

Although Kriya Yoga is not about living in poverty or doing without material goods like the "sky-clad" yogis of India, it is crucial to relinquish attachment to the worldly matters (physical, emotional, intellectual, and spiritual) that surround us. This non-attachment needs to be applied to the "things" of the mind and ego such as revenge, love, greed, aspiration, jealousy, and anger. Non-attachment includes anything, physical or mental, that we might grasp out of attraction or in response to an aversion.

Non-attachment is indicated in *The Yoga Sutras* and the *Bhagavad Gita* with the Sanskrit words *samācara* and *vairāgyam*.

Why do I think is *vairāgyam*/non-attachment a good thing? There is the obvious answer hinted at in *The Woman at the River*: Extremes of anything tend to be uncomfortable places to be. The extremes of attachment and detachment both have significant downsides in terms of peace-of-mind and in our interactions with others. The Teacher demonstrates the extremes to his classes by spreading both arms, palms towards us, as in crucifixion. He then brings both hands together in front of his chest, palm to palm, with the fingers pointing up to demonstrate being centered—the balanced and receptive state of being.

Just as being in the middle between hot and cold is more comfortable, being non-attached is a more balanced state than attachment or detachment. We may shatter the chain that links happiness with success. Pleasure must be in the opportunity to work and not in a reward when the task is done. My Teacher says, "If I lose my job tomorrow, why should I be upset? Absolutely nothing should be clung to."

Non-attachment allows us to see the triviality of the every day irritations we all deal with. Non-attachment helps us to live in the present and to see things with the eyes of a child. That pile of dry autumn leaves may be hard work, mean dirt under the fingernails, and bring a backache, or it could be a source of pleasure and beauty. Non-attachment allows a fresh perspective.

Non-Attachment may bring increasing contentedness as we leave swings of emotion behind, and live increasingly in the present moment, with a life simplified. As the old joke goes:

Henry David Thoreau: Simplicity, simplicity, simplicity!
Ralph Waldo Emerson: I would have thought one "simplicity" would have been enough.

When we are non-attached, the link between material goods and our happiness is broken. It becomes gradually easier to walk away from the new toys of our civilization and even discard or give away the physical baggage that is weighing us down on this journey. Freedom fills the storage space thus emptied. Non-attachment can deliver us from the mood swings that plague and complicate our relationships. Non-attachment is our counsel to remain silent when the ego is making a racket.

My Teacher repeats a quote, "I feel much better now that I have given up hope. Now I can stop thinking about the future [unattributed]." The quote contains an important truth: Hope is a passive attachment to an imagined future outcome. The contentedness that non-attachment brings—with its simplicity, emotional balance, and living in the moment—has a very important spiritual side effect... a *siddhi* of sorts according to the Teacher, "If you are content you will bring good things to yourself."

When we are content, the creative power of the mind becomes more focused and the world may resonate with us now because now *we* are resonating. We are no longer a cacophony of unrealized expectations and bellowing insecurities. We now broadcast the long, clear note of the creative power of consciousness.

Non-attachment holds the promise of spiritual evolution by bringing enhanced insight, freedom of perception and movement, and expanding awareness. How does insight come with non-attachment? Non-attachment neutralizes the

The Woman at the River

attachments that cloud our perceptions and the ability to see things as they really are.

Non-attachment to suffering, to pleasure, to the external, and to the results of our actions is considered vital on our quest towards expanded consciousness. Ancient traditions and modern teachers go so far as to link non-attachment to the quality of our journey after physical life ends. In his fine book, *The Tibetan Yogas of Dream and Sleep*, the Tibetan Buddhist Tenzin Wangyal Rinpoche links grasping and aversion as hurdles to be overcome in order to remain present and undistracted in the *bardo* (to Tibetan Buddhists, the *bardo* is the first spiritual realm encountered after death). The non-attached spirit is more likely to remain aware and in control of their fate than the soul who acts under the influence of attachments, drawn into a grasping fantasy of dream-like visions.

The Monk Who Howled Like a Wolf

CHAPTER FOURTEEN

Is That So?

One day a mob of villagers crowded about the Master's simple home on the edge of the woods. A woman shook her fist at the monk while holding a bundle to her chest with the other arm.

"You have fathered a child with my innocent daughter! You have ruined her fine reputation and brought dishonor on your Order!"

The monk blinked and said quietly, "Is that so?"

"Yes, it is so, you old Billy goat! She is marked with this unnatural red hair just as you are marked with that crazy blue eye! You wanted to be a father. Here, now you are a father! Here is your daughter!" And the furious woman thrust a bawling wad into the master's arms.

The monk looked down at the infant girl. "Is that so?"

Before the angry people left some of the young boys tore down one of the walls of his hut and scattered his rice among the eager chickens.

The master surveyed the ruin of what had been his peaceful

The Monk Who Howled Like a Wolf

home since he left the mountain monastery to teach among the valley people. He rocked the child and began humming a mantra until the girl stopped crying. She was not so young as he had thought at first—she was almost old enough to walk. Her reddish brown hair was thick, but cut short, like a monk. He looked for something to feed her.

Over a year went by and most of the villagers shunned the disgraced master, but the girl thrived, and she and the monk were company for each other. Now life was less comfortable for the graying master because not so many local people came to him for instruction and advice as before. The offerings were fewer, but he had his garden and pilgrims still sought him as stories were still told of the mystic in far places.

As soon as she began to speak the girl started to call him "Da-da."

The monk didn't correct her. He just said, "Is that so?"

Almost two years later, the monk was in his vegetable garden, the spring weeds thick in the rows. The girl played in the flowers nearby. The master looked up to see a group of villagers carrying baskets and packages, approaching him with their heads respectfully bowed. At the front of this group was the same woman that had been so angry with him before.

"Sir, I have done you great harm. I beg you to forgive me." She could not meet his eyes and, trembling, she stared at the ground. "My daughter confesses that you were not the father of my grandchild after all. She lied to hide her shame."

"Is that so?"

"Yes, it is so, good Master. We do not deserve your forgiveness, but we have brought you a few gifts."

"Is that so?"

She gestured commandingly at the same boys who had scattered his rice for the hungry chickens. The boys set down bags of grains and blankets and other packages wrapped in brown paper carefully tied with string. There was more in the pile than the master had ever hoped for or ever wanted to have.

"Now, we will take my granddaughter. It was so wrong of me to burden you with her. You won't have to care for her or see her ever again."

Is That So?

"Is that so?" the master said, a little more quietly than before.

That afternoon the Master found himself alone. He meditated for hours without having to stop even once to care for the child. The hut was silent that night.

But the next day the grandmother and her sheepish daughter came back, led by the tear-streaked girl.

"Master, this child spends all her time crying for you. The silly thing believes you are her father after all."

"Is that so?"

And that afternoon, and most afternoons to follow, the Master tended his garden while the happy girl played nearby, her unusual auburn hair shining in the sunlight. Soon the grandmother and her daughter asked to become students of the Master, saying that he was the wisest and strongest man that they had ever met.

The Master just said, "Is that so?"

Teachers and sources from my instructor to Pema Chodron, from the *Bhagavad Gita* to *Be Here Now*, mention eighteen attributes of the non-attached being.

The ancient texts tell us that the non-attached person doesn't dwell on the past and carries no baggage with them. They are not tangled up in any *thing* of this world. Things include social entanglements and excessive obligations that prevent flexibility of action and movement. They are always free to do what is best for their spiritual development. They also have an internal tranquility that is not distracted by external sensual attractions and aversions.

Instead of looking towards the past, this non-attached person lives in the present moment. My Teacher says that we need to have the ability to have everything come to a stop in a single breath. And for the span of that single breath, everything is fine in the world. The non-attached live more and more in that single breath.

The non-attached do not feel that they have to *do* anything. The importance of this attribute is stressed in the *Gita* with its focus on reducing or avoiding *karma* (derived from actions in the world). Less doing means less acting and less *karma*.

"If your joy is self-derived... there is no need for action."

—*Bhagavad Gita*; Chapter 3, Verse 17

The non-attached should have no expectation of profit from their actions. For the non-attached the key is their attitude toward action, not an imagined reward as a result of those actions.

Not surprisingly, having no desires is a quality of the non-attached. Summarized from Chapter 6 of the *Bhagavad Gita*, characteristic of yogis is non-attachment to the objects of the senses (BG6.04, 08), no cravings (BG6.10), longings, or selfish desires (BG6.18, 24). And from later in the *Gita*, "...conquering attachment... with desires deflected. Released from the dualities of happiness and suffering (BG15.05)."

Neither the "good" nor the "bad" things in life rile the rare non-attached individual. The non-attached are not unbalanced by good or bad fortune. Often, the one hides behind the other. Knowing that good and bad offer nothing real to the immortal spirit, the master in the story was not stirred by the things happening to him. If we lose our balance at good fortune we are just as misled by the *maya* of the physical world as when the "bad" things in life upset us. The *Gita* says, "Remain the same in success and in no success." (BG2.48)

The non-attached being is also peaceful, forgiving, and loving since they do not depend on the actions of others for their happiness.

The non-attached live harmoniously, changing course in a flash as circumstances dictate, but leave only a trace in their passing. They do so little to disturb the rest of us that we may not even realize that they are there, "pursuing their *dharma* without grief."

Again, the *Gita* (Chapter 6, verse 17) tells us that those who have ascended to yoga leave suffering behind. The harmonious yogi is disciplined in speech, satisfied with whatever comes of its own accord, steady of mind (Chapter 12, verse 19), and

Is That So?

without pride or bewilderment, having conquered the faults of attachment (Chapter 15, verse 05).

The non-attached master does not identify with the things of the world. Though they may stop and play for a few minutes, they don't hang onto shiny toys. In his excellent translation of the *Bhagavad Gita*, Graham M. Schweig explains the meaning of the Sanskrit term, *nirahamikara*—"without, 'I am acting'" (used in Chapter 2, Verse 71).

In a realized state, a person without the notion of 'I am acting' (*nirahamikara*) no longer identifies with anything temporary, including one's gender, family, country, race, etc., nor does one claim ownership or possession of anything (*nirmama*).

The *Gita* reinforces this message by telling us that among the characteristics of yogis is a freedom from possessiveness (BG6.10) and a lack of attachment to the home (BG12.19).

Other characteristics linked to non-attachment include the quest for knowledge: "Learned is the person whose action is both without desire and consumed by the fire of knowledge" (BG4.19). And includes freedom from extremes: "A steadfast renouncer neither hates nor desires and is without duality (*nirdvandvo*), easily freed from the bondage of action" (5.03). Non-duality/*nirdvandvo* means that we are not subject to or influenced by extremes of emotion or sensation.

The non-attached is also ego-less as indicated in Chapter 2, verse 71, "The results of enlightenment: Freedom from worldly longings, the sense of 'mine,' and the notion of 'I am acting." Again in Chapter 6, "Characteristic of yogis—thought and self subdued." (BG6.10)

My Teacher says, "Renunciation is not renunciation of life. It is renunciation of the ego." To be ego-less is not to withdraw from all of the things of this Earth. The ego can be controlled and still allow an effective and dynamic community life. To be ego-less means that we do not succumb to emotional impulses that interfere with our relationships. We are comfortable in whatever surroundings we find ourselves in, no matter how opulent or how meager. We do not need reinforcement from the outside world in order to feel a sense of personal value or comfort.

The Monk Who Howled Like a Wolf

Finally, the non-attached being lives in a state of bliss. You may have experienced this bliss for periods or moments in your life—an ecstatic joy that comes from within. This bliss needs no external fueling, but wells up inside until the heart is overflowing with diffuse love and all is good in the world, even while the bills go unpaid, the baby is colicky, and the sky turns gray with clouds. For most of us these moments of bliss are fleeting or last for ten or twenty minutes on a good day, but for the accomplished non-attached being (the modern mystic), it is more and more a stable feature of their life.

CHAPTER FIFTEEN

Watch Your Adverbs!

In early 2015 I received excellent advice from my freelance editor, Erica, on the first two chapters of the initial ponderous 550-page manuscript of this book. At the time I was reading Jim Harrison's book, *True North*. You might not think that Erica's editing and my reading for pleasure would directly interact, but they did.

Harrison's absorbing novel follows decades in the life of one man. He toils for two of these decades writing a non-fiction book. He can't seem to find an approach to his subject that he is comfortable with, but he has huge amounts of source material and keeps on writing and writing and writing. Eventually he has a thousand pages of rambling, pedantic, lecturing, tedious text.

Knowing he is in over his head, he asks a poet to edit the stack for him.

Anxiously he waits for her thoughts and opinions. They come a few days later in the form of a short note.

"You have about thirteen good pages in here."

Back to Erica: With her first batch of careful edits she included a multi-page assessment of the "project." The assessment is filled with many technical details, and some of her philosophy about the writing process, but what caught my eye can be paraphrased into a few of my own imagined sentences.

"Norm, for whom are you writing? I presume that you are trying to write an intertwined personal narrative of spiritual discovery for the person with a mild interest in yoga, but who doesn't know much about it. A book filled with anecdotes and stories, and light on the jargon and obscure details that only the true believer would be interested in.

And watch your adverbs!"

"An '*intertwined personal narrative of spiritual discovery*?'" I thought. " There's been some kind of mistake: I'm writing a reference book. *Nobody* writes 'intertwined personal narratives' about Kriya Yoga! *Nobody* has done that with Kriya Yoga!"

Then the obvious thought hit my painfully dull awareness. I spoke out loud, "Nobody, except Yogananda..."

The Paramahansa Yogananda from the wall of A Teacher's Kriya Yoga Center of Denver. The very same Yogananda I have revered and looked up to for many years. The Yogananda who published *Autobiography of a Yogi* in 1946—the book that did more to spread awareness of Kriya Yoga in the western world than anything before or since. Millions have read that book.

The next day I got started on the re-write.

And I'm watching my adverbs.

> "To start the process of non-attachment,
> you ought to know what your life philosophy is."
>
> —A Teacher

In our magnificent Western world the point of life is to get stuff. At the core of my culture's programming is the message that if I work hard and cleverly, I will earn all the trappings of an upper middle class life, never be hungry, never be poor, and have all the sex I want. That message walks hand in hand with the apocalyptic warning to expect poverty and loneliness if I relax my guard or interrupt my striving.

I wasn't told very often that having a rich soul is more important than being famous. I wasn't told that it is better to have love in my life than a car in a garage. I wasn't told that it is

Watch Your Adverbs!

better to have compassion for people than passion for things.

Instead we are told that our jobs, homes, relationships, gadgets, and even pets define us. Without the things we have, who are we? Tell someone they need to get rid of their stuff and they feel like you are asking them to cast loose into interstellar space without a space suit. That trust in God stuff is fine for a Mohammed or a Buddha or Jesus, but this is the real world and in the real world we need stuff to survive.

What programming have you accepted as truth? What limitations do you lug about?

We make a home here on planet Earth because our egos tell us that this is all there is. We dig in defenses. We hang on. Our egos react to attractions and aversions by generating emotions that cloud our judgment. These emotions push us ever further away from non-attachment to the physical world.

Yet the Denver Teacher asks, "Why are you making a home *here*? If you believe in the immortality of your spirit, you will accept change. If all is change, and you relate to that and you subscribe to that, how can you be attached to anything?"

We must be clear with ourselves as to why we are looking to walk the non-attached path. Non-attachment without a spiritual basis for that practice is dangerous. One of the core values of Kriya Yoga is that this physical world and all it contains is not our true "home." To dig in and build a home here, surrounding ourselves with all of these things in a mistaken belief that they will make us "safe," is missing the point: We are here for our *enlightenment*. Consider that word, "enlightenment." It is not a stretch to suggest that part of the process of enlightenment is to *lighten* our load. We lighten our load so that we may take flight from this nest when we are ready.

> "Look at the things you are attached to now—
> the good and the bad.
> How many of them are ego-oriented?"
>
> —A Teacher

Much of what drives our individual attachments comes

through our unconscious drives and insecurities. These weapons of ego fly under the radar—influencing us profoundly. Dealing with the creations of ego is a precondition of becoming non-attached. How do we uncover these unconscious drives and insecurities?

My Teacher says it starts in the meditative state. Kriya Yoga uses the stillness of meditation to see the grasping and fear that drives us to attachment. When we see these patterns with greater clarity they often evaporate in the light of examination. If attachments persist, conventional therapy or analysis may ferret out and neutralize their root causes. However, we must be on guard against the tendency to relive our traumas endlessly. I have found that my friends have less tolerance for stories about my difficult bosses and ex-girlfriends than I do, while I never seem to tire of the process of telling and re-telling these stories. Talk therapy goes nowhere if the lessons, benefits, and pain of our experiences aren't processed and left where they belong—in the past. The goal is to leave our ex-girlfriends behind, not to let them live on in our heads, rent-free. Consider consciously releasing your traumas with a ceremony or an affirmation.

My Teacher says, "Realize how affected you are by your childhood, then let it go. Stop talking about it. If you stop talking about it, eventually you stop thinking about it."

> The undisciplined elephant [the ego]
> swings its trunk and grabs things.
> The *mahout* [*guru*] gives the elephant
> a bamboo pole [the *mantra*]
> to keep the elephant busy and out of trouble.
>
> —Teaching Metaphor

We can consciously counteract our attachments once we uncover them. When we feel fear or attachment gaining hold, *mantra* can be used until the vulnerable moment passes.

Consistently derailing the mind as soon as it starts down the attachment path may be effective. When we anticipate the grasping of the ego we can do what parents of young children

Watch Your Adverbs!

do—distract. Find something else to think about, do a chore, write that message, clean the car, do some yoga, listen to sacred music, watch a comedy.

We have these tools to neutralize the ego's moves away from non-attachment—meditation, analysis or therapy, the conscious release of past trauma, the conscious counteraction of attachments, strengthening the spirit, and starving the ego.

Remember the Thornapple tree? My Teacher says, "First you have to recognize, 'I am clutching this thorn bush.' Recognize your own Thornapple tree. Be conscious of your attachments." What if we could remove even the roots of our personal Thornapple trees?

It is not enough to catalog attachments, although it is an enormously promising start. We must also dig up the roots of these attachments so that they do not continually sprout new growth. *Why* do we need to have lots of food in the house? *Why* do we insist on receiving gifts in order to feel loved? *Why* must we have alone time every day in order to stay on an even keel? We are gardeners weeding our plots. If we just pull the tops off the weeds, new shoots will reappear in a few days. But if we pull up the roots of the invasive plants, the tasty vegetables we like will grow strong and fast.

> "You can practice non-attachment even in your dream state,
> if you are aware enough.
> What are the limits really?
> They are self-imposed."
>
> —A Teacher

Spiritual practice is a powerful tool for fostering non-attachment. We plant the seeds for conscious non-attachment in our meditations and reinforce the value of non-attachment through our spiritual studies. The *Gita* and the *Yoga Sutras* encourage us in this process. As each day unfolds, we can catch ourselves in the act of attachment and give congratulations when we see improvement. We may look at life through a spiritual perspective and identify what serves us on the path and what holds us back. We may begin the process of letting go of obstacles and devoting increasing energy to what nourishes.

Contentment lies in the inner life rather than in external things like a new boyfriend, a two-for-one sale, or a sunny day after a week of rain. The non-attached being recognizes the external as ephemeral and subject to change. What is sunny today is cloudy tomorrow. If we base our happiness on the transitory, our happiness will be transitory.

"You have to start getting rid of a lot of things in your life if you want to walk the path... you just have to do it gently."

Going lean, if it flows naturally from internal simplification, is part of non-attachment. As Kriyananda has said, "In all your getting, get rid of stuff." The Tao te Ching says, *"In the pursuit of learning, every day something is added. In the pursuit of the Tao, every day something is dropped."* (Chapter 48)

We must evaluate each thing that we allow into our lives. Is this book helpful to my spiritual growth? If I do not read this now will I be missing something that I need to hear? Will these *Mardi Gras* beads enhance my home and focus my thoughts on *samadhi*? Will these plastic bowls help me surrender to God? Will a friendship with this person sharpen my focus on enlightenment? Discrimination regarding each new item that we allow into our homes and lives is part of an effective practice of non-attachment.

> "If you resist the winter, then you are in trouble.
> Be at peace.
> That's all."
>
> —A Teacher

As I write, it is minus 27 degrees Fahrenheit outside of my cabin in Interior Alaska. I have been anything but content this winter. This is *my* winter of discontent. Across this small room, I feel the cold creeping in through the window glass and I chafe at the gross amount of clothes and protective gear I must wear to go outside. Even though I am warm enough here where I write, I dread the errand that I must run later. Will it be colder when I go

Watch Your Adverbs!

out to start the truck? Will the truck start at all? Why can't I live in New Mexico?

Living in the moment, however cold it is, is key to my non-attachment. No matter how much I dream of temperate climates, it won't change the temperature outside. Spring will come without my help. When my thoughts find a home on a past beach or in a future trip to New Mexico, I lose the present reality and its splendor.

We are spirits in body. The body is the vehicle, not the driver. The driver (spirit or soul) is allowed to borrow this vehicle for a time, but must be prepared to exit at the destination and switch cars or find some other means of transport. Too often we mistake the vehicle for who we *are*. It's great if our car looks good, but what is really important is the state of our *Selves*. When we recognize the cars as just the useful tools that they are, we take good care of them, but do not confuse our identity with them. Cars get dinged-up and scratched over time. That's okay. Focus on the spiritual reality underneath it all.

Do not build a home here on planet Earth. A grasping commitment to the physical world is the ultimate attachment. We should be comfortable, but comfortable as we are in a hotel room—without the illusion of taking-up permanent residence. We are travelers moving through this earthly landscape.

> Renouncing all actions in me...
> without longings, without a sense of "mine."
> Fight without grief.
>
> —*Bhagavad Gita*; Chapter 3, Verse 30

Finally, our actions will not contain personal attachments if they are sincerely dedicated to the divine. If we act for something greater than ourselves, all attachment to the outcome of those actions evaporates. Just as we release a gift once given, so a dedicated action becomes someone else's fruit. We do not work with efficiency and thoughtfulness to get a pat on the back or special recognition. Our work may be approached as a physical prayer, once uttered, gone. Our daily tasks are no more ours than the doll we gave to a toddler or the meal we served to a guest. We place our intentions on a respected divinity and act without attachment on behalf of that divinity.

And don't forget to watch your adverbs.

CHAPTER SIXTEEN

Dust Rising

"Emotions are a lust for things we want."

—A Teacher

Two quiet knocks on the door.
I took one quick look through a gap in the limp cotton fabric draped across the dirty glass. A crying woman with familiar brown eyes stood on the covered porch that ran the short length of my shack. She was wringing her hands against the front of her dress.

I eased the curtain closed so she couldn't see in and so I couldn't see out. I retreated into the gloomy interior of that one musty room, hardening my heart against the creeping advance of any treacherous feelings of compassion.

Listening to her bawling, I could tell she was out of options, but I wasn't going to open the door. I locked myself into the dark with my anger and bitterness.

So, she was back. The last time she had run off she was gone for so long my soul grew colder every week. Sometimes in the evenings I looked across the flat brown fields between my shack

The Monk Who Howled Like a Wolf

and the town. The buildings stood like a line of white and gray toy blocks by the muddy river, kerosene lamps flickering the little square windows with a feeble yellow light. I would wonder what she was doing and what man she was with. My fury would grow until I had to look away and swear that I would never *ever* let her in again.

So, she was back, outside my door.

Something was different now from all the other times she returned to my creaking old porch. She wasn't crying to get me to soften. She hardly ever cried; too damn proud to cry for me and she never had to. I was always chasing her, begging for attention. But this time she looked different out there in the shadows—pale and weak.

There was something new in this crying. Maybe there was a baby involved.

I didn't care if there was a baby. It sure as hell wasn't *my* baby.

So, she was back, outside my door, crying on the porch.

I knew if I let her in I would still be the older man that couldn't keep her interest. The one she said was hiding from the war in his broken down old shack. After a month or two she would just wander off again, looking for the excitement I couldn't give her. I would still need her more than she needed me. I was the one who *wanted* the most. I hated her and I hated myself for that weakness.

That old wind-up clock with the brass hand that I found at the town dump ticked louder and louder as I waited. All that tinkering to get the ticking started again, but it still couldn't keep time and now the blasted noise of the useless thing grew louder and louder in the gloom and wouldn't let me think right.

After a long time she took her crying and left my porch.

I stayed inside a little longer in case she came back.

Finally, I couldn't stand sitting and hiding in my own house. I had chickens to feed and hogs to look after. I tiptoed to the door and peeked out on an empty porch. I crept out onto squeaking boards and peaked around both sides of the shack. I scanned the tree line across the grass and the red dirt road out front.

Gone.

Again.

I got back to work and tried not to think. I tried hardest of all not to think about her.

It was best to be on my own. Being around other people got me thinking about the war. I didn't want to think about those times hunkered down in the holes trying not to hear the screams, waiting for the charge order, praying to die in bed with the war an old memory, or better yet, forgotten. It was best to just take care of my little place on the edge of the hills and visit with my buddy back in the woods. He understood what it was like fighting in the war that tore the country apart without wanting to talk about it all the time.

I never saw her again. I never even knew what happened to her. Not many people got close enough to say two words to me and I made sure it stayed that way.

I grew older. Once in a while I would look into my little mirror and curse the wrinkles and the gray and my damn homely face that wasn't good enough for her, and I'd curse the man that did bad things in the war. And I kept on living and living and living.

It's funny—I did die in bed. But it wasn't old age that got me. It was fire. Or smoke, anyhow. I kept too much paper next to the woodstove. The pile must have slipped over without me noticing.

I was dead. Finally.

*

Of course, I was born again—Australia this time, to a Norwegian father and an English mother. A sister came along and then all of us moved to join my father's brother in the United States in the Ballard neighborhood of Seattle, the Scandinavian capital of the Pacific Northwest.

I had an easy childhood, but as a young boy snatches of memories that had no place in this life floated to the surface in quiet moments. Somehow those places and times were mine and yet not mine: Standing in a trench clutching a rifle, knowing they were going to make me go out there; chickens roosting in the low branches of a tree, silhouetted by an orange sunset; the sad cramped shack; brown eyes on the porch.

As a sheltered and loved boy I still carried the scars of a bitter, miserable man. I clung to the old pain like the man who jumped into the sea clutching an anchor. I was hanging onto old desires and old fears. I still wanted and I still turned away. I was determined to resurrect my ghosts from the past.

I grew up in this new life and went to college and had some loves and lost some loves. I moved to Alaska, married, had two wonderful children—the usual story.

Around age thirty, I became driven by the need to learn all things Lakota. I wanted to be something that I wasn't. First Peoples call people like me members of the *Wannabee* tribe.

My aunt from South Dakota asked, "What is it about you that seems Indian?"

I sure didn't know. My strongest memories from before this life was of a winter tree against a sunset sky and a brown-eyed woman sobbing on the porch.

Driven by a misplaced sense of obligation to get the children closer to the grandparents, my then wife and I moved to Colorado. I had the feeling that my life was like that of a salmon driven to return home. I was pushing up against the cold and silted current of my personal Yukon, turning into the muddy tributary of the Tanana, fighting blind up the frigid grey waters of the Nenana. Onwards I pushed, restless, searching for something beyond conscious awareness. I could feel myself getting closer now to my journey's end. In my dreams animals would come to me and on a footbridge over water a woman handed me the sacred pipe.

In 1999 my wife brought me a flyer: "Make a difference this summer! Come to the Pine Ridge Reservation and perform service work at the first Boys & Girls Club on an American Indian Reservation."

I packed up my old work van with all the tools I thought might come in handy and I started the long drive (that I would repeat many times) from Gunnison, Colorado to the Pine Ridge Reservation, my final clear flowing creek.

Just south of the border from Pine Ridge Village, South Dakota, is the sad little town of White Clay, Nebraska. When I slowed the old van coming into the cluster of decrepit buildings, I saw television cameras and state troopers lining the road. Small groups of people were standing along the edges of the cracked and potholed asphalt, waiting and alert and looking north. It looked like White Clay was suspended in the calm eye of the hurricane.

What the hell am I getting into?

Determined to reach my headwaters, I drove on past the rapids of television cameras and the troopers and across the border into Pine Ridge, headed north down two miles of arrow-straight highway linking the "wet" White Clay with the "dry" Pine Ridge Village of some 7,000 souls. I passed half a dozen plastic flower-adorned crosses beneath tall highway department signs warning, "Think! Why Die?"

In Pine Ridge I found the storm when I idled past a parking lot filled with the milling blue jeans and flannel of a couple hundred people waiting for the start of a protest march on White Clay. I found the Boy's & Girl's Club on the east side of town, but I'd arrived early so I parked at the Club then walked back to the rodeo grounds and the summer powwow under a hazy blue sky and ninety degrees. Drums beating, fancy dance dresses jingling with a hundred bells, whirling bright color in the dust rising above hand-stitched moccasins. A sweating Lakota man asked me to hold part of his costume while he adjusted his leggings.

I was here!

Back at the Boys & Girl's Club parking lot, I noticed the sporty red car with Illinois plates. Inside, I met Roxanne with her familiar brown eyes.

The Monk Who Howled Like a Wolf

CHAPTER SEVENTEEN

Tawapaha Olowan

Tunkashila yapi, tawapaha kin han
Oihanke sni he najink telo
Iyohlataya, oyate kin han
Wichichagink ta cha, le chamun welo

—*Tawapaha Olowan*, the Lakota Flag Song

At the start of the second week on the Rez during that Unitarian Universalist service trip in 1999, the group had moved to Kiza Park, the ranch of the traditional White Plume family (traditional in the sense of maintaining core Lakota values from the pre-*washichu* days), north of Manderson—the country of the renown *Oglala* Lakota *wichasha wakan* (holy man), Black Elk. We were building an outdoor basketball court for the local kids.

As was my involuntary habit each morning, I woke before dawn. This morning was clear with just a hint of chill that would soon burn away as the summer day grew hotter. I rose with the idea in my head that I should climb the low hill near the lush grass clearing of tents, campers, and my van, and say the Four Winds Prayer at sunrise.

The Monk Who Howled Like a Wolf

There was one other demand insinuating into my consciousness: I should ask my new friend Roxanne to go up that hill with me. Though daunted at the thought of trying to wake her in the tent she shared with two other women, the idea wouldn't go away, so I crossed the dewy grass clearing to stoop at a large tent and whisper her name.

"Yeah?" came the sleep-clouded reply through the thin nylon.

I explained my plan to go up the hill and Roxanne said, "Give me a minute."

I turned around once on the walk back to my van to see her skipping through the tall weeds towards the outhouse in the trees.

With the eastern prairie sky growing brighter, we found the trail up the hill and soon reached the top, breathless with this dawn adventure. In the few minutes before the sun breached the pine-covered ridge to the east, I told Roxanne what I'd learned about the symbolism of the four directions: The black West where the thunder beings and the spirit world live; the white North, home of the buffalo people, where prayers for strength and endurance should be directed; East, symbolized by the color red, home of knowledge and the illumination we were about to experience with dawn; and the South, where lives trust and innocence. Even though she already knew, I mentioned the fifth direction, downwards—*Maka Ina*—Mother Earth; the sixth direction—*Wankatkiya*—the heavens looking down on us; and the seventh—*hochoka*—the center. The divine Self within us all. As the *Chandogya Upanishad* (one of the two earliest Upanishads) says: "The *Atman* is hidden in the lotus of the heart." (VIII.3.3)

In the cool pre-dawn air, I traced a circle on the sage-studded hilltop and explained to Roxanne that I would say this Four Winds Prayer in Lakota, stopping at each cardinal point, and then moving back to the center to address the fifth, sixth, and seventh directions. As the sun silhouetted the distant pines, I began the prayer in the center of my circle before moving to the West, to do honor to the spirit beings. I translated for Roxanne before moving on clockwise to the North. As I spoke the sacred Lakota words, a drumming came to us from somewhere in the near distance and a single male voice began a song: *Tawapaha Olowan*—the Flag Song, used to begin powwows, dances, even basketball games. The coincidence of hearing this song—one of only three Lakota songs I knew—there on the hilltop, at dawn, during my prayer, almost had me stumbling over my words, but I continued, feeling a power in the sage scented air. The familiar words, sung in the country of its speakers, were more powerful for me than ever before.

Prayer over, I stood in silence for a few moments before I looked to the northeast, the direction of the drumming and singing, trying to find the source. Half a mile away, in flat grassland, I saw a trailer house below us. There were no cars at the old building and I couldn't see anybody outside the trailer, but I theorized that someone might be out of sight on the other side, greeting the dawn, the words somehow carried to us there at the top of the hill through the still air.

The singer reached the end of the verses and all was quiet as the red-orange sun broke free from the horizon and began to warm our grateful skin. We enjoyed the subtle influence of the hilltop ceremony for a few more minutes before we walked back down the hill for a day of pouring concrete.

That evening, as we sat at a worn picnic table in the gathering darkness, I asked some of the local Lakota teens about the drumming and singing that we had heard from the top of the hill and if there was someone living in that trailer off in the distance. The three boys exchanged quick glances. One of them shrugged his shoulders at me. Whatever they had to say about our dawn singer they decided was better left unsaid.

The Monk Who Howled Like a Wolf

CHAPTER EIGHTEEN

Reunited

The Yoga Sutras say that relationships may be a means to experience the sensual delights of the physical world, or they may serve the purpose of spiritual liberation (YS2.18), bringing you closer to Self-realization and enlightenment. Unfortunately, sensual experience is the attractive and obvious choice. I spent years walking down dead-end paths of unhealthy sensual relationships.

"The trouble with wives or husbands is that they are true *gurus*. They show you what you don't want to see."

—Kriyananda

A good place to start the journey towards being a better person is in the "fiery crucible of relationship," as my Teacher terms it. Relationships may be a source of distraction and risk or they may also be environments of self-improvement and transformation. Relationships can expand our awareness and encourage us to exceed our comfort zones as we get to know someone that has a unique way of looking life.

My Teacher says, "Try to be with someone who is different.

We are always trying to be with someone who is compatible with us. We should try to be with people who require us to stretch."

According to Kriya Yoga, the most important benefit of relationships is that of spiritual growth and a way to balance *karma*. My Denver Teacher has told me that he thinks that the best friend that we can have is someone who will speak the truth to us about our lives. These special people force us to confront our blind spots. Kriyananda (who speaks often on relationships) had this to say on one retreat: "If you want to grow, and be spiritual, and rapidly unfold, get married."

Generally, people are happiest when they experience *good* relationships. So my Denver Teacher asks, "Why be alone and malcontent?" Sometimes rocky relationship dynamics will smooth if given effort and focus. It takes hard work and time to forge an enduring friendship. Rather than looking for something new, our happiness may be better served by digging in and cultivating our current social ties.

The needs of our spirits are sometimes the excuse we are looking for to leave a relationship. However, walking away from a messy relationship to focus on the spiritual life may be missing the point. Relationship problems are often a mirror of our internal issues. The Teacher explains:

> Well, sure I can just get that person out of my life. But I will find another one just like that one. Until you get it right, you will keep pulling the same kind of person in. Ask yourself, "What am I trying to teach myself with this person?" and figure it out so that you can say goodbye and not do it again.

Our relationships are where we learn our major life lessons. If we turn our backs on this learning experience we miss the opportunity of uncovering karmic heritage and gaining insight into our true nature.

My Teacher says, "Be grateful for the biggest pains in the butt. If you don't balance the issues with them in this life, you will probably have to deal with them in the next life." The pain of difficult relationships may conceal valuable spiritual lessons.

Reunited

We don't gain the wisdom that the bumpy road has to offer if we turn and walk away. Hanging between Roxanne and I is the rare mutual awareness of a stale story line we could have resolved this time around.

Past *karma* may drive relationships. That irresistible pull we feel towards someone else may be the delight of recognizing an old friend (or enemy) and the desire to fall back into the timeless groove that feels so familiar, comfortable, and natural. I renewed arguments with Roxanne in this life that had persisted from beyond the grave. These *samskaras* (past life patterns) were unhealthy relationship habits that should have died with that pig farmer.

Relationships present an opportunity to balance *karma*. *Karma* postponed is *karma* that still needs to be dealt with. Perhaps we will escape the inevitable in this lifetime, or even several lifetimes, but eventually we must face the dynamics we avoid. There is value in persisting with difficult lessons until understanding and love inform our decisions.

My Teacher believes that this is a particularly hard time in history for relationships. Adult roles were more rigidly defined just a century ago. Now, with greater personal freedom and potential, we can no longer default to traditional values. Relationships aren't the settled and comfortable places we might fantasize about. We move and change just like our world does and sometimes partners drift far apart. Sometimes we let go of people that no longer harmonize with our value systems or lifestyles.

> "There is a razor's edge
> between non-attachment and indifference.
> Don't be indifferent."
>
> —A Teacher, 2009

As a toddler, I would get frustrated with my parents and push them away, telling them, "I don't need you!" Of course, I did need them, but channeling through me was the old man in the shack. As I grew older I cultivated the less confrontational indifference of detachment.

Remember the master of "Is That So?" He didn't use non-attachment to justify neglect or emotional distance from the girl child. As yogis, we must provide aid when the neighbor calls for help. We still need to fish the moth out of the cat's water dish.

> "Speak or act with an impure mind
> and unhappiness will follow you
> like the wheel of the cart that follows the ox."
>
> —A Teacher quoting Buddha

In the course of four months, my father committed suicide, I separated from my wife, and my mother was institutionalized. There was little I wouldn't do then for the security and comfort of a relationship, but the Teacher says, "If you get into a relationship for the wrong reason it's going to be miserable."

Kriyananda describes asking a class of women which they would choose: Happiness? Or marriage? This happened decades ago, but it is still a shock to hear Kriyananda say that every woman in the room chose marriage over happiness. Why not put happiness first? Kriyananda's point was that we grab onto what our culture values rather than reaching for what is best for us.

> "She's looking for a knight in shining armor.
> But there is no more armor.
> There are no more horses.
> We are in big trouble."
>
> —Kriyananda

Relationships have risks from a spiritual point-of-view. A relationship may take us miles off the path, often in unexpected directions. Relationships may push us to spend less time on the meditation cushion and more time trying to work things out with a partner. There is nothing like a relationship—even a happy one—to turn a world upside down. We need to ask ourselves if we can maintain the momentum of spiritual growth and exploration while in a close relationship. Or will we gain a partner only to lose ourselves?

I once had an affair with a married woman. There were children involved and her marriage crashed to an end soon after her husband confronted her with his suspicions.

Ours was not a "good" affair. We fought a lot. She found me needy, and I found her cold and distant. I was ironically unable to acknowledge her profound lack of commitment when that was exactly what got the two of us together in the first place.

Her emotional distance and lack of connection encouraged me to value intimacy as I never had before. For almost two years I worked hard to keep us together. Otherwise, what was the point in wrenching her from her husband? Failure would mean that the whole sordid affair would prove to be a horrible mistake.

It was a horrible mistake.

If possible after the inevitable breakup I was in worse shape than I had been when my father died. At least I had known my father loved me. It was a kindness when she broke off the relationship because I didn't have the strength or the wisdom to do it myself.

Afterwards I considered the mistakes I had made and what I could learn from the experience. The first lesson: Never get involved with a married person.

*

On an unusually warm day in December outside of Seattle in 2001, I paused on the handles of a wheelchair, my mother's white hair thick and untidy in front of me. We were taking a spin around the courtyard in the fresh air before I was to take her back inside to the smell of urine and the unsettling sound of an Alzheimer's resident down the corridor repeatedly calling "Help!"

My mother raised an age-spotted hand and extended a trembling finger, joints enlarged with arthritis, to point at a white post supporting the flat canopy roof over the ambulance entrance. She started to speak and I leaned forward to hear her better.

"Is that Norman over there?"

"I don't think so, but I'm sure that he's around here somewhere."

In the nine remaining years of my mother's life that was the closest she came to recognizing me.

*

Whatever spiritual gains we make in this life we bring with us into the next stage. A teacher says, "Death is a continuation of this plane, not a rupture. If you want to be happy in heaven, be happy here." If we are unhappy and quarrelsome here, we will find ourselves with these same inclinations once we leave the physical. Kriyananda tells the story of people in the working class Chicago neighborhood of his youth eagerly getting together to hold a séance after the death of a particularly irascible neighbor. They hoped to make contact with him on the other side and get winning lottery numbers out of him! Kriyananda pointed out, "This man was an idiot when he was alive, why did they think he was going to be smart just because he was dead?"

"Anything that is born of a moment shall die."

—A Teacher

The traditional texts and our contemporary *gurus* warn us that all is change. Death is a natural part of this *maya*—this illusion of physical world. In two hundred years, virtually every living being around us now will be dead and very, very few remembered. All is change.

My Teacher says, "Why do we grieve when we lose someone? Because we have grown attached."

Grief is a form of attachment. We want a return of something or someone that has brought us comfort and we miss its absence. Naturally, we grieve when we lose a love. Very few of us are capable, as was Kriyananda, of giving a eulogy for his mother, smiling and content in his certainty that her spirit lived on, released from some of her *karma* and moving towards ever-

Reunited

greater Self-awareness.

From the *sadhu's* point-of-view, grieving for the dead is a mistaken perception. The Kriya Yogi believes, as the Teacher says, "Each of us has chosen our moment of birth and death. Why would you grieve for someone getting what they want?"

The *Bhagavad Gita* counsels that grief for the dead is an uninformed response (BG2.11) and that we should not grieve for any once living being (BG2.30). We've convinced ourselves that death is a permanent separation from our loved ones. We falsely assume that the container of this mortal body is *us* and once the container is broken the contents lost.

However, we lose nothing in the great wheel of time. We shall all be reunited in the hub that is spirit.

The Monk Who Howled Like a Wolf

CHAPTER NINETEEN

Brahmacharya

LeAnne asked if instead of our usual two or three rounds of shamanic journeying she might do Reiki work on all of us. A Japanese Buddhist, Mikao Usui, developed Reiki in 1922 as means of facilitating healing in clients, using the effects of "Rei" (divine spirit) released through the extended hands of a trained practitioner. The practitioner is thought to be a conduit for universal life force energy or "ki" (also known as qi or chi). We were all game for the experiment. LeAnne and her sister owned the Wellness Center that the shamanic journey group used one evening a month. We usually met at the front of the yoga studio across the street from the Court House, but for this Reiki experiment LeAnne led us through the back yard to the old brick carriage house on the alley. The building had been remodeled into an elegant private studio for LeAnne to do one-on-one work, but there was enough floor space for the half dozen of us to spread out on yoga mats while LeAnne lit a few candles in the darkened room.

She guided us through a relaxing meditation and then instructed us to visualize any one color that we gravitated towards. We closed our eyes and focused on that color until it filled our awareness.

The Monk Who Howled Like a Wolf

Having no personal experience of Reiki, LeAnne's work was mysterious to me. Since I was looking at a field of unbroken color in my mind's eye beneath closed eyelids, I didn't know what she was doing as she knelt besides each of us in turn. When she came to my side with a creaking of the hardwood floor, I imagined her holding her hands over my body, palms down, doing mysterious "energy work." Trusting LeAnne completely, I was relaxed and feeling profound comfort and peace. When she left me a couple of minutes later, I continued to focus on my chosen color behind lidded eyes, awake, yet so deep in a blissful state that I could have lain there in the warm dark for an hour without complaint.

I was surprised to feel a presence with me again after I thought LeAnne had moved to others at the far corner of the room. I felt the reassuring light touch of a hand on my shin. Seconds after the hand withdrew, I experienced for the first and only time in my life a pulsing of waves of energy (for lack of a better word) coursing up and down the entire length of my spine, starting at the coccyx, rippling to the base of my skull in one or two seconds, then back down to the base of my spine, and then back to my skull, for six or seven transits. An almost indescribable feeling of ecstasy washed over me along with the sensations. The feelings could be described as sexual in intensity, but more satisfying, and located entirely within my spinal column with no physical arousal. I wondered what LeAnne had done to trigger such an explosion of what I presumed to be *kundalini* energy.

Immediately after the feelings in my spine died out I heard LeAnne's voice from the far end of the room. In an even deeper state of bliss and tranquility now, I wondered as I smoked a metaphysical cigarette: How had she gotten way over *there*, after she touched my leg, without any sound from the old complaining floor?

"So what happened to you all? Can you tell me what you felt and saw?"

The others described varying abilities to maintain the color in their meditation and pleasant sensations of tingling and heat in their bodies, but no one reported anything like what had

Brahmacharya

happened to me. I'd been journeying with this group for months, so when my turn came I was more embarrassed to admit what color I had picked than to describe my sensations.

"My color was wisteria—kind of a lavender with a little red mixed in. LeAnne, after you put your hand on my shin I had the strangest experience: Pulses of bliss or joy running up and down my spine. It was some kind of spiritual... *orgasm*. I've never felt anything like that before."

The only other man in the class immediately piped-up "Next time I want Norman's color!"

As people drifted into the warm evening after class, LeAnne made time for a few private words with me. "Norman, I didn't put my hand on your leg. I would never touch anyone in Reiki without getting their permission first."

> "Most people aren't fit for *brahmacharya*.
> I think that *brahmacharya* is, for most people, irrelevant.
> *Brahmacharya* is appropriate in the monastic life.
> *Brahmacharya* is a part of yoga,
> but for most of us,
> our goal is sensual moderation."
>
> —A Teacher

Many of the old teachings call for celibacy (*brahmacharya*) in order to advance on the spiritual path. S*utra* 38 of Book 2 of *The Yoga Sutras* tells us why:

> With *brahmacharya* established, power is gained.
>
> —*The Yoga Sutras of Patanjali*; Book 2, *Sutra* 38

I have a couple disclaimers (rationales?) to interject here. As my Teacher says, the *brahmacharya* concept may be irrelevant to our place and time. Although, the Sanskrit term and its usage in the traditional texts is applied to men only, my suspicion is that this was a sexist oversight, *not* a policy, and that women are not exempt from sexual restraint. Also, as with most translations of Sanskrit, there is some wiggle room in the interpretation of the word, *brahmacharya*. It's meaning varies, depending on the context.

However, *brahmacharya*, in its most literal interpretation, focuses on the complete cessation of seminal discharges. In other words: Men should not have ejaculations. In traditional yogic thought, the discharge of semen is linked to the discharge of spiritual energy (*kundalini*). Retain semen and the spiritual energy is kept and magnified within the vessel of the body.

There is a clear connection between the *kundalini* force and sexual energy—I can personally vouch for a connection from my experience with the Reiki master. It is possible that *kundalini* energy is discharged in the sex act.

What's a yogi to do?

"If you are still thinking about sex—that's not celibacy."

—A Teacher

I mentioned contextual wiggle room in our translation of *brahmacharya*. Kriya Yoga bills itself as the mystic path for *householders*. Householder implies that there are families and children, husbands and wives involved. *Brahmacharya* as a personal choice may have different manifestations just as a label of "Republican" doesn't clearly define the person. In some contexts *Brahmacharya* is interpreted as meaning "sacred conduct" or even "student of the *Vedas*." The *Vedas* are four ancient collections of *Sanskrit* texts (the *Rig*, *Sama*, *Yajur*, and *Atharva Vedas*) with contents believed to originate from the meditations of advanced yoga masters of ages gone by. We could also make a defensible argument that *brahmacharya* as sacred conduct is living the credo of the Eight Limbs of Yoga.

Still...some of these texts clearly refer to having no sex, and even going so far as to specifically suggest huge spiritual gain only after TWELVE YEARS of abstinence!

I prefer the sound of "sacred conduct."

CHAPTER TWENTY

Echoes of the Past

"The people that you love, you will always love.
The people that you love will always be in your life.
Those whom you have loved will come back to you."

—A Teacher

Kriya Yoga tradition teaches that we tend to reincarnate with people we have spent time with before as an echo of the past. Family dynamics are played out over and over again as we gravitate across time to the familiar and to the loved. We may as well settle our problems with the people close to us now because we won't wiggle out of the chore by refusing to talk to our children or by banking on death to remove the obligation of healing old wounds. Sooner or later we face these unhealthy dynamics.

Reincarnation means we *have* to say we are sorry, if not in this life, then in the next.

The unmarried Teacher cautions us that relationships are often based on need. We see relationships as a way to "complete" ourselves, as if another person can somehow make us whole. "Love is usually possessive and based on getting something in return," he says.

We are capable of outrageous treatment of the people we say we love. Sometimes this maltreatment is due to a frustrated (and misguided) sense of not getting what we need and deserve from that person. This is not love—it is greed driven by fear. We "love" as long as we feel that the lover can fulfill our urgent drives for attention, sex, shelter, food, or protection. When we sense a faltering of the supply the love turns sour.

Not only do we use and abuse relationships for the sake of completing unfulfilled desires, but we also use relationships for sensual experience rather than as an aid to liberation. Love may be all about the kisses, the hugs, and the sex. Very nice things, to be sure, but would we still love our partners without these bonuses? Would we love our boyfriend if we found him unattractive? If we can answer, "yes" without hesitation, then we are making progress on the path. But we must be on guard against relationships based on gratification of physical and emotional drives. The Denver Teacher points out that, "For most people 'good' emotion is just stimulation to inflame the senses." Will the relationship still burn strong when the passionate fires cool?

On a positive note, relationships can be the calm in the storm; a place of refuge to keep us on the right track when the entire world is competing to distract us from the spiritual. Ideally, relationships support our *dharma*.

We each are the creators of our relationships. At a very deep level we guide our life circumstances, even to the point of choosing our parents and siblings. *Karma* is the Law of Cause and Effect and the tool of destiny. Each of us are the enforcers of this law for ourselves. We arrange these devilish circumstances that we find ourselves in.

My Teacher says, "Mystically, the people around you probably have the same problems that you do. They wouldn't be here unless they were relative to you." We may hide our issues better or be more sophisticated at making our foibles socially acceptable, but if our husband is a slob that means we have some disorganization at our core. If it drives us up the wall how our girlfriend is always making us late for social events that is probably a reflection of our own unreliability. My Teacher says, "You are not going to be with someone that's not like you. If someone is in your life, you have magnetized them to you."

This is the quality of relationships known in shorthand as, "Like attracts like." Have you ever sworn that you are never, ever going to get involved with *that* kind of person again? And then, years later, you find yourself right back where you started? We may be in the same position yet again if we do not absorb the lesson and address this problem within ourselves—because like attracts like.

Another, esoteric aspect of the nature of relationships is that we see each other through me-colored glasses. The Teacher has observed that, "Everyone in this room is you. The people in your life are really in your head." What does this mean to the modern mystic? It means that except for a few enlightened beings walking unnoticed amongst us regular folk, no one looks at anyone else without the filter of their own life experience, preconceptions, likes, and dislikes. We all stereotype and we all make snap judgments based not on the true nature of the immortal divine being in front of us, but based on our experiences. For all we know that's a Buddha in front of us, or a Hitler. But we project onto them what we expect to see and hear. We are all the poorer for this inability to see sentient beings as they really are.

Our relationships are a reflection of our own growth. The Teacher: "Until you make a connection to yourself, you will probably not make a connection to anyone." Since our experiences of love are limited, our relationships will also have limitations. It is to our advantage to grow in our ability to love because that mature depth will draw in beings that can match that depth.

The yogis also caution us against self-deception in relationships. It is challenging to be clear-headed and honest with ourselves when we are in relationship with another human being. In our need to be loved, we warp and twist our own perception of reality to suit our purposes.

Kriya Yoga has one more important thing to point out about the nature of relationships: They are, along with the rest of this physical world, subject to change. Our controlling egos plot and rebel against this heresy, but change is the natural condition of the cosmos. The world is in motion around us and that motion is reflected in our ever-changing relationships. Our spiritual quest may aggravate this distressing volatility. The Denver Teacher warns:

> If you don't want your life to change, don't meditate. Don't get on the path. When you change internally, people start to leave your life. Everything changes.

Even within a stable relationship that can accommodate our path towards liberation, there are natural cycles. The yogi does not grow attached to good or bad, attraction or aversion, a struggling relationship, or even a loving one. Yogis do not fall into the trap of letting the external rule the internal. The party may be dull, but it is we who decide if we have a good time.

CHAPTER TWENTY-ONE

Give Them Cigarettes & Booze

My Teacher tells a story from his house painting days. [It's difficult to make a living as a yogi in the West: The hours are terrible and the pay even worse.] He was painting from an extension ladder high up the outside wall of a house, when somehow the ladder slid sideways and the Teacher fell into a thick rose bush. The bush saved him from serious injury, but he didn't come out of the experience unscathed. My Teacher says that relationships are a little like that rose bush: They are lifesavers when everything else in your life is collapsing, but you won't get out of them without some cuts and scratches.

It would be wonderful if everything fell into place and went our way all the time, but relationships are complex organisms—in reality an entire colony of organisms—not just wife or boyfriend, but parents and in-laws and step children, friends and neighbors. Inflexibility may make it impossible for a relationship to succeed. Sometimes us yogis can spend a lot of time making our bodies flexible while neglecting the flexibility of our souls and our emotions. We don't always get to keep our toothbrush where we would like to keep it. That's the way it is. In relationships we must sometimes flex ourselves into uncomfortable positions.

The Monk Who Howled Like a Wolf

The Teacher sums up the crucial role of flexibility:

> There's nothing wrong with being strong, but there's a difference between being strong and being aggressive. Life always wins. The oak tree is rigid, but the wheat, bamboo, or willow will bend and right itself when the wind has passed.

The first marriage among my peers was that of my closest friend, a next-door neighbor when I was growing up in Seattle. At a get together for the men before the wedding, my friend's father gave some advice that I have not forgotten.

"In a healthy marriage the husband has to put the needs of the wife before his own. And sometimes the wife also has to put her husband before her own needs."

This idea of putting the partner first is key to any happy marriage or relationship.

> To become strong in such things as friendliness, compassion, joy, and equanimity
> concentrate, meditate, and attain *samadhi* upon them.
>
> —*The Yoga Sutras*; Book 3, Sutra 23
> (with reference to YS1.33 & 3.04)

Chapter 2, *sutra* 22 of *The Yoga Sutras* points out that the world does not cease to exist when we aren't there. The people we know have lives and experiences independent of our aspirations for them. We need to rise above the tendency to project ourselves onto everyone else and instead perceive the others in the room with eyes unclouded by programmed beliefs. We can start by listening more and talking less.

Verses 26 and 29 of the third chapter of *The Bhagavad Gita* suggest (paraphrased):

> One should not confuse the uninformed
> that are attached to action.
> A wise yogi performs actions while in yoga,
> Leaving the others to pursue their own actions.

Give Them Cigarettes & Booze

> People, deluded by the illusions of our physical reality,
> Are attached to the actions of this reality.
> One who understands the nature of reality
> Should not disturb those who do not understand.

My Teacher and Kriyananda sum up the gist of this *Gita* text with the phrase, "Do not disturb the dreams of others." Our challenge is to let people be who they are even if we feel we know a better way.

Kriyananda says, "I used to give my family books for Christmas. I found that when I gave them cigarettes and booze they liked me a lot better." Kriyananda's dreams were filled with books, but his relatives' dreams were filled with tobacco and alcohol. As Kriyabans, we will sometimes find ourselves in the company of people dreaming a different dream. Let them dream. If they want to hear about our dreams they'll let us know. In the meantime, if they want cigarettes, we give them cigarettes.

*

After the destructive relationship with the married woman, I embarked on a new experiment—big city dating. I was over forty years old, but had never been on a typical first date. Until then my relationships had evolved out of friendships.

Big city dating wasn't natural for me, but this period of almost seven years did serve an important purpose: I honed my relationship skills to become a better partner. Honing was required—it's survival of the fittest out there!

I was not a good partner in my marriage to the mother of my children. The divorce may have been the inevitable conclusion of unformed people growing in different directions, but in our seventeen years together I could have been more supportive, more involved, and a more pleasant person to be around. Dating made it harder for me to ignore my shortcomings and increased my motivation to be a better mate.

> "Becoming a loving person is how you manifest love."
>
> —A Teacher

I had interesting experiences during my big city dating—watching my Teacher's mouth drop open when he met one of the beauties, dating a former flight attendant, and dating women quite a bit older and quite a bit younger than me. One of the best things about my big city dating days were the gaps between relationships. Those breaks gave me time to think about what I was looking for in a relationship, how I could be a better partner, and what that might look like.

At the end of this dating period, I stepped away from romantic relationships for a few months. Eventually I listened to the persistent call of the cold North Country and got back in touch with an old friend in Alaska. My life was to change dramatically once again.

CHAPTER TWENTY-TWO

Making the Call

Despite my Kriya Yoga practice, life was not going well. I had a home and enough to eat, but I was starting to wonder how long my savings would last. The economic downturn of 2007/2008 had brought construction and my manager-level position at the university to a stop. Now I was doing odd jobs—returning to the maintenance and remodel work I did when I first moved to Colorado from Alaska—but I was far from the only out of work carpenter. My severance check didn't last long and each month I spent more money than I earned. A roommate moved out and my expenses increased, but I hung on stubbornly to the big house because I felt I needed the room when my children stayed with me.

In a fit of unwarranted optimism and despite my Teacher's muted cautions, I partnered with a younger couple to begin an indoor aquaponics business in a warehouse near downtown Denver. Aquaponics combines aquaculture and hydroponics, using the rich aquaculture water to grow vegetables. While we did grow some Tilapia fish and basil, we were unsuccessful at raising cash. I plunged further into my retirement money to equip the hungry aquaponics business and to pay the rent.

I joked about making a bumper sticker: "Practicing

Involuntary Simplicity."

By late spring of 2011 it was obvious that changes in my life were ahead. I knew that the six-month old aquaponics business would not continue long at the rate things were going. We were getting a lot of attention from the growing urban farmers' community, but we had no nest egg for a necessary expansion and the business had made almost no income so far. I had few other commitments so I was able to spend a lot of time at the warehouse, but my partners were busy with their urban gardening.

I grew wistful when I heard that my ex and our oldest son were going back to Alaska to visit the old places and friends for the first time since we left fifteen years before. Despite many wonderful experiences in the Lower Forty-Eight, I still missed those wild places and the close community.

My love life entered a new phase with lack of pocket money for courting. I changed the text of my imaginary bumper sticker to, "Practicing Involuntary Celibacy." If only I had marketed some of these bumper stickers I might have made some money and attracted a steady girlfriend.

I knew there was a contradiction between my lack of financial and relationship success in those years and the promise of Kriya Yoga. Shouldn't the true yogi's spiritual success be reflected in a stable outer life? I believed the answer to that question was, "Yes." The problem *had* to be in my application of the Teachings. I felt more and more of the contentment and non-attachment that I sought, but any balance I achieved was in spite of my troubled outer circumstances. I was well familiar with the concept of "Path Opens" when one is walking in *dharma* (obstacles melt away and circumstances helpful to your endeavors fall into place), but there was no sign of a clear path in those days.

The Teacher warned me not to be stingy with my money—he believed that generosity brings abundance and miserliness brings scarcity—but I became rattled as I felt my financial situation get worse and worse. I was in my early fifties and I would soon have no retirement savings at all, like millions of the middle class caught up in the housing bubble and financial scandal. Instead of

Making the Call

making sensible cost-cutting measures to big budget items, I cut corners here and there on inconsequential things.

My ex-wife, Kellie, and my son came back from thew trip to Alaska. I called her to get news of the Great White North. Her visit was to have a huge personal impact on me.

"We went out to the old cabin," she said. "It was strange. It was like you were still there."

"What do you mean?"

"Well, even though the new owners have added on to the original cabin, our place is still pretty much like it was, but it was more than that. Your old wood toolbox was still sitting on the deck you built. And the greenhouse was there and inside of it were the old plastic diaper wipe tubs you saved, with your block letter printing for the different types of screws and nails. They were still stacked up on the shelves you built in the back of the greenhouse. It was strange. It felt like you had just left for a bit.

"And so many of the old friends were there and they all asked about you. Like Susan and Dave, of course."

"Huh..."

I didn't know what to say about all this. I had made a conscious effort not to think about Alaska. I became wistful thinking of that life in the wild and feeling trapped in a big city.

"Susan and I were talking one day and we both had the same idea about you."

Kellie frequently had ideas about me. They usually weren't the kind I enjoyed.

"Yeah?"

"We think that you should move back to Alaska and marry Gail."

"What? That's crazy! I haven't talked to Gail in fifteen years and I have a life down here and the aquaponics and the kids and everything. That's just screwy. Where did you and Susan come up with that?"

"You always were sweet on her."

I sputtered, disarmed, "Well, I...unh..."

Kellie and I had never spoken of my attraction to Gail, but she was right—I had been sweet on Gail even while married to Kellie and working with Gail at the hotel in Denali National

Park. But I was certain Gail had never picked up on my feelings and I never acted on the attraction.

Later that day my son talked to me by telephone.

"Mom and I think that you should get together with your old friend, Gail."

"Well, that's just nuts."

"You miss Alaska and you could go back now. We'd be okay."

For three days I went through all the reasons in my head why it was a terrible idea to act on my family's matchmaking efforts.

I had an aquaponics business (that was headed for inevitable failure).

I had two children (adults who wanted their father to be happy).

I had my repair/remodel business (that was making almost no money).

I had my Kriya Yoga studies (that I could take with me anywhere).

I was renting a home (that I couldn't afford).

I might have to leave Denver (where I didn't like living).

I might have to move to Alaska (which I really wanted to do).

I would have to make a dramatic commitment to a relationship with another person...

I searched for Gail on the Internet. I found her picture in an article about an environmental organization. She looked as good as I remembered. I continued my Internet stalking and found a phone number that might belong to her.

There is no way that I am going to call her! I thought as I wrote the number down on a scrap of paper and put it in my wallet.

The whole stupid idea drove me crazy. It was all that I thought about for three days. Trying to spark a romance with Gail was obviously a crazy, mixed-up notion that had absolutely no chance of a happy conclusion.

But deep inside me there was a voice insisting that all I needed to do was telephone Gail to trigger events that would transform my life for a long, long time. Somehow I knew that I was at an important fork in my path. I could hear my name being

Making the Call

called from up the mountain.

On Father's Day of 2011 I spoke to each of my kids and then headed to a coffee shop for my bi-weekly pick-up of coffee grounds and scrap vegetables for worm composting at the aquaponics warehouse. I told myself that before I went inside the shop I was either going to call Gail on my cell phone or forget all about the darn idea.

I called.

The Monk Who Howled Like a Wolf

TWENTY-THREE

The Soul Picks the Mother

"It's coming! It's coming!" Kellie braced herself against the cold brick wall flanking the dimly lit entrance of the hospital as another wave of labor agony swept over her.

"I can feel the head!"

I jabbed again frantically at the buzzer next to the glass doors of the emergency room. I couldn't hear anything from inside the darkened reception area. It looked abandoned.

I searched in the dark for a rock to hurl through the glass.

*

Sometimes we yogis slip past the gates of *brahmacharya* and find ourselves with children. Never mind our planned or unplanned descents into sensual pleasure, Kriya Yoga has a few things to say about those darling bundles of *karma*.

Children, and their parents, have much more than nature versus nurture to contend with. My two children exited the birth canal with personalities firmly established. The cosmology of Kriya Yoga grants the possibility of thousands of prior lives that stamp the character of each newborn. The Denver Teacher says, "They are separate souls. You really have very little control over them. You didn't make them what they are."

Moms and dads should be proud of allowing a soul the

priceless opportunity at growth or even enlightenment in the physical. My Teacher says, "It is a sacred act for the mother to allow another to come through her into being."

However, the whole process is an ego buster for the father when he hears Kriya Yogis talk about fatherhood. According to Kriyananda:

> The soul picks the mother. The man isn't very important. The soul checks out the environment by going up and down the spine [of the potential mother]. The soul will eject itself short of three round trips up and down the spine if it is not compatible. If the soul makes three loops it is stuck there until miscarriage or birth.

The Denver Teacher confirms, "The father has some influence, but the child goes through the mother's *chakras*, not the father's."

In this spinal tap, the incarnate soul cruises through the *chakra* system of the potential mother, checking out her karmic background, and seeing if the mother's *karma* is a good fit. The soul will consider factors such as home life, educational level, major life themes, past life connections between the new soul and the mother's world, etc. If the soul doesn't like what it sees, it will skedaddle. If the mother's spiritual and physical environment provides what the soul needs for a good learning experience and a way to express its own *karma*, then it might hang around.

Kriya Yoga teaches that the child's birth environment—nurturing or neglectful—is no accident, but chosen by the soul of the child before birth. That karmic underpinning is in no way a justification for indifference to the circumstances of any child. The course a child has chosen may have been their selfless sacrifice to provide the people in their lives with the opportunity to gain good *karma* by providing them support. Children are a physical embodiment of divinity, receptive and open to our compassion and intelligence. Help, offered with wisdom and good intention, is always appreciated in the bigger picture and reflects back on the helper with positive *karma*.

The Soul Picks the Mother

My children were born into a household in which they were read to every night; they had a mother who concerned herself with their every need; and they had a father who modeled focus on the spiritual path. But they also had to contend with the growing tension in their home of a marriage slipping apart and, ultimately, ending. It will be one of their challenges to find personal meaning in the circumstances of their births and childhoods.

*

Kellie and I had reason to believe that her second labor would be fast. The labor of our first child, was only four and a half hours. (At the conclusion of that birth Kellie summarized the experience as a "piece of cake.") Second labors tend to go more quickly than the first. Our cabin on Stampede Road in Alaska was over two hours from the nearest hospital in Fairbanks in good weather conditions. A March birth would require that my wife ski or snowshoe over half a mile to our old Ford pick-up truck while in labor. And if the weather were cold enough (below zero degrees Fahrenheit), I would have to direct the hot exhaust of a propane weed burner at the underside of the oil pan through sheet metal chimney pipe. After fifteen or twenty minutes of this treatment the oil could be counted on to be warm enough for the motor to start. *Then* it would take two hours to get to the hospital in my old two-wheel drive Ford pick-up, *if* the roads were clear. Longer if covered with snow and ice.

One local expecting couple ran out of time on the drive to Fairbanks Memorial Hospital and had to pull over in the hills thirty miles shy of the city to have their healthy baby. Half way between the village of Nenana and the "big" city of Fairbanks they stopped at the pullout of the only business in that stretch of highway. Their child earned a permanent passage in local lore as the baby born in the parking lot of Skinny Dick's Halfway Inn.

Not surprisingly, we accepted my parents' suggestion that we housesit for them on Whidbey Island in Washington State while waiting for the baby to come. They would snow bird in Arizona that winter, but return in plenty of time for the birth of their second grandchild.

On Whidbey Island we only faced a twenty-five minute jaunt

from the detached garage to the hospital to the north in Coupeville. We would be starting our warm Datsun in a warm garage before driving on snow-free roads. Still, in the months before Kellie went into labor, we had joked about a car birth and prepared an emergency kit of towels, blankets, and a shoelace and scissors for the umbilical cord.

That fateful night when Kellie's labor pains started, we left our first born with my parents and bustled into the old station wagon. The labor pains accelerated to once every two minutes as I accelerated the car through the dense island fog. We *needed* that hospital! Gone was our cavalier attitude about catching the baby in the back of the station wagon. We wanted a doctor!

Before I could find my rock at the entrance to the emergency room, a nurse bustled up and unlocked the doors for us.

Kellie told her, "I'm having a baby!"

"I know you are, dear."

"No you *don't* know. I'm having a baby, *now*!"

We were in the hospital no more than twenty minutes before the baby was born. By chance our pediatrician was already on site for another birth, but was nowhere to be seen for the first few tense minutes. The nurse from the door eventually got into the spirit of things, racing frantically in and out of the room, gathering instruments and supplies, and preparing the headstrong mother-to-be.

"Don't push! Don't push!"

"I'm pushing!"

Our second child was fine—asserting needs from the start—but the quick birth was hard on Kellie and there was some non-life threatening but dramatic tearing of flesh involved. Afterwards, while three Sollies were recovering at the hospital in their own ways, a custodian pushed a mop bucket in front of her as she came in the door. She slowly shook her head.

"I've never seen so much blood."

TWENTY-FOUR

Who Are We?

As the drums' deep voices and the alarm calls of the rattles dwindled and died, I ended my shuffling steps and opened my eyes to the candlelight and stared, unfocused, at the floor, hanging on as long as I could to the wild ecstasy of the shaman's dance. Six of us padded in socks or barefoot across the narrow oak boards to find our places. I slid my drum and drumstick into a fleece bag and arranged them gently on the floor next to my coarse woolen blanket. The journey guide stood alert in the center of the circle holding a large elk skin drum. We lay stretched in an arc around her and closed our eyes to the shadowed ceiling.

I groped for the beanbag at my side and used it to seal my eyelids from the feeble light. The journey guide began a simple, fast beat resonating in my chest. My waking mind latched on to the sound, leaving another, deeper part of me free to explore the world inside.

The sound became a spiral of energy my spirit could travel on. Soon, all thoughts of my body receded into formless dark. I expected the dark to form into sagebrush and grass around my faded brown work pants and scuffed leather boots as it had in many journeys before, but instead of blue skies and a breeze, the walls surrounding our journey group came back into focus on the pulses of the drum. This image was not of the physical space of wood and plaster, paint and trim that I knew from many nights, but was instead a spiritual shade—the imprint of the creative power of consciousness in that place fashioning a parallel world of ethereal walls, floor, and ceiling, glowing and trembling with the awareness that sustained this ghostly reality.

Gone were my fellows in shamanism. I seemed to be alone in this mysterious space.

Why was I here? Why wasn't I walking through the sage towards the stone that I would touch before climbing the steep, rocky slope to the cave above in my middle world of journey space?

There was someone with me.

Not one of my journey partners, not the drummer. In fact, now even the drumbeat had receded into another place. But someone was here with me. I could feel it.

My inner eye searched the room and in so doing brought sharper focus. I found him. A tall, slim young man in a heavy army surplus parka, hood down, his back against the north wall ten or twelve feet from me. His hair wild, he stared blankly, his eyes seeing some invisible horror, fear holding his entire body stiff as the oak floor. He was trapped.

"You're safe here," I called.

No reaction. The horror didn't leave his face. He didn't flinch at my voice. I realized that the young man was locked into the moment of his physical death.

"Hey, you're okay. Let it go."

I didn't know if I could make a sound that he would be able to hear, but I had to try—his suffering seemed ghastly.

I remembered what I had read in books about the after life journey.

"Do you see a light? You'll be safe in the bright light. Find the light."

My calls and advice weren't doing anything for the man. There had to be something I could do. I couldn't leave this poor guy frozen in fear.

"Hey! Someone! Does anyone know this guy? A relative?"

Who Are We?

I didn't question my ability to broadcast a call for help into the land of the dead; anything was possible in journey space with my logical mind elsewhere, busy chasing the far off beats of the drum.

"This guy needs someone to help him move on! Is there anybody out there that he trusts?"

First, at a great distance, and then advancing closer as if I was zooming in on them through a video camera, two brightly lit human figures appeared opposite the young man: A seated man and a standing woman, both middle-aged. They were smiling and waving. His body began to relax. He could see them!

Like the ring of an alarm clock calling through deep sleep, the abrupt change of the drum beat into the "call back" rhythm wormed into my consciousness. The drummer was pulling me back from the journey. I couldn't resist the call. I flowed back into my earth-bound body.

> "Common belief is that there is no difference between the *purusha* and the intellect. However, they are totally distinct from each other."
>
> —*The Yoga Sutras*; Chapter 3, Sutra 35

Beyond the surreal environments, I find it perplexing that during shamanic journeying I find a *self* in the trance, but this self is different from my waking self. This self can talk to the dead or soar like an eagle. Within journeys I am "I" and yet afterwards I look back as if recalling a movie. Journeys have much in common with memories of past lives—there is no emotional attachment to the events. It's like the journey happened to someone else, and yet, these are my memories.

Who is having these journeys? Is it the soul or spirit? Is it a part of my personality stripped of its earthbound ego? Are there parts of both mixed into the experience? Can Kriya cosmology answer these questions?

The traditional texts of Kriya refer to the *purusha* (also *Ishvara*, *Atman*, and *Vasudeva*) or soul (Self, cosmic Self, indwelling Self) as the building block of immortal consciousness in the universe. It is perfect, divine, and complete; omniscient, omnipotent, and omnipresent; the source of all life (*Isha Upanishad* 15); without attachment and unaffected by the *karma* in the lives of its physical incarnations; unaltered by the *maya* (illusion) of the changing fortunes of its splintered and deluded personalities. The *Katha Upanishad* offers in II.2.11: As the sun looking down is untainted by the flaws of the eyes looking up at it, the transcendent Self is not tainted by the evils of the world below.

The *Yoga Sutras* declare that the unchanging *purusha* is fully aware of the changing manifestations of the mind and is, in fact, its master. (YS4.18) However, the mind is rarely consciously aware of *Atman*. It is beyond the senses and cannot be seen. (*Katha Upanishad* I.3.15 and II.3.9) In fact, the *Upanishads* warn that the Self cannot be grasped by the mind, existing as it does beyond thought.

You can think of the relationship between soul and these changing manifestations of the mind as similar to the relationship between your brain and your hand. The brain has a very good idea of what is going on with the hand. It sees and directs the hand, sometimes making it work hard, grip objects, perform various tasks. Sometimes the hand is consequently bruised or cut. Sometimes the hand gets to relax as the brain is distracted by other concerns. The brain sees all these manifestations of the hand both as an observer and as a director of the hand's activities.

What does the hand think of all this? Well, we prefer to believe that the hand doesn't think at all. But the cells of the hand have ways of sensing and experiencing their environment first hand (so to speak), though they can't see in any way that we consider vision. If the individual cells can think at all, they must find life a series of events that happen *to* it—incoming nervous system signals and hormones; nutrient levels rising and falling; caloric demands fluctuating wildly; extreme variations in ambient temperature, etcetera.

My hands on this keyboard, right now: What does this experience mean to them, all this hunting and pecking? Are they

Who Are We?

making up stories to explain and rationalize their experience? Do they feel that they are in control of their fates? Or do they believe that their life is arbitrary and cruel?

And how much do I, the master, care about these hands and how they feel? And do my hands yearn to know the brain? Do they wish to merge into this mysterious consciousness that they sense directs them from above, imbued with powers and abilities that they can only imagine? Do they strive for ways to share the journey of the brain?

Who are we? Are we DNA-determined biological circuitry, with mortal consciousness centralized in the grey and white spongy tissues of our brain? Or are we spiritual beings, trapped in the physical? Or, as shamanic journeying suggests, is our consciousness part of a spectrum spanning both the physical and the spiritual?

Kriya Yoga teaches that each of us shares an association with unchanging, immortal souls. These souls are very much aware of us. Yet we are usually painfully ignorant of our souls much as the hand is ignorant of the brain. But perhaps, in certain heightened states, such as in prayer, meditation, devotion, or in the shaman's trance, the hands rise up to experience as much of the world of the brain as they are able to perceive with their limited senses.

The foundation texts describe our mortal consciousness as the "internal organ" the *antahkarana*, or as *prayojakam chittam* (master mind), or sometimes simply as *chitta*—mind. It is taught that this *antahkarana* is composed of four distinct forms of consciousness: *Buddhi* (intelligence or discriminating intellect), *manas* (that part of the mind occupied with the senses), *ahmkāra* or *asmita* (the troublesome ego), and the *avacetana* or subconscious.

Buddhi/intelligence is an unfocused, conscious energy that originates in the divine *purusha*. *Manas*/mind can then utilize that energy to perceive and catalog its physical environment (to the extent that it is able through its native and learned abilities). Much like *prana* may be utilized by living beings to build and maintain the body, *buddhi* is used by *manas* to interpret the sensory environment. *Ahamkāra* (ego) is the part of us that has

"I" awareness in the physical journey, reacts to the information of *manas*/mind, and directs action (*karma*).

According to these Teachings, mortal consciousness (intellect, mind, ego, and subconscious) and immortal consciousness together experience four states or "quarters." The first quarter is *vaishvanara*, the waking state (represented by the "a" sound in the *aum mantra*). The second is *taijasa*, the dreaming state (represented by the "u" sound in *aum*). Third is *prajna*, the deep sleep state (represented by the "m" sound in *aum*). The final and fourth quarter is *turiya*, the Self that is both beyond and within the first three quarters. *Turiya* is symbolized by the *amatrah*, the no-letter, no-sound that follows in the silence after *aum*. (*Mandukya Upanishad* 02-11)

Another metaphor that may help us to wrap our minds around this day trip into Kriya Yoga cosmology is that of *purusha* being the film projector and bulb. *Buddhi* is the light emanating from that bulb. *Manas* are the images on the screen. Ego is the audience, absorbed in the illusions on the screen, forgetting all about their "real" life outside of the theater. The audience members have their backs to the source of reality and are so emotionally involved with the illusions (*maya*) on the screen that they have no awareness of the projector behind them and have forgotten their true identities for the 90 or so minutes that they are in the theater. Absorbed in this *maya*, the audience believes that they are a part of the action in front of them.

My Teacher reminds his students frequently that, "You are not your ego. You are not your mind." We are much, much more than ego and mind. Journeyers and meditators may discover the truth of the *Gita's* words, "yogis can see that Self exists within the self." (BG15.11)

That's what the journey of the *sadhu* is all about—the journey towards Self-knowing or Self-realization. There is a *purusha*— what we can think of as soul—that transcends the ego, which transcends this lifetime. There is some part or parts of us that touch a consciousness not tied to the physical plane. We may turn from the movie screen and look into the light behind us, but first we must shake off the fear binding us to this fleeting life.

Sananda Lal Ghosh, again, quotes Yogananda in *Mejda: The*

Who Are We?

Family and the Early Life of Paramahansa Yogananda, "God is the ocean of light out of which have come the waves of human form."

The Monk Who Howled Like a Wolf

TWENTY-FIVE

The Student & the Demon

"The key problem is, we're bored.
Boredom is one of the most dangerous things to the spiritual life.
When you are bored, you will get into trouble."

—A Teacher

A student heard from another disciple that their guru had the ability to conjure up a genie that would do anything asked of it. Wanting a genie like this for himself, the student begged his guru for such a servant.
"You must do exactly as I tell you," the guru warned.
The student eagerly agreed to all the guru's requirements and waited impatiently for the instructions. With great reluctance the guru gave the student the meditation ritual for the spell. As soon as the guru finished speaking, the disciple hurried off to conjure his very own obedient genie.
Unfortunately, the impatient student took shortcuts in the ritual and found that the powerful genie was a demon with a voracious appetite for tasks. It soon became clear that if he couldn't keep the genie busy that the genie would turn on him!
The man grew exhausted trying to keep the genie occupied

and began crying for the guru to come to his rescue.

The guru came quickly.

"Do exactly as I tell you or this demon will devour you."

"Yes! Yes, of course!" cried the man, desperate to extricate himself from the bondage of the never-sated demon.

The guru told his student to instruct the demon build a bamboo pole that would rise to infinity. Then the student was to tell the demon to climb up and down the pole until asked to stop. The demon leapt with his usual impatient energy and violent tension to satisfy this new command, but after many days it grew exhausted and pleaded with the man to allow him to end the pointless task. The vanquished demon promised that he would be the humble servant of the disciple from that day on.

In this story of *The Student and the Demon* the demon represents the ego/mind and the pole is the spiritual energy well of the spine. This is a story about conquering the untamed ego by keeping it occupied; otherwise its frenetic activity distracts us from focusing on our important life goals and *dharma*. It is vital for the mystic to understand and to tame this ego demon that lives within us all.

In Kriya, the ego is an integral part of the greater spiritual being, but the ego may be blind to the soul that observes, just as the hand is blind to the eyes that watch the fingers. The ego believes (mistakenly) that the body itself is the source of intelligence (BG3.27) and feels that it is fundamentally isolated in an arbitrary and indifferent universe. It's no wonder that we act in reaction to this nihilistic sense of isolation. We need to keep the ego demon busy climbing up and down the bamboo pole so that we are free to cultivate our spirits.

We can't consider the nature of this demon without mentioning its primary orientation—fear. Fear is at the core of the untrained ego, clouding our perceptions. This core fear must be soothed or it will push us ever further from the end goal of *kaivalya* (also variously described here and elsewhere as liberation, *nirvana*, illumination, enlightenment, *turiya*, transcendence, *moksha*, or Self-realization).

The ego sees itself as a victim and uses this perspective to

The Student & the Demon

justify grasping for security and pleasure. Spiritual growth is seen as a luxury made irrelevant by the need to contain the threats of the physical world.

Gail and I went to Fairbanks, Alaska, to see a screening of the movie *Awake: The Life of Yogananda* about Paramahansa Yogananda's personal journey to Self-realization and how he brought Kriya Yoga to North America. I had looked forward to this movie for months and had already narrowly missed showings in Hawaii and Colorado. I was so worried that some mishap would keep us from this sole showing in Fairbanks that we got to the theater much earlier than we needed to. And then I couldn't bear to wait outside for the other couple that we were to meet. Gail reluctantly followed me into the dim and empty theater. We saved two seats next to us on the aisle, close to the entrance where we could spot our friends and save them the trouble of searching for us.

"I am going to sit furthest in because I don't want to have to talk—I want to focus completely on the movie," I said to Gail in my best pompous ass impersonation.

So there I was, in the fourth seat into the row, with Gail on my right in the third seat, with two empty seats to her right for our friends, Sarah and Tom. I fretted about them arriving late, disrupting the movie with the nuisance of greetings. This movie was all about me, of course: It *was* about a Kriya yogi in my Teacher's lineage and I was writing *the book* on Kriya Yoga, right? Why couldn't everyone see that it was *very important* that everything be perfect for me?

Gail, who had been watching for our friends, suddenly called to a tall slim man hesitating on the stairs, "Hello, Samuel."

Gail was talking to someone that I didn't recognize at first. Then, with a shock, I realized that this was Gail's ex-boyfriend, whom I had not seen in years—since before Gail and I got involved. And now he was edging into our row of seats! He was going to sit with us!

I tried in vain to move one seat further down the row, in a desperate bid to maintain some autonomy and cushion from the tedious conversation that was doubtless going to spring from this horrific turn of events, but Samuel (damn him!) did the decent thing and said, "Oh, no, I wouldn't dream of splitting up the party. I'll just sit on the end, next to you, Norman."

My world had been turned upside down in seconds. One minute I was about to watch a glowing tribute to my man Paramahansa Yogananda and in the next minute I was sandwiched between Gail and her ex-boyfriend. As the credits began to roll I was *forced* to make pleasant conversation and do my best to make Samuel feel welcome. It didn't help that he seemed at ease and relaxed. I found out later that the friends we were waiting for had forgotten to mention that he might join us.

After a few moments of credits and chitchat I was faced with a new problem—trying to contain the laughter building up inside of me. What a funny joke the universe had played! I had been so determined that everything should happen at that theater exactly the way I wanted, but look at how events had conspired to make a fool of me. I was forced to face so many of my insecurities and fears, attractions and desires in that one moment. I could almost believe that Paramahansa Yogananda himself engineered that afternoon as one hilarious teaching lesson.

The ego wants control. We believe that if we are in charge of the world that our lives will move along predictably with no surprises. Ha! Until we have neutralized or balanced all of our *karma* we are subject to the patterns of the past.

Just as the demon motivated the shortcutting disciple to try something new, the ego may be an effective motivator. Our egos give us the fortitude to stick with tedious tasks that we would not complete if we weren't under the whip of fear or reaching out with greed. My Teacher describes the well-trained ego as an ally on the spiritual path. Kriya Yoga does not demand the death of the ego, only its allegiance.

> "Isn't the goal of life, unity?
> Doesn't ego separate us from everything else?"
>
> —A Teacher

While the ego's ability to motivate is a silver lining, the ego also separates us from other sentient beings, just as I first felt separated from Samuel at the theater. Ego inspires us to reject the spiritual truth We Are One and that rejection leads to many problems. Social isolation is one result. Fortunately, once I was able to laugh at the humor of the lesson I got at "Awake" I was able to wake up and get my priorities straightened out. Samuel and I ended up having a great conversation there, and at dinner afterwards, learning that we had many things in common.

I had almost fallen prey to another quality of the ego that my Teacher identifies—self-absorption. Excessive interior focus can happen even to those who are actively on the path. This intense work may strengthen the ego's protective barriers. Transcending the ego requires dropping self-absorption and expanding awareness to encompass the Other.

The ego, in all its striving to protect itself, may be staggeringly dishonest. Have you noticed that anytime you look in the mirror you are already posing before you even see your reflection? We pose all the time, consciously and unconsciously. It is seldom that we let anyone (including ourselves) see us in the unguarded moment. That's one reason why the Denver Teacher appreciates the people at rock bottom—they have nothing to lose, so they have nothing to hide. "The mind is a liar. People on the Path are trying to be spiritual, so they are not honest," he says. "Give me an addict anytime."

Unfortunately, most of us are like school kids wanting to stay out of the Principal's office. We will resort to astounding self-deception before facing psychological defeat in the form of admitting our own weaknesses.

Ironically, in the ego's need to assign blame for its unsettled place in the world, it will sometimes pick the nearest target. Self-incrimination from our egos can be debilitating to forward movement and prevent awareness of our positive qualities—erecting high barriers to truth and spiritual contentment.

Another side effect of our ego's blindness to the truth is our immaturity. Much like how the pleasant side effects of alcohol can keep someone from facing their problems head-on, the ego works tirelessly to protect us from the honest self-examination that could strengthen our character and deepen our compassion.

My Teacher cautions students to avoid focusing on data like a "donkey carrying books." I think of the donkey as my ego, and the endless notes and lists I make are the books this donkey carries with it. My dim-witted donkey is ever-striving to make meaning out of chaos and force order onto a mystical world beyond its understanding. All the data in the world is of no help to me if I can't convert these facts and figures into an intuitive understanding of deeper spiritual reality.

> "The mind has no relationship to reality whatsoever. We have to suspend the mind."
>
> —A Teacher

Ego obscures reality and stands in the way of the truth by constantly distracting us with attraction and aversion. As *The Yoga Sutras of Patanjali* warn, "Ego mistakenly identifies the means of perception as the source of perception." (YS2.06) The ego causes a confusion of mind and body with the true Self, blocking the path to Self-realization. Swami Nityananda Giri writes, "immortality is impossible for an ego-bound entity finding multiplicity and differences." To Nityananda, Self-realization comes only with "annihilation of the ego and removal of the ignorance that exists as a barrier between individual self and the Cosmic Self."

In the Kriya world, *samskaras* are the continually reinforced psychological patterns, beliefs, and imprinting of our personalities, *chakras*, and egos through repeated lifetimes of experience and *karma*. My Teacher says that, "the ego is a *samskara*." He is pointing out that the ego is the mob voice of all of our angst-ridden *samskaras*, reacting continually to manifesting *karma*, as every event it encounters in the physical world is perceived through the filters of the past. The untrained ego reacts to everything it encounters as an incarnation of past *samskaras*. Through the ego's reactivity, it then becomes the generator of new *karma* in this self-defeating and self-perpetuating process.

The untamed ego prevents serious self-examination and growth, puts itself at the center of the universe, has its judgment clouded by emotionality, and is so busy reacting to its *samskaras* that it has little time for anything besides getting us in and out of trouble.

So how do we master this demon ego if there is no *guru* to rescue us?

The Monk Who Howled Like a Wolf

TWENTY-SIX

The Rabbit & the Cobra

On a warm spring day, the master was sitting in meditation beside his cottage. In his stillness, all of nature forgot he was there and went about its business. Through his lidded eyes he was aware of a rabbit wandering to his right, nibbling contentedly at the new grass shoots twisting up through the cobble bricks of his little courtyard. The master felt the rabbit's happiness as it devoured the sweet green leaves.

Hearing a rustle to his left, the master opened his eyes. An old cobra swayed back and forth, hood splayed wide, staring unblinkingly at the rabbit. The rabbit lifted its head from the grass and then froze in terror. The chubby young one hadn't sensed the cobra until it was very close. The rabbit seemed under the spell of the snake, unable to look away or flee, rigid as the hungry serpent inched closer and closer, maneuvering for the fatal strike.

Unhurried, the master reached down to grasp his wooden staff and extended it, waving it into the space between rabbit and cobra. The rabbit blinked and seemed to shake its head as the staff broke its trance. In an instant, the rabbit whirled and darted to safety.

The furious cobra swung its head towards the master.

The Monk Who Howled Like a Wolf

"Don't even think about it."

With one brown and one blue eye gazing down at him, the snake sank defeated into the grass and slid toward the trees, looking again for lunch.

Closing his eyes, the sitting master murmured, "Always the guru is asked to break the spell of ego."

> "The mind is fallible, so is the ego.
> Why use that as a source?
> Get rid of the loyalties and the prejudices and strive for the truth.
> What we are trying to do is get rid of past patterns.
> Transcend your mind.
> You are not the mind.
> It is an instrument, a tool.
> It's the mind that torments us.
> It's the mind that can save us."
>
> —A Teacher

A war with ego never ends, but it is possible and desirable for our ego to be an ally instead on this path. The ego is our child that must be gently distracted to keep it out of trouble. Giving the ego a task so it stays out of the way may buy no more time than a father does by giving a toddler a new toy to play with. Still, this is a useful short-term tactic for the yogi and may allow a spiritual practice for those who had none before. In shamanic trance journeys a drumbeat is often used to keep the ego occupied so that the primal core can do its work without ego interference. The same goes for the beat in dance and in traditional music. For the more conventional Eastern-leaning *sadhu*, *mantra*, meditation, service, renunciation, ritual, *pranayama* breath work, and yoga *asanas* are all effective techniques for keeping the ego busy.

To move beyond distraction, the ego must be enlisted on the quest of the spiritual warrior. As my Teacher says, "The mind should become the servant rather than the master." Repeatedly, the *Gita* refers to the need for training of the ego and to instill discipline on our thoughts, desires, anger, and fear. The Denver

Teacher has identified six emotions that must be confronted and soothed in order to attain any sort of control over the ego—craving, rage, arrogance, anger, pride, and envy. My Teacher gives the group an acronym—CRAAPE.

In earning the trust of the ego it may become a useful servant. The Teacher says, "Treat your mind/body/ego as if it is your friend." Give that frightened ego the love it needs. Reassure it. Tell it that everything will be okay while you meditate. The goal is to coax our egos along gently to contentment—a state with no extremes of attraction or aversion.

The *Gita* tells us that the ego can be controlled with repetition and objectivity (BG6.35) and that the mind can be stilled with the efforts of the heart (BG8.12). These non-violent approaches are much more effective than striving to submit the ego to our will through force.

My Teacher suggests a specific *mantra* to release the hold of fear on the ego and allow it to focus on success. I use it frequently after I heard Kriyananda growl it out slowly and powerfully in a deep voice during a video lesson:

"Hai Ram. Jai Ram. Jai, jai Ram."

"*Hai*" and "*jai*" rhyme with "guy." "*Ram*" rhymes with the "am" in "Amish." Translated, "Go forth (*hai*), supreme consciousness (*Ram*). Victory to (*jai*) the supreme consciousness (*Ram*). Victory (*jai*), victory to (*jai*) the supreme consciousness (*Ram*)."

Repeat as needed. Fifteen or twenty minutes of repeated chanting may not be too long a time to spend with this *mantra* when we feel anxiety getting the upper hand.

The ego must be distracted, soothed, coaxed, reminded, cajoled, reasoned with, teased, and humored—whatever it takes to relax its grip. Otherwise, it may grow into our very own insatiable demon. My Teacher quotes the Buddha: Defeating the mind is like defeating 1,000 warriors one after another. Daunting, but Kriyananda points out that no matter how many times we fall, we only have to get up one time more after that last fall in order to succeed.

The Monk Who Howled Like a Wolf

In meditation we may shift the seat of our consciousness from the monkey mind of the ego to the dispassionate Observer. The Observer is called many things—the soul, the Self, the over soul, the higher self, the guest, the spirit, or the watcher. The Observer is the calm voice that can't help but laugh when our ego carries on about being too fat or too hungry or too angry or too bored. Focus attention on the lower middle of your forehead in meditation to find the Observer or concentrate on slow and even breaths. When we feel that fussy ego getting the upper hand and devolving into CRAAPE, we may shift away and upwards into Observer consciousness.

> "A fully-developed ego
> is comfortable with itself
> in all its humanness."
>
> —A Teacher

According to the *Gita*, contentment comes with a trained ego. It's only when the desires of ego are channeled or dissipated that contentment flourishes. Chapter 9, verse 18 of the *Bhagavad Gita* says that liberation comes when the self is absorbed in renunciation. The concept of renunciation is recurrent in the *Gita*. My Teacher frequently quotes Osho, "Renunciation follows awareness like a shadow." As the ego relaxes and loosens its hold on us, it is natural to become content with less. Renunciation is not deprivation. It is a refocus on the spiritual, with the physical no longer an end unto itself, but as a reflection of the pure, lean spirit within.

> "You can be wealthy and still be a renunciate.
> Renunciation is not renunciation of life.
> It is renunciation of the ego."
>
> —A Teacher

The spiritual being is a psychologically balanced being. When I say "*Namaste*," I first bring my hands together palm-to-

The Rabbit & the Cobra

palm in front of my body, then I lift my hands up to tap the outsides of my forefingers at my third eye—the *ajna chakra*—at the center bottom of my brow. Finally, I drop my pressed hands down and push my thumbs firmly against the center of my chest—the *anahata chakra*—the heart center. This signifies to me a union (*yoga*) of mind and heart inspired by my Teacher's advice, "Take all this head stuff I see people doing on the spiritual path and make it heart stuff."

Moving past ego-centered consciousness is a priceless step for the seeker. One of the most important final results is liberation from both attraction and aversion. In the story of *The Rabbit and the Cobra*, the rabbit's actions were controlled both by the sweet grass (attraction) and by the hungry cobra (aversion). The master broke the spell of the ego, liberating the rabbit from the consequences of its actions.

The *Gita* teaches that when we pry loose the death grip of the ego, the karmic consequences of actions may be avoided, a sense of union with other beings achieved, and enlightenment draws closer. Liberation from ego nourishes our sense of compassion as we move from a self-absorbed state to an expansive state in which we realize that all beings are of one consciousness. Inner spiritual evolution requires this outward expansion of awareness and identity.

As ego training takes hold and we are no longer manipulated by our emotions and *samskaras*, we find new freedom. We then are free to slide back down the steep slopes of this mountain to rejoin our friends and loved ones or we may take flight from the heights into the unknown.

The Monk Who Howled Like a Wolf

TWENTY-SEVEN

What Are You Doing & Why Are You Doing It?

"What we are trying to do is to become super-conscious.
Become a spiritual warrior.
Be still.
Be silent.
Pay attention to dream symbols.
Be an astrologer.
Be a mystic."

—A Teacher

After her experience with the man at the Thornapple Tree, the auburn-haired yogi wandered into a meadow. She arranged her legs into the seated lotus position in a field of fragrant flowers, cooled by the light breeze off a large pond.

But soon there came a disturbance as birds took sudden flight from the trees across the still water and the air carried a beating of drums and the earth a growing shudder. The thick foliage on the far bank of the pond quivered, then parted to let the noisemakers through into the bright sunlight.

There were servants on foot and officials on horseback; donkeys pulled small carts of supplies; a few thin dogs slinked

The Monk Who Howled Like a Wolf

on the edges of the commotion.

On a fine snorting stallion rode a man in his early forties, stiff and tall in his gleaming gem-studded saddle. He wore the finest silks and a golden crown with yet more jewels perched on his jet-black, carefully oiled hair. The largest and finest jewel of all was a crimson ruby set over the center of his forehead.

The yogi remained still in her samyama, unnoticed across the pond.

The kingly man handed his reigns to a livery boy and dismounted with an appreciative sigh. The servants burst into action by unloading rugs, cushions, jugs, and food baskets onto the bank of the still pond.

While the servants prepared a place for him and the other officials, the nobleman made his way out into the pond by hopping from one sun-warmed rock to the next. He held his fine robes above the clear water while two servant boys hovered anxiously nearby.

On a flat-topped boulder surrounded by water and smaller rock islands, the King lowered himself to hands and knees and bent forward to look at his own reflection. The grand centerpiece ruby of the crown came loose from its setting and dropped, bouncing between smaller rocks before disappearing into the pond.

Oh, what a commotion!

The man bellowed and jumped to his feet, gesturing wildly at the mortified boys and the water. The boys leapt into the pond as the man first pointed to one spot, then another, as excitement clouded his memory. The boys clawed through the mud of the pond bottom, fingers groping for the large gem.

Soon, a dozen others had joined the search including two bespectacled officials who re-mounted their tired horses and spurred them into the water, hoping to spot the jewel from the height of their saddles. Horse hooves churned the mud on the bottom, turning the water opaque. No one could see anything in the roiling soup that had once been clear as glass.

The yogi released a sigh.

The anxious leader retreated to the bank during this frenzy of useless activity. He spotted the meditator on the far side of the

What Are You Doing & Why Are You Doing It?

pond and dashed around the shore to the yogi, her eyes now closed again.

Breathlessly, the man said, "Yogi, I beg your pardon for interrupting your meditation, but I have great need of your attention."

The yogi cracked one eye open. "Is there a problem?"

The man flushed with anger then controlled himself enough to wheedle, "Oh, Omnipotent One, I hardly need tell you that I have carelessly lost the center ruby from my crown in that cursed pond."

The yogi opened both of her eyes.

He brought his hand to his forehead to show the gaping hole where the ruby once rested. She saw the change in his eyes as he noticed her unusual hair color and how he reached unconsciously towards his more common, jet-black hair.

"This ruby is very important to the lineage of my kingship. I fear if it is lost, chaos will follow in the Province as pretenders to the throne fight over the chance to rule. Oh, Wise One, will you help us to find this stone?"

"I will help, but you need to do as I say."

"Yes, of course."

"Then instruct your servants to leave the pond and all of you please wait well away from the water while I finish meditating."

"You want us to just wait while you meditate?" the King asked, incredulous.

"You would like your pretty stone back, wouldn't you? You must wait until the time is right for me to help you find your rock. Now, please return to the other side. I will be with you soon enough."

The King and all his party waited impatiently on the other side of the pond for the yogi to rise up from meditation. After about an hour, the yogi opened her eyes and stood. Waving off the hovering King, she made her way out to the flat rock where she had seen the vain man kneel to admire his reflection.

A jewel glinted in the now sparkling clear water.

The Teacher asks his students, "What are you doing and why are you doing it?" The problem for us mystics is that we often don't know the answer to this question. This obliviousness to our own motivations cripples our search for truth and expanded consciousness. Our ability to expand awareness and make crystal clear the waters of consciousness is crucial for Self-realization. Expanded consciousness is expanded awareness.

The old story of *The Pond and the Jewel* illustrates one aspect of awareness: How can we expect to have clear vision if we muddy our minds with wasted efforts and desires? A still mind sees what is truly important. Sometimes awareness directs us to wait.

The Teacher's questioning of his students' motives leads to yet more questions: Are we cultivating a clear life and spirit or have we stirred up the muddy bottom, clouding our awareness and concealing the jewel within?

Awareness is our ability to perceive the true nature of reality. My Teacher and his lineage are discouraged by the human inability to move beyond lives of reaction and pre-programming. Shelliji once lamented to his disciple, Kriyananda, "We are the walking dead."

> "There may be a reality outside, but the form is subjective. You, your universe, and how you interplay with it— that's all there ever will be."
>
> —A Teacher

A friend of mine suggested considering reality as a dream to be interpreted with the language of symbolism. With this perspective, I divined a deeper reality underlying an experience I had one winter night, while I still worked for the University in Denver. I was biking home in near dark on a wide asphalt path along the shore of a frozen lake. My mind was absorbed by the latest intrigues of my high-pressure job. My boss required that I be the enforcer of policies I didn't support. I didn't like being told to threaten contractors with legal action when those contractors were doing the best they could in difficult situations. In my self-absorption, it took a few moments to notice the commotion of honking geese scrabbling on the ice beyond the

What Are You Doing & Why Are You Doing It?

cattails. I slowed my bike to a careful crawl on the icy trail and heard something crashing through the brown stalks as I passed. The source of the disturbance leapt out of the reeds behind and quickly turned its attention on me. A pit bull!

The dog sprinted on an intercept course. Knowing I would never out-pedal the dog, I swung off my bike and used the frame as a barricade.

A woman with a leash rushed up to restrain her pet. My "Aries-rising" hot-blooded side took command and I gave her an earful about her unleashed dog chasing wildlife and bikers. Any apology she might have considered evaporated in the heat of my angry words and the woman and her now leashed dog stalked away in one direction and I rode off fuming in the opposite.

On the surface, the experience was just an ill-behaved dog let loose by its master that rushed a nervous bicyclist trying to get home after a hard day's work. But I intuited that this disagreeable outer reality was somehow a reflection of my own inner reality. How?

A couple days later the uncomfortable truth hit me: *I* was the mad dog released by *my* master to inflict havoc on the innocent. By allowing myself to be sicced on those he felt had mishandled projects, my boss was using me as an attack dog. Now I knew what it felt like to be rushed from the darkness. A morsel of awareness slipped past my type A executive foolishness and moral compromise.

As we uncover layers of ourselves and gain greater awareness, we develop new wellsprings of empathy as it sinks in that we literally share one consciousness. Sometime this growth comes with wisdom and insight and sometimes it rushes forward on four feet!

> "My beloved—a harsh truth—they are us.
> Mystically speaking, there is only one being."
>
> —Kriyananda

The Monk Who Howled Like a Wolf

TWENTY-EIGHT

Iwa Awareness

"For how many moments are you aware?
The rest is mind.
Some shift has to happen.
The real revolution has to happen within us.
We are so rarely present that we are almost not alive.
We're all self-strung puppets.
But *we* have the scissors!"

—A Teacher

In one hand I clutched my travel mug and a brown paper bag. I shrugged out of my daypack and lowered it onto the carpeted floor and myself onto the black naugahyde airport seat with a sigh—I was through security and I had a mocha, something to eat, and time to read before boarding. At last I could stop worrying about making connections and schedules. Tension drained out of me as I settled in, the airport's bustle fading from my consciousness.

I carefully set down my stainless steel mug and the bag with a bagel and bent to wrestle a book out of my overstuffed pack. A flash of motion caught my eye: A little gray bird swept up to an overhead beam as another dropped from a tall fichus tree to the concourse floor, gathering crumbs brushed off laps. Among the boarding announcements and muffled footfalls on carpet I could now hear the sharp twitters and chirps that had been with me all along. The sterile world of glass and steel came to life.

Too often, I begin my day from a position of weakness—of being barely present in my own life. How many birds do I miss?

I am still a child in the process of becoming fully Self-realized. I aspire to be a mystic, but spirit revolution comes only with persistent efforts to expand awareness.

The masters suggest that we can start our journey towards awareness by practicing *iwa*, translated "as if." Act *as if* something were true and our mind gradually aligns with the fiction until we begin to take on the qualities of the attribute. In other words, "Fake it till you make it." Obviously, we need a mental concept of what it is to be aware in order to begin our important acting role. By examining the attributes of the *sadhu*, we may begin to practice this important *iwa* exercise.

Zen Buddhism teaches the importance of increasing awareness of everyday activities. This is the familiar goal of being in the now. That goal can be difficult to achieve as the mind slips back into the past or hops forward into the future due to attraction and aversion. The monkey mind of ego is an obstacle to being aware in the now. As my Teacher says, we can always worry about our job or boyfriend later. For now, just be.

Balance is another attribute of the aware yogi. Balance is a union, a yoga holding us at the spiritual center—the place of creative power. The Teacher illustrates balance by bringing his palms together, fingers up, centered in front of his body in the *namaste* greeting. He illustrates lack of balance by spreading his arms wide, reaching out to the extremes. The Lakota cry out in dance and ceremony, "*Chokata hey yupo!*" Go to the Center!

Childlike wonder at the birds in the airport or at this marvelous universe is the natural state of the aware Kriyaban. The beauty of the universe is reflected in the enthusiasm and curiosity of a child stopping to climb a tree or to watch the clouds. Teacher says, "Learning takes place only in a mind that is innocent and vulnerable. We never taste this moment fully, so we don't taste its sweetness."

Kriyananda notes, "We have been stuck for thousands of years with the either/or perspective—if I am good, you must be bad—a dual system. It is a *damnational* patterning."

Our duality pushes us to categorize everything in the world into black or white: Good or bad, human or animal, spirit or physical, truth or lie. To reject duality is to see the good in the bad and the bad in the good, embracing all, maintaining our childlike wonder, and insisting on the right to be innocent and vulnerable, and wise and strong all at the same time. This transcendence of duality is part of what it is to be reborn as an aware Kriyaban.

Creativity is another attribute of awareness. The power of creation exists in each of us, whether or not we guide it consciously. The creativity of an artist has the power to turn tragedy and ruin into wild and gentle art. Creative awareness perceives the beauty and hope in the broken brick and glass of urban decay or in lives weighed down by grief and years of pain.

Discernment is linked closely to both awareness and enlightenment in the *Bhagavad Gita* and *The Yoga Sutras*. The *Sanskrit* words *buddhi* (favored in the *Gita*) and *viveka* (used in *The Yoga Sutras*) are often both translated as discernment. Discernment is the active practice of wisdom, insight, and intelligence. *Viveka* is also the first of the *Sadhana Chatushtaya*, the Four Pillars of the Spiritual Aspirant.

Book 2, sutra 26 of *The Yoga Sutras*, tells us that experiencing the freedom of the soul comes by replacing ignorance with uninterrupted discernment. The *Gita* describes discernment as seeing the difference between bondage and freedom (BG18.30). Expanding awareness brings this ability to see the difference between what is real and what is unreal, shining a light on the illusions that tempt us from the path.

Another aid to greater awareness comes through imitating the masters that have walked this path before (*Iwa!*). My Teacher advises, "Emulate someone that isn't hanging onto that Thornapple tree." Read their books, study what they studied, and listen to their words.

The Teacher says, "If there's a bad taste in your mouth when you go to do it, then don't do it." "Follow your gut" is cliché, but there is effectiveness in listening to the visceral communication of intuition. Awareness through intuition may come in a flash or carried on pleasant or unpleasant body sensations. If we want our intuition to bear fruit, we may encourage it by listening for its quiet voice and accepting its council.

Logic and wisdom are allies of awareness in the challenge against emotion. While emotion can change our lives suddenly and harshly, logic and wisdom are more likely to change it for the better and keep us out of trouble. Emotions spring into being as a reaction to *samskaras*. Logic is sourced in the *buddhi*—the wisdom originating in the *parusha*/soul—granting us the opportunity to make helpful decisions that nurture our growth.

> "Hardly anyone is tilling the garden.
> You have to till your garden."
>
> —Kriyananda

A quality of awareness related to the last of the Four Pillars is perseverance, *Mumukshutva* (the intense desire to attain enlightenment). *Mumukshutva* is the motivation to weed and water our gardens when it seems more pleasant to sit in the cool shade with our familiar *samskaras*.

To be aware, we must question the way things are. The Denver Teacher says, "Always the key word is, 'Why?' Loyalties are hard to see as an attachment because you think of them as positive. But they will blind you more than a prejudice." Rather than blame their actions on loyalty to a boss or spouse, the spiritually aware accept responsibility for their place in this world. Kriyananda put it this way: "Everyone is right where they want to be. Look at your life—that is what you want. If you didn't want it, you'd stop it."

The everyday mystic must employ self-examination—the study of our internal reality. Without knowledge of the internal reality we miss most of what makes up our very *self*-centered reality.

Self-examination relates to the self-study of the fourth

Iwa Awareness

Niyama of the Eight Limbs of Yoga. This self-study can include the nature of Self, life events, the unconscious, dreams, or *dharma*. My Teacher sees the study of the inner universe as a way to study the outer universe, in an "as below, so above" sort of way.

Both Kriyananda and my Teacher suggest an end of day practice called *tarka*. This is a reflection on the day's events, often performed in bed just before going to sleep. *Tarka* is a review of the day to assess how we have done in our jobs, our relationships, our spiritual practice, within our households, etcetera. *Tarka* gives us the opportunity to affirm how we would like to handle these issues tomorrow.

Self-examination for awareness needs to extend even to the workings of the unconscious mind. The Teacher explains, "The unconscious patterns are what we are trying to get greater access to because that is where we are stuck." Self-knowledge must include the vast hidden bulk of our psyche existing like the hidden mass of an iceberg. Often in the meditative state personal insight will spring into being, providing primal material to expand our personal awareness.

The teachers tell us that we must practice self-protection for the sake of our awareness. Kriyananda and my Teacher both warn us to take care of our bodies. When our bodies are out of balance our spirits suffer as well.

"The good mystics are all really simple."

—A Teacher

If you ever find my Teacher's Kriya Yoga Center you will see that while all the furnishings are clean and well maintained, they are simple, if not austere. He doesn't have a lot of stuff.

We aren't likely to have clarity of purpose if we have trouble walking through our living room. A cluttered apartment may mean a cluttered mind. A simple mind (in the Teacher's sense) lends itself to orderly thought and focus on the divine. Simplicity of surroundings and soul is a quality of awareness.

My Teacher says, "To improve your earth life—break free

from your limitations. You must be able and willing to shed this skin." Move beyond old patterns and attempt a journey through uncharted territory. Awareness and life are both enhanced by the challenge of living outside the comfort zone.

Study of the external world (different from the self-study of self-examination) is another element lending itself to greater awareness. Kriyananda says that through this study, "We see how to live and how not to live." This study may happen with nature, history, science, biography, and philosophy.

Finally, if we wish to grow in awareness we need to be still and watch and listen. Spend less time trying to get other people's attention and more time paying attention to them.

The Denver mystic's advice:

> Learn by watching other people. Listen to life because it communicates what you need to hear. Be still and listen. Practice the ultimate *mudra*: Put the hands over the mouth and open your ears.

CHAPTER TWENTY-NINE

Awareness Exercise

> "The more aware we become,
> the more free we become."
>
> —A Teacher

A self quiz with no scoring and no wrong answers:

1. How relevant are matters of the spirit in your everyday life?
2. Where do you conduct your spiritual practice?
3. How important is the spiritual to your perception of the world?
4. How happy are you with the world?
5. How many possessions do you need to be happy?
6. How much do you like the people around you?
7. How much do you have in common with the world you see in videos, movie theaters, and on television?
8. How much control do you feel you have over your life?

These questions skirt some significant attitude changes we

experience as we gain wisdom in life. Behind each of these simple questions is a profound yogic truth.

The first question: "How relevant are matters of the spirit in your everyday life?" approaches the idea that the life we lead in the physical world is still a spiritual life. The physical is a solid projection of an underlying spiritual reality. As our awareness and sensitivity to this other reality grows, what was once mundane becomes mystical.

> "Every moment is an opportunity for your spiritual practice. You can do it anywhere."
>
> —A Teacher

"Where do you conduct your spiritual practice?" The *sadhu's* answer is that we carry our spiritual practice with us everywhere. Sometimes I am asked how long I practice or meditate each day or what I do in my practice. I usually hesitate before answering because a complete answer would either be book length or confusing in its simplicity. The short answer: "I practice all the time." Kriya practice is not just conducted on the meditation cushion or while singing *mantra* or while in the bliss of *samadhi*. Once we "swallow the Teachings" they are a part of all we do. The goal is to remain aware during every moment our everyday lives: In a restaurant; during a movie; while taking a shower; while walking to catch a bus. This is a continuous practice.

In the "Gorillas in Our Midst" study by psychologists Christopher Chabris and Daniel Simons, participants were shown a video clip and instructed to "count how many times the basketball ball is passed by players wearing white." Subjects did a great job of counting the passes—awareness of passes was at a fever pitch. What approximately 50 percent of those who viewed the video did not notice was the woman in a gorilla suit entering the scene, beating her chest, and walking off stage again!

A follow-up study instructed participants to watch for a gorilla. But in this new video morphing curtain colors were overlooked, leading the researchers to quip, "When you're

Awareness Exercise

looking for a gorilla, you often miss other unexpected events."

Realistically, we probably miss 90% of what is under our noses (such as the birds at the airport) due to a lack of attention and a preoccupation with other things. Expanding awareness may drop that percentage to 80%. Ever finish a meal and realize that you did not consciously savor the food in front of you? I can't recall if I sampled the smells on the wind the last time I walked outdoors—though I am certain my dog did. Did I watch the clouds?

We can't perceive everything in our world, but we can do a better job of exercising our awareness throughout the day and keep an eye out for gorillas.

You may guess the importance of the third question: "How important is the spiritual to your perception of the world?" As we first begin to sharpen awareness, there may be a period of frustration with the sleepwalkers we perceive around us. Increasing awareness can drive us to feel less content, not more. This is not a problem of awareness, but instead is a problem of incomplete awareness. Planet Earth is not here to be comfortable. It is a learning ground for souls that have room for improvement. We are given an opportunity for that improvement just by being here.

> "How you see the world is an internal concept.
> If you see the world being violent
> there is something inside of you that is violent."
>
> —A Teacher

The spiritual precept that the outer world is a reflection of the inner world is contained in the question, "How happy are you with the world?" We are unable to perceive something outside of ourselves unless it is another variation of something that we know and understand intimately. If we are happy with the world it is probably because the promise and joy that we see in the world is a reflection of the promise and joy that we carry within us. If we are unhappy with the world, we are likely seeing or projecting our own self-dissatisfaction onto a more acceptable focus.

"How many possessions do you need to be happy?" The Teachings tell us that the spiritually aware are content. The *sadhu* knows that there is nothing to be fixed, nothing to be made whole again in this world. Everything here is a reflection of the divine and every day is another opportunity to heal, to serve sentient beings, and to experience the wonderland of inner consciousness. Knowing what is truly important, the mystic doesn't become attached to the *maya* of this life, but remains focused on the goal of *kaivalya*.

> "Did you feel one with that *Ficus* plant when you walked in? If not, why not? We are one."
>
> —A Teacher

A man sat on his porch in a small town, enjoying the morning air, when a car with out-of-county plates pulled up in front of him. The passenger window slid down and a couple peered at the sitting man.

"Excuse me, sir, but we were thinking about moving to this town and we wondered how are the people around here to live with?"

"How are the people where you come from?"

The couple both scowled, "Oh, they are horrible people! Always gossiping and backbiting! We can't wait to get away from them."

"Well, they're about the same here."

"That's what we were afraid of!"

The window rolled up as the car sped away.

Twenty minutes later another car pulled up and a window was rolled down and the engine shut off. Two smiling faces beamed out.

"Excuse me, sir, do you mind if we visit with you for a few minutes?"

The man on the porch stood up politely and walked halfway down his steps.

Awareness Exercise

"Not at all! I could use a little company. Why don't you take a break from that car and come on up here?"

The three of them sat together and chatted about the weather and then the couple asked the homeowner about his life.

After the man was done talking about the fruit trees out back and how his elderly aunt was doing, one of the couple said, "This seems like a fine place to live. We were thinking about moving to this town and we wondered if you could tell us how the people get along with each here?"

The man replied, "Well, how are the people where you come from?"

The second person said, "Oh, they are the best people—so friendly and open! Always willing to give a hand or stop and say hello."

The first person worried, "We can hardly stand the idea of moving because we would miss our neighbors so much. Anytime we need something, someone is happy to loan us a mower or collect the mail. We are so happy there—are people here like that too?"

The man smiled, "I think that you are going to find that the people here are about the same."

The seventh question, "How much do you have in common with the world that you see in videos, movie theaters, and on television?" is a reference to the *maya* of this earth. As we become more aware, we find worldly concerns less absorbing than they once were. The spirit begins to gain ground, convincing the ego that we are in the world, but not of the world. Sometimes this realization can create a sense of distance from the hustle and bustle of society that we once found so engaging. Some days, as my Teacher warns, we may feel more like a *misfit* than a mystic.

Consciously directing one's life is one of the great promises and challenges of the mystic and that is why I asked the final question, "How much control do you feel you have over your life?" As the Teacher said in the quote at the beginning of this chapter, the more aware we become the freer we are. We become conscious that the sum total of who we are and what we have experienced controls our destiny.

The Monk Who Howled Like a Wolf

"You have the power to create what you wish to create, even if it's bad."

—Kriyananda

The *yoga siddhis* will beckon to all of us at some point in this journey. Some of these *siddhis* we are encouraged to exercise. One of these *yoga siddhis* is to manipulate our reality. This manipulation should be done to the benefit of our evolution towards enlightenment and for the benefit of those sharing this mystical journey with us. Unfortunately, attraction and aversion encourage the practice of creative power towards other ends, resulting in more *karma*.

The ability to be the creative force in our lives is a neutral *yoga siddhi*. We determine how far we take it and in what direction. With determination, we may influence our destiny even after death.

THIRTY

Awareness & Death

Before I moved from Gunnison to Denver and discovered my Teacher and his Center, a friend told me about a house in the county where something dark was rumored to have happened. She felt the old farmhouse was haunted. Knowing a little about my shamanic work, she hinted that maybe I could do something about it.

I was uncomfortable being linked with death and hauntings. The trapped young man who showed up uninvited in my shamanic journey a couple of months before was a peculiar, but passive brush with death. It was a different matter to go out *looking* for the dead, but I didn't want to turn my back on a sincere request for help.

Driving by the property a few times in the next couple weeks gave me the opportunity to think carefully about what I should do. It was probably my imagination, but the two-story house in pastureland felt like it had a secret—as many old houses do.

> "Death is a continuation of this plane, not a rupture.
> If you want to be happy in heaven, be happy here."
>
> —A Teacher

The Monk Who Howled Like a Wolf

A longtime Kriyaban experienced a death in her immediate family. Even though the teachings specifically suggest that before birth we each agree to the time and manner of our deaths, this Kriyaban was struggling with loss, survivor guilt, and remorse months later. I experienced the same feelings after my father's sudden death.

The *Brihadaranyaka Upanishad* explains how the *Atman* or Self gathers the *prana* of the failing body and slips away to rejoin Brahman (IV.3.35 - IV.4.7). Although we are taught that souls are immortal and that physical death is just another step towards enlightenment, this can be difficult to accept when death is close to us. Kriyananda reportedly spoke with joy at his mother's memorial service, celebrating a life lived well and the opportunity for his mother to advance spiritually. Not all of us can swallow these Teachings so completely, but if we prepare ourselves, we may find that death does not bring as much fear as it once did.

The mystic's reaction to death may seem unnaturally detached, but is a natural outcome of a deep acceptance of the Kriya Yoga belief system. Awareness of our culturally ingrained assumptions about death gives us the opportunity to question those assumptions and begin to assemble alternatives.

"All is change" is a foundation principle of Kriya Yoga. Everything on this physical plane has a birth and a death. The Teacher reminds us, "All the things you own will be scattered. Those that you love will leave you or vice versa."

To hang onto life for all it's worth makes about as much sense as refusing to get off the train because we like our window seat. It's our stop! We have enjoyed the ride, but when the train pulls into the station it is time to get off and begin the next stage of the journey.

Another principle for the yogi is that we are not automatically handed a ticket to enlightenment when we get off this train. Who we are at death is pretty much whom we are when we move into this next stage, whether we think of it as heaven, an astral plane, the bardo, or even purgatory. The good news is that we will move into this new phase of consciousness with the same

Awareness & Death

amount of awareness that we had in life. If we are wise, then we will be wise, if we are happy, then happy... and so on. All the ground we gain in this lifetime will serve us well and we will find that ethereal world after death pretty much as we expect to find it.

"You will be learning in this life to live without your body."

—A Teacher

As we reach the end of a train ride it is time to collect ourselves and begin to plan what we will do at the train station and beyond. Likewise, the yogi needs to compose herself for the transition of death. As Kriyabans, we visualize what we would like to find at the station on "the other side." We work to be conscious of what we are expecting because that is probably what we are going to get.

Krishna said to Arjuna (Kaunteya) on the battlefield:

"Kaunteya, when the body gives up at the final moment of life,
whatever state of mind the soul is in
is definitely what the soul will become thereafter,
having been absorbed within that state."

—*Bhagavad Gita*; Chapter 8, Verse 06

We have been taught in the West that a lifetime of misery and suffering will be rewarded in heaven. Kriya Yoga cautions that this is not necessarily the case. If we accept misery and suffering as our natural state, we, naturally, expect the same on the other side and in so doing create that new reality for ourselves. Kriyananda warns us, "We will take all our unhappiness with us."

Kriya Yoga has a layered view of reality, with "the other side" claiming many of these layers. According to the Teachings, the astral planes (sometimes numbered as seven) are separate dimensions of reality beyond this physical plane. We can think of these planes as flat layers like sheets and blankets on a bed, or stacked pages, but I prefer to think of a sweet onion, with a great mystery at the center, and our physical plane near the surface.

Consciousness tethers itself to the physical in our corporeal layer although during sleep our spirits may drift into one of the "lower" astral planes. Unfortunately, most of us do not stay sharp in the dream state and this sometimes-accidental astral travel tends to be aimless, unfocused, and unaware. The adept may consciously visit the astral during *mantra* and meditation, and in astral projection (mental projection of the ego or the spirit from the physical plane into the astral). The astral is sometimes also traversed in near death experiences and is also taught to be the home for most of us after death.

These astral planes are thought to be less earth-like as one shifts further from the physical plane(s), but places in the lower astral are hard to distinguish from Earth. I believe the astral is a place where conscious intention can manipulate the energy pervading these planes to create whatever environment individuals or groups would like or expect. Expatriate earthly souls use their conscious creativity to mold the all-pervasive malleable energy of the astral into a familiar environment. This new home may be cheerful or banal or even torturously unpleasant, depending on the inhabitants' inclinations. The combined focus of many souls serves to create and maintain "consensual realities"—including astral realms in imitation of the residents' concepts of heaven and hell.

Middle astral layers are thought to have regions that consistently resemble more traditional religious concepts of heaven; whereas astral layers closer to the spiritual source and nearer the causal planes (the *causing* planes) are so ethereally based as to be beyond comprehension to earthbound egos.

After death in the astral we find that our thoughts, conscious and unconscious, have instant creative power. Kriyananda points out that knowing something of how the astral works can be used to the advantage of those of us that can establish a good attitude now. "Be happy now and you will be happy over there." The departing soul naturally and easily moves to the place it is most in harmony with.

Awareness & Death

*

After spending a couple weeks thinking about the spooky old farmhouse, I was back with my shamanic journey group as we prepared for the third and last journey of the evening. I decided to attempt a visit to the farmhouse to take a look around.

The drumbeat began. I closed my eyes.

This was a vivid journey to the "real" world. Although I had never set foot onto the property, when I found myself on the front porch everything was solid and detailed. The only insubstantial element was I. I didn't have a body. I was a point source of awareness hovering on the porch.

I moved this awareness through the front door and into the entryway. I listened without ears. Hearing nothing, I examined my surroundings.

Just inside the door was a flight of stairs. To the left, a tight hall led towards the back of the house. I hesitated.

"Is anyone there?" I sent out.

Nothing.

"Hello?"

Nothing.

I didn't know what to look for. For all I knew there could be something malevolent lurking in the house, but I trusted my friend not to send me into ambush.

I sensed movement upstairs where it felt *darker*. There was a gloom hanging in the air, and lingering fear.

"I'm coming up the stairs now. I'm friendly." My body formed instantly into being so that my legs could lift my feet, one after the other. I climbed effortlessly.

"Hello? Is someone here? My name is Norman."

I stepped up into a hall and saw the two bypass doors of a closet on my left. One partly open door revealed a dark jumble of clothing and boxes. I sensed this closet held the secret I was here to uncover.

"Hi... Will you come out?"

A long silence.

"It's not safe," whispered a small voice.

"It'll be safe with me."

"No. It's not safe out there. It's safe in here."

"I won't let anything hurt you. I *promise*. Why don't we go outside, into the garden? It's beautiful and sunny out there."

I could feel the battle between hope and fear as an agonizing decision was made in the dark closet.

A small form hurtled out of the clothing and leapt up, wrapping skinny arms and legs around me, burrowing a brown-haired head into my neck.

"Let's go outside, *now*."

We went out, into the light.

CHAPTER THIRTY-ONE

Happiness Unshakeable as a Shadow

The Island Mystic was agreeable and eager to please the older monk, but there was also a stubborn streak in him—he got results by doing things his own way. His effective spiritual practice did not come from a rulebook or memorized instructions. He was a true mystic, finding his own path accompanied only by a deep joy more miraculous even than the act of walking on water.

Happiness operates on a spectrum. At one end is common happiness (residing in a world of mood swings, dependent as it is on the external), working into contentment (a general, non-localized feeling of well-being), transmuting in its highest manifestation to *ananda* (a spiritually-based state of bliss).

In Chapter 13 of the *Gita* the "field" and its manifestations are introduced. The *Gita* describes corporeal bodies as a type of restricting field that the *parusha* (soul) finds itself trapped within. Although trapped, the soul finds that happiness is an elemental part of the nature of this field (BG 13.06). To be human in body is to have happiness within reach.

The Sanskrit word *santosha* is defined as "contentment." My Teacher begins to clarify the distinction between happiness and contentment when he says, "People confuse contentment with pleasure. It has nothing to do with what happens in your external life." This rarefied feeling is devoid of outward focus or external source.

A step higher than contentment on our Kriya scale of happiness is *ananda*. *Ananda*, unlike happiness, has no flip side. There is no un-*ananda*. The Teacher says, "Bliss is like the Mount Everest of happiness."

Obviously, being happy feels good, but the Kriya Yoga teachings have other reasons to cultivate happiness. For one, happiness helps to keep us out of trouble. In Chapter 3, verse 17 of the *Bhagavad Gita* it describes how the person who looks only to themselves for happiness and contentment has no need to accomplish anything. No ice cream cones, no drugs, no sex, no roller coaster rides. This yogi is happy all by himself with no help from the outside world.

When we are happy—and not looking for external things to fill a gap—our lives becomes more stable. Happiness has a feedback effect. The happier we are, the happier we tend to become. In fact, negative elements tend to start moving out of the happy person's life as the negative become increasingly irrelevant. My Teacher says, "If an angry person is in your life and you become content, the angry person will leave."

> "You want to improve this world?
> Be happy."
>
> —Kriyananda

When we are happy, this happiness rubs off on the world around us. We create a sphere of peace with ourselves in the center. The *Gita* is specific when it explains that if we are content then we will act unselfishly towards all beings in both our actions and inactions (BG 3.18). This is a small example of how cultivating our own happiness is one of the best services we can perform for the world. The Denver Teacher speaks of how, "Subconscious, conscious, and super-conscious become permeated with wisdom, insight, compassion, and sensitivity because your mind is content. As the higher mind begins to permeate your three levels, you begin to know what actions to take to benefit the beings around you."

> "Speak or act with a pure mind and happiness will follow as unshakeable as a shadow."
>
> —Attributed to Buddha

Happiness lifts the mind closer to the rarified wavelengths of *ananda* and transcendence, but Kriya Yoga is *"the path of action,"* not a philosophy of wishful thinking, sitting in blissed-out meditation, and waiting for happiness to follow. Blissed-out meditation doesn't hurt, of course, but it is not a basis for a happy and fulfilling life. There are active elements of self-discipline and study in Kriya Yoga. Happiness does not come just by wishing it so.

One action for enduring happiness is healthy motive. The Buddha's urging to, "Speak or act with a pure mind" is an excellent definition of healthy motive. If you are not inflicting pain on the world, the world is much less likely to inflict pain on you. One of the best supports for your happiness is to be the type of person that other people enjoy being with.

Conscious choice is another route to happiness. Begin the process by making a decision to be happy. This is no easy realignment of perspective. We all hold things against ourselves: The times that we have been cruel; the negative messages we have been given; a deep familiarity with our own arbitrary pettiness. It's a wonder we can look in the mirror! But we must look in that mirror and we must begin to like what we see to bring about a shift to personal happiness.

We may act with discernment to support our growing happiness. My Teacher suggests, "Do what you feel will bring yourself joy and don't worry about what anyone else thinks." And as Kriyananda said, "The first step towards *samadhi*: Lock yourself out from the negativity of your culture." However, much like when an alcoholic stops drinking and upsets dysfunctional family dynamics, there may be subtle pressure to drag us back down into unhappiness.

Gratitude is another element of happiness. Over thirty years ago I injured one of my knees while downhill skiing. Since then I have managed to keep myself limping along. I still cross country ski and I am more mobile than many, many people. What do I really have to complain about? I hike, I bike, I walk, and I climb stairs (slowly sometimes). My own bad attitude is my worst enemy. I should be shouting with joy that I have two strong legs that will get me outdoors or allow me to walk the dog. So what if my knee twinges now and then?

Another one of Kriya's actions for happiness that should be taken seriously: Get your Earth life in order. Kriyananda puts it this way, "Happiness is a byproduct of a lifestyle." Every problem, every bad relationship, and every closet that needs cleaning out is a distraction from our happiness.

"If what you do doesn't bring you joy, then don't do it."

I work to bring my areas of attention down to a handful of broad categories. My narrow list of what is important to me includes spirituality, health, learning, relationships, and career. The list is a conscious way for me to focus on happiness and identify what I need to jettison as excess baggage.

"You're here to serve. In that service is happiness," explains the Teacher. Compassionate service, with appropriate motivation, is an excellent way to support individual happiness and to share it with the world.

Happiness is a focused mind. The yogis and the *Katha Upanishad* (I.3.11) say that our life should be single-pointed. My Teacher explains that focus helps us to stay on the spiritual path: "Have a goal in your life so that you are not automatically influenced by the world." Multiple desires splinter our potential happiness.

Our goal should be chosen wisely. If our focus is on money, we will require money for happiness. I once heard that, "The secret to happiness is wanting what no one else wants." I've noticed that there aren't a lot of people out there elbowing each other aside to seek spiritual growth. And so far there isn't a way to tax it!

How do we maintain focus in this world of electronic images

that scream for our attention? The Island Mystic had his remote retreat without wireless or even a cell phone signal to distract him. There is much the Kriyaban can do to maintain focus on the happiness of spiritual growth. Utilizing *shama* for serenity and tranquility from the *Sadhana Chatushtaya* (the Four Pillars for the spiritual aspirant—see Chapter 9) we may support our happiness if we:

> - Avoid karmic impulses that pull us into the patterns of the past
> - Resist control of our emotions by *external* senses, objects of the physical world, and the pull of attractions and desires
> - Avoid upsetting things and situations
> - Cultivate surroundings that enhance contentment
> - Focus our minds on our source of serenity
> - Engage in activities such as meditation, prayer, chant, *mantra*, exercise, singing, *asana*, and *pranayama* to enhance contentment
> - Dedicate our actions as prayer in motion

Meditation is an excellent starting point for establishing happiness. It aids focus, fosters peace of mind, and prompts insights into the root causes things that disturb our equilibrium and happiness.

My Teacher points out an important component of happiness, "When you're happy, the mind is your friend. When you are unhappy, the mind is your enemy. That's why training the mind is so important." We must get the wild horse of the ego under control for our spiritual benefit.

Spiritual awareness is also important to our happiness. "The more aware you are, the happier you will be." The more our awareness of how the physical and spiritual worlds work, the more capable we are of skillfully staying out of the way of trouble and our own *samskaras*.

This journey towards happiness closely resembles the approach to *kaivalya* or enlightenment. Both happiness and the spiritual path lead to bliss. I like to think of "enlightenment" as "lightening up."

The Monk Who Howled Like a Wolf

Non-attachment, not surprisingly, is also a strategy for happiness. My Teacher says, "Your Inner Self is bliss. That bliss is available when you stop the striving."

Non-attachment may extend into isolation for some. The *Gita* mentions the isolation of accomplished yogis, living apart from others (18.52). Social isolation, though tempting for householder monks like me, is not a sure path to happiness. Although happiness is derived internally, unhappiness dwells internally as well. If we never rub shoulders with the world, our character flaws simply remain dormant for lack of opportunities to bring then to the surface. Prudent isolation should maintain happiness, not conceal unhappiness.

> "Don't try to improve others.
> Improve yourself."
>
> —A Teacher

The everyday mystic must go within to find the true sources of contentment. As everyday mystics, it is reasonable to suppose that a Kriya Yoga practice will lead to greater personal happiness, but whatever personal devils we harbor must first be booted off our howling monk's island. In the peace and contemplation that follows, we may find what we search for.

CHAPTER THIRTY-TWO

Ananda

> "We need to have a partnership between consciousness and bliss."
>
> —Kriyananda

There are limitations to how far happiness will take us. We live in an imperfect world and we express our divine souls through the limitations of mortal bodies and imperfect intellects. Our approach to happiness is flawed due to its dependence on mind and its constant distractions of attraction and aversion.

The Denver Teacher says, "Everybody is striving to be happy. They may be beating their head against a wall, but they are just trying to be happy." His use of the word "striving" points to one of the problems with happiness: We grasp for happiness because it feels good. *The Yoga Sutras* go so far as to identify attachment as a consequence of happiness (YS 2.07). In *"The Thornapple Tree"* (Chapter 12) attachment keeps a man hanging onto to what hurts him the most. Attachment is the primary force that keeps us marooned on this hard rock of planet Earth. Happiness inspires attachment to the objects, people, experiences, and circumstances that bring pleasure our way. The allure of happiness may inspire us or it may mire us in pursuit of the physical.

There is a state of mind beyond ordinary waking consciousness that goes by many names such as expanded awareness, *samadhi*, Self-realization, or Christ consciousness. This higher consciousness is one of the goals of Kriya Yoga practice. It is commonly believed that a union with the higher Self brings abiding contentment, but does this "partnership" bring us sustained happiness in this world?

Physical incarnations are subject to the effects of *karma*. Shoots of old *karma* spring up like weeds from tough old roots buried deep in our fields; seeds of new *karma* blow onto fertile ground to germinate and burst forth into blooms of sudden and surprising intensity. However, the fertility of *karma* is not the curse of our lives—it is the promise. On this world we are granted the opportunity to balance our personalities and to learn to rise above the *karma* that would otherwise have us on behavioral autopilot. Ultimately, happiness is irrelevant to the greater spiritual context of our lives.

If we set ourselves the goal of personal happiness we find that behavioral attachments stand in the way. Fear is one of these behavioral attachments. The fear that we will do something wrong in our pursuit of happiness makes us fainthearted. This is aversion (the flip side of attraction) at work, but to experience happiness we must take risks.

My Teacher says, "We need to focus on what we need to do rather than on hoping." Hope may cause us to passively wait for prayer or circumstance or an unlikely benefactor to bring happiness our way rather than to stick our necks out and do the work ourselves.

Our persistent attempts to control the external world are also barriers to happiness. The external cannot be controlled. If we stake our happiness on external reality we will be disappointed again and again. Everything of this world will end. For happiness to last, it must come from within. There is nothing in the external that we can count on throughout our lives. True happiness, like unhappiness, comes from within.

The company we keep may assist or hamper our movement

towards happy. People in our lives looking for validation of fearful or insecure perspectives push those perspectives on us. If we aren't careful, we misdirect our creative capacity from magnetizing good things into life to attracting strife and imbalance.

We have to wonder, "Why are these negative people in my life? Are they a reflection of my own tendencies?" It may be necessary to weed out our own negative aspects before the negative people in our lives move on for more receptive ears.

Mixed motives also come into play when we consciously or unconsciously sabotage our own happiness. This is instant *karma* at work. We expect bad things to come our way so we engineer events to confirm our suspicions. We think that our partner will betray us so we put her under such intense scrutiny that eventually she flees our obsessive control for healthier relationship pastures. Or perhaps we do not expect to succeed at work and our poor expectation is echoed in our performance. Consequently, we get passed over for recognition and promotion.

These stories we tell ourselves are our internal *mantras*. What is your internal *mantra*? What is the inner narrator of your life whispering in your ear? An internalized unhappiness may have its roots in previous lifetimes. We can begin to take conscious control of our lives by changing our attitudes towards ourselves and finding a new *mantra* that will serve our goals. If we begin to chant to ourselves, "Happy, happy, happy," happy will come.

With attention to these barriers to happiness—grasping for happiness, fear, passively hoping for better days, trying to control the external world, surrounding ourselves with bad company, our own mixed motives, and internalized unhappiness—we begin to improve our lives and even find ourselves moving into occasional states of bliss, or *ananda*.

We have all experienced bliss at some point. The experience may have lasted for only a few moments or minutes. These experiences may have nothing to do with what is going on in our "real" lives. In prayer for one precious, timeless moment warmth and a sense of deep peace and satisfaction fills our body; the intimate connection looking into a baby's eyes; standing on the top of a craggy mountain, still breathing hard from the climb, we take in the 360-degree view and know that all is right in the world; or bliss may come while locked in loving embrace with our partner, feeling a timeless connection tingling where warm skin merges.

This is *ananda*.

The Teacher says, "Real joy is placid and deep and still and abiding. Mystic bliss has nothing to do with this world. Nothing to do with good or bad, happy or sad."

Ananda is not based on emotion. Strong emotion may be involved at times, but we may also have bliss sweep down on us while sitting quietly in deep meditation far from the pulls of this world. *Ananda* is not a worldly experience—it is a spiritual experience. Kriyananda (note the last six letters of his name) points out that "enthusiasm" is literally derived from the Greek, *"en"*—in, *"theos"*—God, and *"ism"*—state or condition. In its original Greek usage, an "enthusiast" referred to someone possessed or directly inspired by God. Enthusiasm is the bliss of the God state.

Kriya yogis don't seek an external God (while not negating God). The Kriyaban's enthusiasm or bliss is internally generated from the god stuff within. Bliss lies within us all, carried eternally within the divinity of our own souls. Our moments of *ananda* come when we slip into soul consciousness or *Self-realization* as Yogananda described it.

Kriyananda, in his coyote trickster way of getting our attention, suggests that to find *ananda* find a path in life that brings contentment. "Just be happy. Go rob banks if that will make you happy." He describes a unique state of conscious needed to feel this type of happy—s*amadhi* consciousness:

> When you are down to one thought and there is nothing to measure time against and you are in the timeless realm. Suspended animation. Breathless. Timeless. The path for you is simple: Bring that which brings you joy. Find your bliss and follow it. That's it. That's your Path.

THIRTY-THREE

Meditate, Meditate, Meditate

One of my most intense meditation experiences was at a job in a Montana sawmill. I stacked newly planed lumber as it was disgorged from a huge planer. The constant deep howl of the planer, the repetitive movements of my legs and arms, the smell of pine in the air, the absorbing focus required to pull boards off of the "plane chain" and slide them into the correct bunk, neatly and tightly stacked, one on top of the other, all while watching for the next boards advancing towards me down the conveyor belt—it kept both body and mind occupied. Spinning and turning in my worn work boots, pacing up and down the line, breath loud and deep in my ears under the hearing protection muffs—that was my meditation in those winter months.

Another meditator sits on a yoga blanket in a darkened room, with a lit candle on the floor in front of her. She closes her eyes, slowly intones *"aum"* three times, and feels her breath move gently and deeply in and out through her diaphragm. She gradually loses her *self*.

This also is meditation.

Another may sit against a rock for ten minutes, feeling the first warming of the spring sun while looking out over a mountain glen. Drinking in views of forest, snow, and rock, content in the moment, she is without a care in the world.

A runner, striding forward, leg stretching, foot reaching, toes feeling for the rough pavement ahead, body carrying over the foot on slightly bent leg as the other muscled limb comes forward, the second foot reaching for its own patch of asphalt, breath rasping, sweat beading, eyes on the horizon, no distractions. The world narrowed down to movement, breath, body, and the path ahead.

This too is meditation.

Meditation is much like the word "yoga"—its meaning depends on its context and definitions vary widely. In Chapter 8, *Tending the Fire*, we surveyed the linguistics of the word "meditation" as it exists in the Kriya Yoga world. What we found was that meditation in traditional Kriya Yoga may be any one of the last three of the Eight Limbs:

> ➤ ***Dharana***—concentration of the mind upon an object (physical or mental).
> ➤ ***Dhyana***—control of the mind in meditation.
> ➤ ***Samadhi***—dissolution of the self into the object of meditation and, ultimately, union with everything in the universe.

I think of meditation as described in the seventh limb, *dhyana*. Meditation is control of the mind. With this perspective, concentration, or *dharana*, is an element in meditation and *samadhi* is an advanced state of meditation. Concentration is the tool, meditation is the action, and *samadhi* is the result.

Look back on the examples of meditation that open this chapter: Working in the sawmill; the meditator on her blanket; gazing on a mountain scene; the long distance runner. What of these was *dharana*? *Dhyana*? Do any of the activities have the potential for expressing *samadhi*?

No matter what definition we choose or where we are in the broad spectrum of meditation activities, Kriya meditation has common elements. One element is that meditation should be effortless and non-resisting. My Teacher suggests, "Watch your thoughts without evaluating or judging them. Watch them come in and go out."

Part of this effortless state, according to the *Gita*, is meditating with our ego under control (BG06.14). *The Yoga Sutras* in Book 3, Sutra 2 state that while in meditation we need to be focused on only one concept, image, or thought. The Teacher gives specific, esoteric instructions for attaining this focus:

> The state of consciousness that is related to the *ajna chakra* [at the third eye point in the center of the brow] is in command. The *ajna chakra* is where the mind is held in the meditative state.

The awareness of the meditator should be focused away from the external world, though we may concentrate on an external object such as a candle flame or even a mountain. That external object is a mirror in which we perceive the nature of our inner Self.

In the jargon of our New Age of spiritual exploration, we are trying to lift our vibrations up (which is to say, to increase the operating frequency of our mystical selves). Successful spiritual ascent grants us an enhanced perception of the deeper, non-physical reality underlying this physical world.

If we are successful in our quest for enhanced perception of the deeper reality, we may stumble upon that rarified result of meditation—*samadhi*. It's easy to assume that *samadhi* is a type of meditation. However, *The Yoga Sutras* describe *samadhi* as distinct from both concentration (*dharana*) and meditation (*dhyana*). The hierarchy of concentration/meditation/*samadhi* suggests that one must first learn to concentrate before one can meditate, and one must meditate before one can experience *samadhi*. Meditation guards the gate to the important state of *samadhi*.

If meditation guards the gate to *samadhi*, *samadhi* guards the gate to enlightenment. This means *samadhi* deserves special attention from the everyday mystic. In fact, *The Yoga Sutras* and other traditional texts devote a great deal of attention to the spiritual and practical benefits of combining concentration, meditation, and *samadhi*.

Schweig (a *Gita* translator and commentator) defines *samadhi* as, "perfect meditation... the attainment of total absorption in which the meditator becomes self-forgetful and is only aware of the object of meditation." In the *Bhagavad Gita*, *samadhi* is described as "unchanging discernment." (BG 2.53) My own translation of the description of *samadhi* from Book 3, *sutra* 3 of *The Yoga Sutras* sounds a lot like Schweig's: *Samadhi* happens when meditation becomes the thought and the mind is empty of its own nature. There is no distinction between the meditator and the object of the meditation.

The Denver Teacher points out that the ego resists surrender to this process of temporary oblivion:

> You have to release that base fear before you can go up to subtler states of consciousness. Defense mechanisms hide that fear, but it is always there.

The challenge for the modern *sadhu* is to allow the fearful personality to be absorbed into pure, unchanging consciousness, the ultimate source of all awareness, beyond individuality. We must allow our personalities to dissipate in meditation as the morning mist above a river dissolves with the rising of the sun.

The rising of Self.

> "If you don't want your life to change—don't meditate. Don't get on the path."
>
> —A Teacher

For most people, most of the time, meditation is the fastest way to move forward on the path—a proven route to enlightenment. As I wrote earlier, when Shelliji was asked what were the three most important steps towards enlightenment, he answered, "Meditate, meditate, meditate." The *Gita* also says that we will attain *yoga* (union with the Self) when we

Meditate, Meditate, Meditate

experience perfect meditation (BG 2.53) and that an effective route to avoiding the cycle of death and rebirth is through meditation as the personality comes to know the soul hidden within the personality (BG 13.23 & 24).

> "When you're happy, the mind is your friend.
> When you are unhappy, the mind is your enemy.
> That's why training the mind is so important.
> We are trying to learn how to use the mind
> rather than it using us."
>
> —A Teacher

Moving toward enlightenment is noble, but this far off eventuality may not be sufficiently immediate to keep us on the mat with all the noisy distractions in this world. Fortunately, meditation quickly begins to reward the time spent in daily stillness. Meditation is a means to control the ego. This improves our relationships by reducing the extremes of emotions that lead to conflict and helping us to remain in a loving state even when we do find ourselves in a disagreement. According to my Teacher, meditation also improves attitude by increasing stamina and enthusiasm, and meditation helps change the thoughts that determine whether our interactions with the people around us are stormy and reactive or thoughtful and calm.

The teachings reference meditation's ability to bring contentment (BG 12.12 and YS 1.30, 32, 34, 35, 37, 39, and 2.11) and meditation enhances awareness, allowing the voice of Self to be heard. While meditation can be exploited to attract material goods, the usual outcome is for the grip of physical objects to loosen.

> *Dharana* [concentration] is the binding of the mind to one place.
> *Dhyana* [meditation] is focus on one concept.
> *Samadhi* [meditative absorption]
> is when that same *dhyana* [meditation]
> takes on the identity of the one concept
> and the mind is as if void of its own nature.

The Monk Who Howled Like a Wolf

> *Samyama*
> is when these three
> [concentration, meditation, and meditative absorption]
> are practiced together.
> From *samyama* comes wisdom.
>
> —*The Yoga Sutras of Patanjali*, Book 3, Verses 1-5

The sages of old were known for their wisdom (as are the old sages of today). Chapter 2, verse 69 of the *Gita* refers to the sage as deeply meditative and insightful. This wisdom is born of or enhanced through concentration and meditation. The solutions to persistent problems and difficult relationship dynamics often spring fully formed into our awareness when we settle on the mat or even while reflecting quietly during a shower.

Jerry, who had questions about *yoga siddhis*, shared this inspiration at breakfast at that same Retreat:

> Any deep material that comes up in meditation has karmic weight to it and is likely to be residue from a past life. You should then be able to work effectively with this past life material without even knowing the details of any past lives.

I've wondered before how I might deal with past *karma* before it has a chance to cause more mischief in my current life. Jerry's reminder that meditation intercepts the flow of *karma* may offer a solution. *Karma* manifests first as a thought. Meditation gives us a chance to examine *karma* as a thought before we birth it into the more complicated world of words and deeds.

I do not use many affirmations beyond *aum* and various *mantras*, but I have repeated from my meditation mat many, many times these words from Kriyananda:

> The subconscious and the conscious are united in yoga, creating in focused and effective ways.

Meditate, Meditate, Meditate

The sages say that meditation may help our creativity. Meditation is a portal into the astral world and the astral is where thought energy begins to manifest into the physical. When we fuse *dharana*, *dhyana*, and *samadhi*, we are capable of the effective creation Kriyananda alludes to in the above quote. Here is the punch line: Our subconscious and conscious are already continuously creating, but if we create without focus and awareness, what we create for ourselves may seem like a bad dream. In meditation we can create consciously, improving our lives and enhancing our progress on the spiritual path.

The last benefits of meditation that I would like to mention are finding our *dharma* and union with our souls. As my Teacher says, "To the mystic, proof of consciousness comes when the mind is still. Once you slow down and quiet down and pay more attention you will hear your own inner teaching." As a meditation practice deepens, our *dharma* begins to exert a more active influence in our lives. Through meditation, the everyday mystic comes to know the divine soul within the personality, and the answers to our quest for meaning in this life begin to surface.

However, a comfortable and safe life may not be the best learning experience or natural expression of spirit. The most sublime spiritual progress may also challenge relationships, career, or lifestyle. To the ego, this dislocation of priorities looks like trouble. To the spirit, these changes may be the trivial side effects of approaching liberation.

*

A man came to Shelliji for advice on how to meditate in his over-crowded home with his less-than supportive wife. Shelliji assured the man that he would give him a technique for his difficult circumstances if only the householder would promise to follow the instructions no matter how odd they sounded. The man agreed, though puzzled by the advice.

In a couple of weeks he was back to see Shelley, eager to tell his story.

On the first day, as instructed, the man had asked his wife for just one minute to meditate undisturbed in the bathroom. She agreed. The man meditated for one minute, came out from the bathroom, and then did the dishes, just as Shelley had told him.

"On the second day, like you said, I asked her for two minutes to meditate. She was slower to say okay this time, but she did. So I went in and did my two minutes and then came out and did the dishes *and* vacuumed.

"And so on, day after day, a few more minutes and a few more chores, just like you told me."

"Well, young man, you seem like you are confused." Shelliji asked, "What's the problem?"

"I don't understand it, but now my wife wants me to meditate every day for an *hour*!"

CHAPTER THIRTY-FOUR

The Four Pillars of Meditation

"There needs to be time for stillness, silence, and simplicity."

—A Teacher

The first of the Teacher's *Four Pillars of Meditation* is **time**. He suggests a consistent time each day when we are rested and can focus (even if for only a minute in the bathroom). Find a convenient time and stick with it. The Denver Teacher suggests meditating when the sun is below the horizon—either before dawn or after sunset. Consistency is important for establishing and maintaining a meditation practice. Meditation should be as compelling a part of our daily routine as brushing our teeth. Meditation is our *mental* floss, after all.
Teacher:

> Even if, for some reason, you are not going to meditate during your chosen time, sit in your 'spot' for five seconds before jumping up again. This will help to reinforce the habit even if you do not actually meditate.

The second Pillar is **place**. We begin to establish meditative

The Monk Who Howled Like a Wolf

intention when we have a spot permanently reserved for meditation. This can be a corner in a room—perhaps adorned with a small altar or a candle, mandalas, or pictures of spiritual teachers. The best place I could find for meditation in one of my homes was a closet.

Yes, I was a closet meditator.

Meditation aids may include a cushion, a blanket, a meditation stool or a chair, candles, an altar, incense, or sacred music. Although none of these aids are necessary, they may help set the mood and cement our intention.

The seat may be a chair, a stool, a cushion or a blanket on the floor. The Teacher suggests natural fibers such as wool for any blanket or material we sit on or wrap ourselves in. However, he says, "I'm sure you could get enlightenment using polyester."

Lying down may not be a good idea—it's too easy to fall asleep. Sitting upright in a chair or on the floor (perhaps on a block or low stool) is recommended. I still find myself occasionally falling asleep even when I am sitting up, but I've never tipped over.

A block a few inches high, or something similar, helps me to maintain the sitting posture for up to an hour with minimal squirming. My habit is to put a yoga block flat on a clean floor or on a mat and drape a blanket over the top of the block. I sit on the cushioned block, with the outsides of my feet on the blanket, rotating my pelvis forward (reducing fatigue and discomfort to my back), and sit in half lotus (all my knees can handle).

David Lipschutz sat on the floor with nothing but a folded yoga blanket beneath him.

The Lakota believe material objects gain *ton* (rhymes with "fawn")—a spiritual energy—through repeated use by a holy person. This *ton* aids their healing work by amplifying the holy person's efforts. Your meditation spot and its contents may do the same for you. Your yoga block, seat, blanket, or cushion should only be used by you, and ideally only used for your spiritual practice. Focused mental energy will gradually infuse the material and begin to resonate with the spiritual power of Self.

Whether we meditate with our eyes open or closed (I do

The Teacher's Four Pillars of Meditation

both), a candle may help to set the mood or to provide a focal point, the flame a symbol of divinity.

Facing an altar may be helpful. Altars may be as elaborate or as simple as we wish, but many people add personally meaningful elements such as a picture of a teacher or *guru*. My Teacher says, "Your altar may include a flower, a picture, a book, crystal, or stone."

The Teacher uses incense in a group setting but warns against robust or stimulating scents such as frankincense or *nag champa*.

My Teacher's third Pillar is **technique**. Technique begins with a supple and flexible spine (through *asana* or otherwise) and correct spinal posture while standing, sitting, or lying. The spine should be in its natural gentle s-curve, not slumping to either right or left. The chin should be dropped down slightly towards the chest to straighten the very top of the vertebra. If we are hunched in meditation, or slumped over, curled into a ball, or otherwise contorted, our ability to amplify and conduct natural spiritual energies is limited. This is why the *Gita* advises stillness for the meditator, with body, neck, and head aligned (BG 6.13).

In meditation, and in spiritual practice in general, we attempt to cultivate the spiritual *kundalini* energy that is thought of as a dormant serpent lying coiled at the base of the spine in the first or root *chakra* (the *Muladhara chakra*). The expression, "rising *kundalini* energy" refers to that serpent rising up the spine during spiritual emergence and awakening.

A trained body is helpful to meditation practice. If we can't sit quietly for twenty minutes without restlessness or exhaustion setting in, we are unlikely to achieve any depth of meditation. An *asana* practice may be helpful to establish the ability to maintain a pose for longer periods. Or a vigorous walk before we "sit" gives our restless body a reason to appreciate some down time. Toning and strengthening the core torso muscles that maintain an erect posture may also help the meditator.

The Teacher advises that during meditation we should keep the belly soft, breathe through the abdomen, and relax the tongue away from the roof of the mouth. He also says, "When you sit down, surrender your body to the cushion, and your mind to the method."

Once the body is in shape for meditation, we can begin strength training for consciousness itself. Three basic techniques guide our approach to the desired mental state of meditation—beginner mind, focus, and no expectations. The Denver Teacher speaks about beginner mind:

> When you sit in meditation, there must be innocence. People on the path a long time sit habitually. Go into your next meditation with the belief that it is the first time. That moment will be unique...

"Beginner mind" is a state of childlike wonder: Noticing the birds in the airport and the joy in a spring day. When meditating, sit with the innocence of a child. There is no telling what will happen on that blanket.

The willingness and ability to focus is also critically important to meditation. It may sound simple: Just concentrate the thoughts on one subject or object. Unfortunately, we are forever multi-tasking—driving with the radio on; exercising while listening to music; washing dishes while watching a video. It's been a long time since I just sat out on the porch in Denver at the end of a summer evening and watched the sky grow dark, the neighborhood hush, and the bats come out. We are trained by our world of electronic "devices" to have the attention span of humming birds. We flit from channel-to-channel, song-to-song, or even spiritual path to spiritual path like a hungry bird searching for the latest, greatest nectar.

Any meditation is better than none at all, but for the best results we must build up our ability to focus. My Teacher suggests that we "keep our awareness at the third eye" and that we, "Watch the breath. That becomes the object of meditation."

The Yoga Sutras instruct that concentration/*dharana* is a focus on one thing. Our own breath may be that one thing. We carry it with us, available whenever we meditate. We don't have to have a candle or a *mantra* or *koan*. Focus on deep and slow inhalations through the nose, sliding down the back of the throat, conscious of the workings of the diaphragm acting as a bellows.

The Teacher's Four Pillars of Meditation

Be aware of the short pause at the end of the inhalation and remain aware through the slow exhalation (the little death) as the diaphragm rises up to empty the lungs.

My Teacher coaches, "Sustain awareness for the length of the exhalation. Let the breath breathe you..."

Focusing on the breath gives the monkey mind (ego), something to do. With the ego occupied, the observant Self may pass on guidance or the meditator may occasionally slip into the timeless state of pure awareness and peace known as *samadhi*.

"Do nothing; look for nothing; expect nothing."

—Kriyananda

We may meditate for months and "nothing happens." We go reluctantly to our cushion; our minds wander; we squirm; we mentally watch the clock. Then one day a solution to a critical problem at work floats, pre-polished, into our awareness, or we feel unsought bliss coursing through our body as an electric charge in our flesh, or we realize that we have no recollection of where we were for the last ten minutes and we can't recall the last time we took a breath. That monkey mind was gone. Just gone. As we come back into our *selves*, we pull in a little air, trying it on for size—like it is a choice whether we breathe or not.

Or it may seem like we make no progress at all in our first six months.

But on reflection, we realize it has become easier to sit. We are more creative and healthier. Or we may find ourselves more tolerant of the quirks of those around us and of our own human shortcomings.

The changes in the meditator may be subtle or they may be dramatic, but meditation changes us for the better. Life begins to improve, particularly if we have no expectations of meditation. As Kriyananda said, "You can only truly meditate if there is nothing you want. Meditation is to get rid of stuff—not to get things."

Kriyananda traveled to the Far East many years ago to see

what he could learn and came back with a lesson on the importance of non-attachment in meditation. He found a monastery in Thailand with a pleasing meditation space, but the room adjoined an open market and the windows were typically flung wide open to catch the cooling breezes. The street vendors made a terrific racket right outside the window, making it impossible for the young Kriyananda to concentrate.

Kriyananda talked to his meditation teacher about his difficulty focusing with all the noise. The teacher appeared very concerned and immediately ushered Kriyananda to a small and peaceful room in a quiet place in the depths of the monastery and settled Kriyananda back down again. The teacher played some Mozart on an old-style turntable.

Kriyananda settled down with a sigh of contentment and closed his eyes gratefully.

"Are you comfortable now and able to meditate in this quiet room with the beautiful music playing?"

"Ah, yes, sir. This is just perfect. Thank you so much!"

The teacher then pulled the needle of the record player across the black plastic disc with a horrible tearing sound. Kriyananda's sense of peace disappeared in an instant.

Kriyananda turned to the teacher and blurted, "Why did you do that? Everything was so wonderful here."

The teacher demanded of Kriyananda, "Do you think that the Mozart you love is any different than the noise outside?"

Although Kriyananda's meditation teacher pointed out the value of flexibility in meditation, I find it useful to have a pattern or sequence of techniques. Knowing what I am going to do as I sit takes away some of my performance anxiety and relaxes that insecure monkey mind. My techniques include some focused breath work and repetition of certain *mantras*.

Some start their meditation with the "death breath." After finding your seat, take a deep breath while looking forwards, then turn your head to the left and slightly down, and exhale with two rapid puffs through parted lips (the death), before facing forward, pause for a second or two, then a slow inhalation (the rebirth in meditation).

I find myself occasionally drawing in two very rapid,

The Teacher's Four Pillars of Meditation

involuntary puffs of air—the opposite of the death breath (usually when my consciousness wanders between wake and sleep). The life breath? I feel that this quick double inhale heralds (for myself) the arrival or departure of a layer of consciousness. I have the impression that the state of my own superficial consciousness or ego determines the suitability of mental environment for this other state, causing it to ebb and flow, those shifts in the tide marked by this unheralded life breath.

The Denver Teacher suggests that we not try to force order and focus on the disordered ego. There is a technique he calls "Let the kids run wild" in which we let the mind go where it will and watch, as Observer, with interest and non-attachment. Eventually the thoughts tire and they leave you alone.

Mantras may help quiet the mind. Traditionally, *mantra* was chanted, rather than sung, but Westerners have an easier time remembering the foreign syllables when they are attached to a tune. Today there are beautiful *mantras* arranged by excellent musicians. For a real treat go to a *kirtan*, or "call and repeat" concert. Hundreds of people singing in *Sanskrit* to ancient *mantras* generate an electrifying mystical atmosphere.

Mantra doesn't have to be in *Sanskrit*. It can be in your native tongue or even in meaningless syllables. My Teacher introduced the "E" mantra in one of his classes, saying that it can stun the monkey mind into silence. "Eeeeeeeeeeeeeeeeeeeeeeeeeeeeee," with a sudden cut-off before running out of breath. Repeat as many times as needed. "If done correctly, you will sound as if a smoke detector has gone off."

"*Aum*" (often written "*om*") is the *mantra* that the master tried unsuccessfully to teach the monk who howled like a wolf. It is the *mantra* most commonly used in the West. Often *aum* is intoned three times slowly to start or end a meditation. It is also a popular way to start group events. Most of us have heard *aum* before, but the Teacher cautions that there is a tendency towards mispronunciation. The mother of all *mantras*, *aum* should be sounded as three syllables, "Aaaaaahhhh-uuuuuuuuu-mmmmmmmm," with a gentle slide from the "ah" sound into the "u" sound and on into the "m" sound. Without three distinct syllables, my Teacher feels that we miss some of the beneficial energy of this sacred *mantra*.

Aum forms the core of another monkey mind suppressant technique: We take a long, slow inhalation and then burst out with *"aum"* rapidly and repetitively until we are out of breath. We then duplicate the process as many times as needed. This technique should bring the wanderings of the mind to a sudden stop—like throwing cold water on fighting cats. Instantly, the cats have something else to worry about.

There are *mantras* to conquer fear, battle depression and negativity, or to send compassion to those who are struggling. Find meaningful resonance with the *mantra* or *mantras* that are best for you—you don't need to know what the words mean. Playing, chanting, or singing a *mantra* may be helpful to start or conclude a meditation session or may help bring a distracted monkey mind back into focus.

If *mantras* are not for you, perhaps *tarka*, "intense reflection," would be more effective. I introduced the *tarka* practice in Chapter 28, *Iwa Awareness*. *Tarka* is looking back on how the day went—what we did right; what we wish we had done better; where we might have picked up new *karma* or where we successfully sidestepped *karma*. *Tarka* practiced at the end of the day in meditation may help us to gain greater insight into our patterns and deeply ingrained *samskaras*. *Tarka* can be done while in meditation or, less formally, lying in bed after we have turned out the light.

The Denver Teacher says, "To meditate *on* something is important as an occasional technique." This thing can be a *mandala*—a colorful wheel of patterns or images designed to direct the mind toward specific aspects of spiritual reality. We can also meditate on any beautiful object (the candle flame is a previous example) or may even mentally construct an object, real or imagined. He describes a technique:

Ask yourself what the most beautiful place or thing of beauty is to you. Do not use a person. Perhaps a rose? Recreate all aspects of that thing in your mind. Create beauty and then realize that you are that beauty.

The Teacher encourages students, "In meditation, keep

The Teacher's Four Pillars of Meditation

repeating and answering the question, 'Who am I?' and keep eliminating successively deep answers until you find your core belief." This simple query is one of the basic puzzles of spiritual existence. What is our true nature and what was our origin?

The last of the Four Pillars of Meditation is a **healthy diet** for our practice. A healthy diet allows the body to sit quietly and comfortably while our mind does the same. If our body is calling out for attention, the mind will not be able to concentrate.

My Teacher suggests that it is best to meditate on an empty stomach—with perhaps a little water before sitting to head off cries of abuse from the monkey mind. He believes that spicy food, dairy, stimulants, alcohol, meat, sugar, and impure tap water can all interfere with meditation. Good eating habits include organic food in smaller helpings than the average Westerner normally consumes. Occasional fasting is also part of my Teacher's approach to proper diet.

Commitment to my own health has grown with my commitment to the spiritual path. This commitment includes thoughtful eating choices (greater proportions of organic food, more plant matter, less dairy), regular moderate to strenuous exercise (walking, hiking, skiing, biking), and a consistent sleep schedule. As my body and my interest in spiritual matters have matured, I have become less tolerant of unhealthy choices. These shifts in behavior are not privations—they are changes that I make without soul searching or resolutions. Much like Osho says, you naturally begin to turn towards what works. "Renunciation follows awareness like a shadow."

The Monk Who Howled Like a Wolf

CHAPTER THIRTY-FIVE

Sit Down & Think About That

"If you believe you don't have ten minutes a day to meditate, well... you better sit down for an hour and think about that."

—Duncan Roads

Even when applying the Denver Teacher's Four Pillars of Meditation our *dharana* experience may not be all that it could be. Kriyananda and my Teacher suggest how to improve meditation with a formula:

Intensity x Duration = Force

In other words, if the force or outcome of our meditation is lacking, we may increase either or both of the intensity (concentration) or the duration (time) to improve the outcome.

The intensity of meditation has a big impact on the quality of the experience. Are we focusing on the breath or are we thinking about what we are going to have for breakfast? Drop the mental chatter and listen. It has been said that prayer is talking to God and that meditation is listening to God. It doesn't hurt to listen harder.

The Monk Who Howled Like a Wolf

The other variable in the equation, time, is simple to address. Spending more time "sitting" is another way to get more satisfying results out of our meditation. Instead of ten minutes, try to meditate for twenty. If you feel rushed in the morning, perhaps you need to meditate at night when chores and job aren't competing for immediate attention. Perhaps you need to suggest to your partner that you will vacuum in exchange for more time in the bathroom.

Another method for getting the most out of meditation is to practice techniques designed to control *prana*, or life force, through deliberate manipulation of our breath patterns. These esoteric breath techniques are often referred to as *"pranayama."* The *Sanskrit* word *pranayama* has many layers of meaning, but in this context it means directing life force with breath. One-on-one instruction is best for learning *pranayama* techniques, but written and video information are other options.

The last basic method for improving meditation is the most effective, but also the most difficult to put into place—the adoption of a lifestyle suitable to support meditation. The Denver Teacher points out, "There is a direct correlation between lifestyle and the effectiveness of meditation. Practice the *Yamas* and *Niyamas* and your meditation will flower." This lifestyle support ranges from organized and simple living to less obvious and more fundamental changes such as what my Teacher terms "purification" and "stabilization" which encourage the states of consciousness sought in meditation.

If our lifestyle is characterized by discord and noise, then the inevitable impact on our spiritual life will be to bring that discord and noise to the meditation cushion. Lifestyle should reflect the harmony, peace, and order that we hope to experience in meditation. Meditation is, ultimately, a portal into our Self. We are a reflection of our environment and our environment is a reflection of us. As below, so above. As above, so below. To ignore the external landscape is to unwittingly program the internal. Even if we do not feel peaceful and harmonious we may begin or enhance our spiritual path by creating a lifestyle in harmony with our goals.

Remember: *Iwa*. Fake it till you make it!

Sit Down & Think About That

Duncan Roads' quote at the beginning of the chapter and the story of the man with the small apartment and the uncooperative wife illustrate two reasons why people don't meditate—misplaced priorities and a poor environment. It's hard to justify the time meditating when our "To Do" list is half a page long, but the life improvements that come with meditation are worth twenty minutes a day. We may be willing accomplices to the skewed value system of our consumer-driven culture, or, we can choose to cultivate what is truly meaningful in our lives and spirits.

> "It's better to quiet that mind of yours
> and listen to what comes up
> than to fill it with a bunch of knowledge."
> —A Teacher

As far as having the wrong "place" in which to meditate, look at Shelliji's creativity in finding a path to meditation for the harried man in his small apartment. There is usually a way. Our ability to meditate is limited not so much by circumstance, but by our own lack of initiative, flexibility, and resourcefulness. The solution may be under our nose and as simple as skipping late night television and getting up half an hour early, or walking to a nearby park in the evening and sitting on a bench, or shutting and locking the office door during lunch breaks.

Kriyananda says, "People who are always focusing on other people, other things, are running away from themselves. That's why meditation for most people is impossible until they learn to accept themselves."

Some of us have more complicated barriers to meditation than even self-acceptance. It can be difficult, almost painful, for some people to be alone with their thoughts. If this sounds familiar, don't label yourself as unable to meditate. Our culture is resigned to a cacophony of constant sensory input so going inward is a foreign sensation to many of us. The Teacher points out, "It is a big shift to sit down for fifteen or twenty or thirty-five minutes and not expect anything to happen." But basic approaches can make meditation a habitual part of life.

Meditation takes discipline. Even in the midst of a peaceful and satisfying meditation practice it may be hard to ignore the voice of the self-sabotaging ego. We must be resolute in our meditation. Eventually, we look forward to it as the best part of our day.

When we fall off the meditation horse, we can follow the old advice: It doesn't matter how many times we fall down, only that we get up again each time that we fall.

The Teacher takes a flexible approach: "After almost forty years, I notice people tend to be a little rigid in their meditative practice. They try too hard to get something. They try too hard to get it right. It's okay to let your mind wander, at least initially. Like a dog or a kid, eventually the thoughts settle down."

Trying *hard* to meditate doesn't help outcomes. Of course, we want to make an effort, but effort in the conventional sense is counter to the process and spirit of meditation. My Teacher once showed me a cartoon of two Zen monks having a meditation match, each sweating and straining with the effort to meditate longer and harder than the other. My Teacher couldn't help breaking into laughter as he held the sheet of paper up for me. A meditation competition is ridiculous, of course. Meditation is not Zen monks straining to outdo each other. Meditation is an effortless, non-resisting upwelling of pure, relative consciousness. It is only after quiet contemplation that our sight can penetrate the pure waters and spot the shining ruby within.

Seated in *Satsang* another day, the Teacher said, "The three questions Buddhists ask themselves in meditation: Am I reaching or grasping for something in my meditation? Am I resisting something in my meditation? Am I not being vulnerable enough in my meditation?"

Although interruptions to the daily routine should be avoided in establishing our practice, we *can* meditate too much. According to the *Upanishads*, anyone who spends all of their time in the physical world is destined to a lack of awareness, but anyone who spends all of their time in meditation will go to even greater darkness. We are spiritual beings, but we are also of this world. To turn our backs on the world is a negation of the "now" we have chosen to experience. This now was Self-engineered for our spiritual growth. As aware beings we apply what we learn in meditation to further our effectiveness in the world.

The Denver Teacher cautions us to avoid the ego-trap of using meditation to accumulate possessions through the creative power of harnessed thought or strengthen *yoga siddhis*. The beckoning *yoga siddhis* are a time-consuming detour, not a destination.

The meditator may become aware of sounds in the right ear, said to change as the seat of consciousness climbs up the *chakra* centers: Buzzing, a tone like a flute, the notes of a harp, a deep bell, or other sounds as higher *chakras* become the focus of awareness. In meditation, I first noticed overlapping harmonics in my right ear: A warbling keen, sliding a couple notes up and down the scale in a continuous pattern, while the volume pulses louder and then more quietly, with a deeper hum underlying this pulsing. This is not tinnitus, which I also experience on the rare and brief occasion with no change to these underlying tones.

A new or old meditation practice may also bring erratic and disturbing, or controlled and thrilling manifestations of *kundalini*. Without guidance, awakening *kundalini* through meditation can be a bumpy ride. Rising *kundalini* can bring sudden flashes of inexplicable insight, mysterious physical pain or burning sensations, feelings of static electricity sliding about or in the body, pulsations in the spine, psychological disturbances, restlessness, feelings of pointlessness, ecstasy, or even depression. Obviously, it is best to have an experienced guide through *kundalini* rising. It may advance into a "dark night of the soul"—an existential crisis of potentially life-changing proportions.

> "Meditation is designed to disturb you.
> It will initially expose you to stuff you have tried to hide."
>
> —A Teacher

The first six months of my meditation practice uncovered some of my own darkness. The moral impact of what I remembered of a past life began to sink in and I saw my nice guy persona as just a brittle shell covering a lurking malaise of old pain, moral ambiguity, and frustrated desires. Although my meditation showed me a clearer picture of who I really was, this picture was difficult to face. Eventually, as I absorbed this new awareness, the pace of uncomfortable self-discovery tailed off and I entered a period of balance and self-acceptance.

The Teacher says:

> Do not evaluate. A thought comes in and automatically we evaluate it. *Don't*. Touch a thought gently with your awareness and it will go away. You don't have to take responsibility for the thought—only for what you do with it.

In the Kriya world, thoughts are autonomous, like leaves drifting through the currents of the astral. We cross paths with thoughts, but the thoughts aren't "ours" in a conventional sense, and if we don't grab onto them, they will be swept away on the current and no longer trouble us.

In *Mejda*, Sananda Lal Ghosh describes Yogananda's perception of thoughts in meditation like dirt clouding a jar of water. First the water is a chaotic swirling cloud of color—you might not even see the particles. Soon though, you will pick out individual grains and you might get discouraged seeing that your water is full of dirt. But if you are patient and wait longer still, the dirt begins to settle out, leaving clear water behind.

> "You can't get off your cushion
> and leave meditation mind behind.
> You must live it."
>
> —A Teacher

Meditation is not the endpoint of our spiritual practice. We do not meditate to grow calm, know peace, or to accept our life—though these goals are worthwhile. We meditate to become an effective and *conscious* physical and spiritual being. We meditate to know the indwelling divinity and to become, increasingly, an incarnate expression of that divinity. We meditate to begin to understand, as a *sadhu*, how the world works, why we are here, and where we are going.

The Monk Who Howled Like a Wolf

CHAPTER THIRTY-SIX

Sufficient Unto One Life

Memories of past lives aren't necessarily a good thing—they may disagreeably color a present, as did mine in my relationship with Roxanne. And as a child, I remembered a time that had nothing to do with my life in Melbourne, Seattle, and Kailua: Wood smoke curling out of a small shack's chimney, a hog pen a few feet away; chickens silhouetted in a leafless tree against a sunset sky; red dirt patched with grass; a town a couple of miles away through the fields; a woman crying outside a door. In my memories of that life I was a hermit, raising pigs and chickens; living alone for a long, long time. My Pig Life.

As an adult in the 1990's I tried self-hypnosis and dredged or manufactured a few more details out of the murky depths of my unconscious. A scene of absolute terror crouched in a trench with a long rifle, waiting for the order to advance. I remembered a city name from later in that life and enough of the terrain around the familiar shack to draw a topographical map of the area. One night lying in bed, this incarnation's name popped into my head with enough force that I couldn't forget it. In my focused meditations I retrieved a date of death—over a hundred years ago. I searched atlases and found a small town in Kentucky that matched the town name in all but one letter.

The Monk Who Howled Like a Wolf

I waited anxiously for the USGS map I ordered to come to me in the mail. When it did, my hand drawn map overlaid the printed topographical map almost perfectly: North was north and the hills were as I had sketched them. Even the city was the same distance away and in the same direction that I remembered. The correlations made it even harder to shrug off my memories as fantasy.

Emboldened and hesitant at the same time, I wrote off for birth and death records—with no luck. None were kept from those years in that county. Not giving up, I walked the two miles to the nearest pay phone (yes, still a hermit) and called information for the Kentucky town "I" might once have lived near. I asked the operator if there were any listings under the last name in question (*my* last name?).

She answered, "Oh, honey, half the people in this town have that last name."

Shocked, I politely got off the phone and thrust my hands into my pockets to warm them against the Alaskan winter cold. I wasn't ready for this homecoming yet.

> "Most of us have forgotten the last cycle
> so we think this is new and exciting."
>
> —Kriyananda

Naturally, we wonder why we can't remember past lives. Even uncertain and vague recollections of past lives, like mine, are rare in adults. By the time most of us reach adulthood, the memories we may have had as children have melted away.

I've forgotten a lot about this present life of mine. I mowed lawns in Seattle to pay my way through college. For five years, all summer, every week, I would drive a beat up '64 Chevy pickup with bad brakes to the same lawns and march back and forth; shearing arrow straight rows in crisply cut Kentucky blue grass. Thirty-five years later, I'm not certain that I could find one of those dozens of yards I once knew so well. I even struggle for the names of childhood friends.

Not too long ago, I moved back to Alaska after an absence of fifteen years. When I left Alaska the first time, I left in a big way, packing up everything and moving thousands of miles to a completely different culture and climate. In Colorado there was virtually nothing to remind me of my old life. Names of my old acquaintances didn't come up in conversation. Email and social media had not yet wormed their way into daily life to keep me posted of marriages and break-ups, births, and graduations. With almost no reminders of the old, Alaska was forgotten. I felt the loss of the wildness of Alaska, but I didn't spend a lot of time thinking about it.

Then I came back, drawn by Gail, the old longing to return, and a vacuum in my life that called for a challenge. The homecoming was disorienting, though I remembered the place—the mountains, the land, the animals, even the mosquitoes. All that was familiar, and I maneuvered myself through the landscape with long practice, but the details of my previous life and my memories of people I once knew well were vague and difficult to recall. Even now, years after returning, I run into people I once knew, but I can't recall their names or my former relationship to them. My amnesia embarrasses me—it must seem as if I am senile or uncaring. It's as if a light switch in my brain was turned off, casting the Alaskan files into darkness. But sometimes, if I focus and dig deep into my over-stuffed file cabinet of a mind, the old memories start to resurface through the fifteen-year interruption.

The process in which I have misplaced chunks of my present life through lack of use and relevancy is similar to what happens when we die. The Teacher says, "When we incarnate there is a non-continuity of consciousness that causes us to forget." Death immerses us in a different world (like my move out of Alaska) and begins the steps that lead to a "non-continuity of consciousness." We metaphorically find ourselves thousands of miles away in a "culture" completely alien to that of our former lives. If we don't exercise the memories of what happened before, we lose or misplace those memories. Throw in the possibility that our ego "re-boots" with the birth of a new body (the non-continuity of consciousness my Teacher talks about) and it's a wonder any of us remember anything at all of past lives.

A few people remember their birth, or being in the womb. Some people also claim to remember even further back—to a past life or lives or even remembering a time between lives. Some have inexplicable scenes or events float into their awareness, as I did. In young children these memories may include verifiable details that cannot be explained away as something read in a book or overheard (see the studies of Dr. Ian Stephenson).

For most of us though, we forget our past lives much like we forget our dreams on waking, or forget once daily routines after years down another path.

Our tendency to confuse our mortal roles with our immortal identity creates yet another barrier to hanging onto these timeworn memories. When we introduce ourselves to new acquaintances we tend to say something like, "I am a homemaker," "a plumber," or "retired." We define ourselves based on our role in the physical world rather than by our personality's enduring qualities. Very few of us would tell a new acquaintance, "I am an introvert, with an interest in keeping my surroundings orderly that borders on OCD. I struggle with persistent anxiety issues, and I have a tendency to keep small animals—perhaps to combat that anxiety."

When we die, external means of identifying ourselves are gone. We are suddenly aware that this life we have clung to is just an act. We have jumped into the sea clutching an anchor. Naturally, we release the anchor of our past lives and swim for the light, leaving behind the weight of the labels that we once carried.

During his Sermon on the Mount, Christ said, "Sufficient unto the day is the evil thereof." (Matthew 6:34) These words remind me that the *karma* generated even in this life (one brief day to the immortal Self) is burden enough. I have struggled with memories of a crying woman at the door of a shack and snatches of wrenching war scenes. Paralyzing despair could be the result if I remembered all the times I have hurt other beings. Whatever the reasons for our amnesia, it may be fortunate that we seldom remember more than bits and pieces across lifetimes.

CHAPTER THIRTY-SEVEN

To Love & To Learn

"The *dharma* was the dream.
That was the initial reason we came into this life."

—A Teacher

The two weeks of service work at the Boys and Girls Club in Pine Ridge Village on the Pine Ridge Reservation was the beginning of many trips to South Dakota. Every few months I would contrive a week off and coax my old van northeast on the ten-hour drive from Gunnison and make myself useful at the Club. The Executive Director and founder of the Club was Leatrice "Chick" Big Crow. She became one of my spiritual mentors. Chick was a dedicated and sometimes unnerving Lakota woman who had learned compassion the hard way—through painful life experience. After a rocky start to adulthood, she dedicated many years of her life to her people (Lakota *oyate kin*) of the Rez.

One summer day Chick was driving the van on dusty back roads as we returned to the reservation from a northern Nebraska gathering marking the life and death of Crazy Horse (*Oglala Lakota* mystic and warrior of the 1800's). We were both in a thoughtful mood, pondering Crazy Horse's doomed struggle to protect his people from the westward expansion of European culture.

Breaking the silence, Chick said, "Sometimes Indian souls are born into white bodies."

I thought about that for a minute, reminded that although I was born white I was somehow magnetized to Pine Ridge.

Finally I asked, "Why do you think an Indian soul would be born into a white body?"

Keeping both hands on the wheel as she maneuvered around potholes, Chick glanced at me as she said, "Because they're being punished."

Then she tipped her head back and roared with laughter.

Rather than reincarnation as punitive, Kriya Yoga teaches that any punishment is self-inflicted and not designed to hurt, but instead to heal and broaden the soul's understanding and compassion. The Denver Teacher says, "There is no external control, according to the mystics. *You* have planted the seeds. That's the Law of *Karma*." Still, from the ego's perspective, a hard life might feel like retribution inflicted by an outside force.

Instead of a type of recidivism for penitents, one reason for living over and over is to understand all we may of love. We are also blessed with the opportunity to broaden our knowledge of life on earth in all its incredible variety of forms and systems and sentient beings. These two assignments—to love and to learn—drive our schooling in the physical realm.

Reincarnation is a transition of consciousness from one reality to another, much like from sleep to waking. Transitioning from a dreaming consciousness to waking may be abrupt or slow. The dreams may hang on and insinuate their way into waking life for a minute or two.

What was that sound?

I've got to get away from this monster!

Where am I?

Who am I?

What day is this?

The transition of sliding back into our physical form may be confusing. Sometimes the dream life seems more real than this life.

This is reincarnation—the movement of consciousness from one reality to another.

This movement happens much the same whether we are drifting off to the astral worlds in sleep, or when our heart stops beating, or when we find ourselves in a new physical body. There is a period of confusion or even lack of self-identity as the body (physical or astral) shuts down and consciousness "reboots" into another state.

Evidence from NDE's and After Death Communications suggest that personality and memories often make the transition from the physical plane to the astral, but the astral ego rarely penetrates to consciousness in the new physical incarnation. There is something about the move from the realm of thought to the denser physical worlds that buries the soul consciousness and disrupts the memory track. Usually there is no recall of past lives.

By the time a soul has taken up residence in a new body, only the old likes, dislikes, patterns (*samskaras*), and inclinations make it to the forefront of the new consciousness.

This reincarnation process, according to the *Gita*, applies to all but a very few souls. Almost inevitably, souls take on new bodies a few years after death just as we replace old clothes with new ones (BG2.22). Chapter 2, verse 27 of the *Gita* says that for anyone that is alive, death is certain, and for anyone who is dead, birth is certain.

Entertaining the possibility that reincarnation may indeed be the way of things leads us to yet more questions. Where are we between lives? How do we travel back and forth to that in-between place? Is it possible to go to this other place while still alive? Can the dead travel to our world? Can the dead see us? Hear us? Can we see or hear them? If there is such a thing as reincarnation then there must be much more to reality than what we understand. What else is possible if consciousness is independent of the brain?

We may also ask, even if there is such a thing as reincarnation, what difference does it make? The Teacher explains that there are important reasons reincarnation matters, such as getting another chance to get life right and having time now to prepare to make the next life better.

To the everyday mystic, the spiritual process of reincarnation is a sacred one, supporting us in our search for transcendence. A life that is part of a gradual spiritual evolution is not to be lived thoughtlessly. Reincarnation means that our lives matter. The laws of *karma* will take into account all that happens here. This is not a carrot and stick philosophy. No one is trying to punish us because we bullied someone in third grade and no one is trying to reward us because we gave generously to the poor last Christmas. But reincarnation does mean that the next time around we will gravitate to the life environment that best suits us.

We have the opportunity to change lives—our own. We can envision now where we want to be the next time around; the way we would like to live; the skills we will need; the people we would like to keep company with—and start the groundwork. Some exceptional mystics, such as Shelliji and Kriyananda, literally plan seven lives ahead. We may start by planning for one life ahead. It will be here before we know it.

Kriyananda points out, "We are immortal. Being killed is not going to solve your problems."

I'm tired of hiding in that old shack. I have made mistakes and I have hurt others and myself. There are devastating patterns in my life that I would like to end. I have taken the idea behind a Dalai Lama quote, "*If you make a mistake, fix it as quickly as possible*," and expanded on it from my northern perspective: "Mistakes grow like snowballs rolling down a hill. It's best to deal with them as quickly as possible, because as they roll they're going to getting bigger and bigger." I have seen the consequences of my actions get bigger from lifetime to lifetime.

It's tempting to wail that there can't be a God—just look at the unhappy world that we live in—however, as my Teacher says, "This world is as it is because it's a classroom." Our world is the result of the shared karmic expression of the souls inhabiting it. From the Kriya yogis' point-of-view, this world is the perfect place for us. Until there is an improvement in the quality of the souls marooned here, the world will continue limping along much as it is now. Want the world to be a better place? Make yourself a better self.

A belief in reincarnation means that our priorities shift. This doesn't mean that we should give away our possessions and live in caves. Not even Lahiri did that. We have responsibilities and often have given our word on very deep levels to be a part of a community greater than ourselves. However, the mystic operates under different priorities than most people. The mystic finds the yearnings of the masses trivial and the masses find the mystic's perspective mystifying.

My Teacher believes, "In mysticism you are self-created. To the mystic your life was not created by some god. Only you can fix your life because you made it that way." Reincarnation means we have no one to blame for our troubles and behavioral ruts. We have practiced these mistakes hundreds or thousands of times (possibly with the same partners). These patterns are ingrained on a spirit level.

Awareness of reincarnation gives us our personal power back. We are not victims or pawns of forces beyond our control. We manifest ourselves into the conditions that we need due to the laws of *karma* and due to a resonance with our family of birth. A reincarnationist worldview challenges each of us to rise spiritually from the circumstances we have gravitated towards in the past and to consciously and effectively work towards the life that we would like to experience tomorrow.

We are responsible for the quality of our lives. No one has forced us into anything. We may not be in charge of the details such as how our neighbor feels about us or if it snows tomorrow, but we put ourselves in this place, with all of its stormy weather. If we want to head out in the car for some fresh scenery, we'll have to shovel the snow out of the driveway first.

The Monk Who Howled Like a Wolf

THIRTY-EIGHT

Consciousness Entombed

> "Life is swift and short.
> We are immortal,
> but *this*
> [tapping the flesh of his arm]
> will die."
>
> —A Teacher

Mystical reality intrudes into our familiar and predictable world in an infinite variety of forms for those who notice such things. I am reminded of an odd event on that Kriya Yoga Retreat in Woodstock, Illinois.

Between Kriyananda's talks and meals I would strike up conversations with other attendees or go outside to find a patch of good cell service to update Roxanne on the latest lecture subjects and goings on. Although she lived just forty miles away in Chicago, she wasn't attending the Retreat, but she liked to talk yoga.

Taking a contemplative break from real life, I kept socializing to a minimum. I fell into the habit of exploring the expansive wooded grounds. I wasn't the only one—a few people would head outdoors during free time, singly or in couples. To maintain my solitude in the solitude, I wandered further and further out into the thick trees. A quarter mile away from the Retreat Center I came across a large pond in a break in the leaf canopy. A small boat rested temptingly on the grassy bank. Occasionally I would row out into the middle of the pond and watch the fall leaves drift down to settle on the still, dark water.

One afternoon, thinking I'd walked beyond all the casual strollers, I took a serpentine route through unfamiliar groves to the pond. Deep in thought, it took me a few moments to become aware of a dark figure downhill and a couple hundred feet away, traversing an area choked with brush and downed timber. I couldn't pick out any features or clothing colors, just a black silhouette, although mid-day light suffused the space under the trees. It was slim, appeared slightly fuzzy around the edges, and perhaps five and a half feet tall. The figure stepped stealthily through the brush with absolute silence, attention focused intently on the sound of murmured voices in the distance, closer to the Retreat Center. After a few moments I lost track of the walker as it stepped behind a tree.

At the time, I hardly paid attention to the person, lost in thought as I was. It wasn't until three or four minutes later that I consciously considered what I had just seen and began to wonder at the odd black figure and the misplaced furtive movements of the watcher in the woods.

I wondered then—like Sybil—if Kriyananda was keeping an eye on us, but Kriyananda has better things to do in his astral body than peak at us from behind trees. Was this a meeting of worlds? My world, where consciousness is chained to the physical, and this other world, in which someone is at the same time here and not here, vanishing without trace like the tracks of leaves through still autumn air. Was this a live being or some exotic entity walking on the border between physicality and the astral? How does my apparition fit into the grand scheme of things? The Denver Teacher says, "There is a double nature within us—an ego and a spirit." Was my shade more spirit than ego?

Consciousness Entombed

The Kriya Yogis, while stretching for non-dualistic reality, warn of the dualistic nature of human consciousness. Our normal consciousness is ego-based and tethered to the physical body, but a non-dualistic reality abides within "the secret cave of the heart" as the *Katha Upanishad* (I.3.1) calls it—an inner spark of immortal consciousness. This dual nature is the basis for reincarnation beliefs whereby ego handles the concerns of the physical world and the physical body, and spirit is the captain of the larger and timeless spiritual journey. While restrained in the dualistic consciousness of ego segregated from our shade-like spirit, we are doomed to a cycle of birth, death, and rebirth.

> "Anything that is born of a moment shall die."
>
> —A Teacher

The "I" who writes these words will die. The *Gita* says, "having been born, death is certain." (BG2.27) Perhaps I will die tomorrow. Perhaps I won't.

My Teacher uses the metaphor of an arrow's trajectory to describe a lifetime: "The release of the arrow is birth. Hitting the target is death." That's a short flight across our earthly landscape.

The Tibetans have a term for corpse that literally means "that which is left behind." Bodies soon outlive their usefulness on the astoundingly long journey of the spirit. Our fragile and short-lived bodies are vehicles for the myriad manifestations of these immortal souls.

Kriya Yoga thinks of three different types of bodies (*shariras*) that the spirit makes use of during its many incarnations, closely related to the Hindu concept described in the *Taitomnitiriya Upanishad* of five successively more ethereal sheaths or casings (*koshas*) over the inner core of spirit.

The physical body, "*sthula sharira*" contains both the *annamaya kosha* (the casing made from food) and the *pranamaya kosha* (the casing made of the life breath). The *annamaya kosha* is the familiar layer of flesh and blood created and sustained through physical matter while the *pranamaya kosha* is a parallel energetic system animated by *prana* or *chi* and manifesting physically in the breath.

The astral body, "*sukshma sharira*" (subtle body), is that part of our selves created and maintained through the power of individual ego consciousness and unshackled from the physical world. The astral body is the mental or mind layer—our vehicle of consciousness in dreams and out-of-body experiences—and is also known to the Hindus as the *manomaya kosha* (the casing made of mind).

The third and final body is the causal body, the "*karana sharira*," a subtle spiritual essence at home in levels higher than the astral worlds. The causal body contains the higher intellectual and spiritual identities, the soul memory track, and *samskaras*. It is ageless and timeless, containing both the *vijnanamaya kosha* of higher intellect and discrimination (the casing made of intelligence) and the *anandamaya kosha* (the casing made of bliss) closest to the transcendent *Atman* or Self. The causal body is for most of us deeply buried beneath the facade of the physical and the ego, and is only sensed or experienced during *kundalini*, peak meditation, and deep, dreamless sleep.

Within and beyond all these bodies and layers, as the saints and sages have been telling us for millennia, is the core of higher reality—the spirit that is not tethered to any body or boundary; spirit that exists in a state of pure consciousness.

It may interest pet owners to hear that Kriya Yoga teaches that animals only need to have a brain and a spine to be utilized by spirit. Any vertebrate may be the home of soul and souls may transmigrate between species.

Even though the lifetime of a body is "swift and short," the body serves as a vehicle for the physical manifestations of the spirit and is also our vehicle for ego consciousness and personality. Kriya yogis see our time in the physical body as potentially dangerous—addictive in a spiritually damaging way. The physical world is seen as a trap, a self-imposed detour on the sacred journey to transcendence and enlightenment. The physical state encourages amnesia towards the ascendancy and even the existence of the divine spirit.

The Denver Teacher says, "You have never been born, therefore you can never die." He teaches that, "God created the universe but did not create you. You are infinite. You were not created."

My Teacher's words are an echo of the *Bhagavad Gita*, "The soul was not born and it will not die... it is unborn, eternal, and everlasting..." (BG2.20) The spiritual plane does not have the same relationship to time that we do. The Teacher says, "As I understand it, time is a product of the mind/body complex. Immortality negates time." Spirits exist outside of time and beyond the physical and energetic structure of the universe.

The *Gita* describes the soul/spirit as omnipresent (BG2.24), unalterable (BG2.25), and eternally enduring (BG2.30). As I let these words and their literal meaning sink in (*meditating* on them, so to speak), I am increasingly drawn towards the idea that the soul exists outside of time in an unchanging bubble of pure consciousness, spinning off bits of itself through some sort of inter-dimensional porthole from its world into ours.

My Teacher says:

> We are spirits caught up in the material world. We are consciousness entombed. No past, no future. Mystically, yogically, we are consciousness—period. You have a cosmos within you.

Spirit is our true nature. We have these lives in the physical that seem so real, so permanent, but who hasn't woken from a dream with the sense that they have been in a world every bit as real as our own physical world—perhaps even more vivid and more substantial than this life? As my Teacher says, "When the real world begins to look like a dream then you are becoming a yogi. There is a more real world within you."

In the first seven years of life, according to Kriyananda and my Teacher, the memories of the previous life are closest to the surface. If we want to see what a past life might have been like we can look at our early childhoods. Did we always want to be the one with the bow and arrow when playing cowboys and

Indians? Were we the neighborhood tattletale? Did authoritarian parents intimidate us or were we strong-willed and quick to challenge power? What kind of life-threatening or persistent health problems did we have?

We can't expect to establish a clear storyline with these cues, telling as they may be. We are unraveling a complex cosmic mystery with a plot that has developed over thousands of years.

We are entombed in the physical like flies caught in amber. Though we are trapped on the surface of this rock we have an immortal core, made of the creative building block of the universe—the pure consciousness of spirit. All in the physical and all in the astral finds its birth in this consciousness.

In the beginning there is soul.

CHAPTER THIRTY-NINE

What Haven't You Done?

"We've all been whatever there is to have been under the sun."

—A Teacher

It is a soothing but mistaken simplification to think of reincarnation as coming back to Earth again and again in a brand new body with a fresh start. The Kriya concept of reincarnation avoids oblivion at the physical body's death, but reincarnation also means that *dying* is experienced over and over again. We outlast these physical bodies, so prone to aging and system failure, but our conscious memories, central to our notion of who and what we are, are only marginally more permanent than our flesh and blood. Our personal history dissipates as we establish a new ego consciousness in the next life. Only deeply rooted patterns and neuroses (*samskaras*) and the odd memory persist.

The Teacher's *guru*, Kriyananda, suggests that the average human on the spiritual path has already experienced 800,000 incarnations on the physical plane.

800,000!

If "we" live on, as we think of ourselves now, it is as a buried file in a large drawer, filled with three-dozen other dusty life files, in a four-drawer file cabinet, in an enormous, dim warehouse filled with five thousand five hundred and fifty-five ancient file cabinets.

The Teacher asks, "If you've eight hundred thousand lifetimes, what haven't you done?"

If we really are one life in 800,000, two conclusions are immediately and disturbingly inescapable: 1) Our egos amount to nothing when weighed against the enormity of the whole; and 2) There is likely no experience, no matter how noble or depraved, that is not contained in those cabinets.

The Kriya belief in reincarnation is not a feel-good approach to life. This belief system carries with it the certainty that we are the murderer, the rapist, the torturer, the victim, the thief, the adulterer, the whore, the saint, the hero, the soldier, the baker, the scientist, the farmer, the herder, the spouse, the beggar, the queen, the cripple, the child, the hunter, the monk, the trader, the athlete, the stag, the pig, the dog, the hare, the rat, the eagle, and the mystic...

> The yogi,
> wholly developed after many births,
> goes to the absolute goal.
>
> —*Bhagavad Gita*; Chapter 6, Verse 45

We have done it *all*. And the crushing weight of all these experiences is buried in those file cabinets, moldering in the vast causal warehouse of the spirit. Our spirit. Despite all this weight of experience, *sadhus* dream of transcendence—of leaving that baggage behind and knowing an indescribable bliss free from the consequences of our depravities and our moments of grace.

One unpleasant possibility in the concept of reincarnation that does not receive much attention is the fate of the personal ego. Everything that I remember of past lives is no more personal than recalling a movie or a book. There were hard times in the Pig Life, but I don't *feel* the trauma. I remember something of the death and something of the recluse's heartaches, mistakes, and fears, even mundane details, but the experiences feel second hand.

I do believe in reincarnation *and* I don't believe that I, Norman Sollie, was alive before this life. I explain this apparent contradiction through my understanding of how the reincarnation process normally operates.

Sometime in utero or during physical birth, the causal body—the body housing the higher intellect and the uppercase Self—animates a new being. Since the causal body carries the memory track of all incarnations, as this new child grows, she may have scattered past life memories at the surface of her consciousness, particularly those of relatively recent or traumatic events.

But growing is absorbing work and of necessity this girl devotes her energies into developing and establishing her physical and astral bodies (the astral body being the home of ego consciousness, lowercase self, and the **I**-dentity). She grows and matures and develops an earth-bound sense of individuality with an ego born of this lifetime. The images of past lives that had once been at the forefront of her consciousness are overwhelmed and replaced by a flood of new, vastly more relevant sensual experience.

She grows older until one day her physical body dies one of a million possible deaths. Her astral body, weakly connected to the physical, quickly abandons the worn out corpse, but conveys her identity and ego into the astral planes where she manifests or is drawn to a celestial environment in resonation with her intrinsic nature.

She, her personality and ego, continues to exist in the astral even after physical death, but "she" does not survive through another birth. The spirit/soul/Self of her causal body animates a new being before or during physical birth. Being born again is similar to waking from a dream: The dream ego and sense of self are shattered at the transition back into consciousness. We are born again, but we lose the largest part of that former consciousness at the transition to the physical world. As death kills the physical body, birth normally kills the astral body and the ego within it.

This new physical being may have access to the causal body's memory track of her past life. However, *the old astral body with its ego and personality does not make the transition to the new body*. Her old ego and personality are reabsorbed into the collective, immutable Self and filed away.

The new physical being puts its energies into the process of ego restoration, developing its physical and astral bodies. It grows. It develops a separate sense of identity with a new ego born of this *one* lifetime.

However, nothing is lost. Every moment of our previous lives are recorded in the memory track and available (with a little work) for replay and review, but only with the fleeting emotional connection of an audience member watching a film. My Pig Life is dead and gone, absorbed into the filing system of consciousness that lives within the causal body. Beyond the causal body, the Over Self, the *Atman*, the Soul—whatever we choose to call it—is infinite, unfathomable, and timeless compared to mortal egos.

The ego self is dead. Long lives the Self.

CHAPTER FORTY

Prepare for Death

"It is better to die once than to live 80 years with fear."

—Kriyananda

During the fourteen months I lived in Hawaii as a child, I developed an infection in my ankle from a minor scrape. Warm, humid Hawaii is full of life, even at the microscopic level. The infection became serious enough that my parents took me to a doctor. As instructed, I bent over an examining table with my shorts pulled down a little ways. But that was the limit of my cooperation. I cried and squirmed while the doctor explained that I needed a shot to save my foot from amputation. He grew frustrated with my unreasonableness.

"Would you rather have this shot now or lose your foot later?"

I knew better than to answer that question. I didn't want either one, thank you very much. I continued to blubber and whine about my cruel fate.

In a few moments the doctor interrupted me to announce with disgust, "I already gave you the shot!"

I hadn't even noticed. Sometimes the anticipation is so much worse than the event. After that day I no longer worried about shots. It had been proven to my satisfaction that they weren't all that bad.

Death is much the same: We worry and carry on about how horrible it is, but death can be over in a moment with hardly an awareness that it has happened. Accounts from Near Death Experiences tell of blissful relief and immediate freedom from pain.

The Teacher says, "Mourning is for people that have a different philosophy from a mystical philosophy. How can you mourn when something cannot be separated from life? Death is a continuation, not a rupture."

In our materialistic world there is a great deal of uncertainty, repression, fear, and resistance regarding the dying process. I recall the old joke about the dying man who said, "I know everybody dies, but I thought that God would make an exception in my case." Death is to be avoided at all costs, with the underlying assumption that it is an *end*. To the Kriya yogi it is not an end, but simply a transition to another stage that may be beautiful, may be a learning experience, or may be another wasted opportunity. It all depends on the dying person's state of mind.

The everyday mystic can be a "merit-bringer" when loved ones are going through the process of their own physical death. The Teacher advises us to, "Encourage a dying person to remember their great deeds or joyous moments as they approach death so that they will cross over with a good attitude about their life."

A merit-bringer improves the state of mind of other beings by extending the peace and contentment they feel to those around them. One way to be a merit-bringer when a loved one is dying is by weakening the hold that fear has on them. Ask a dying person to tell about their happiest times. If someone dies with happy memories and a light heart, they will be greeted in the astral in a pleasant place that reflects their own light state of mind.

Prepare for Death

> At death, Kaunteya,
> you will go to the state of being
> you are conditioned to remember.
>
> —*Bhagavad Gita*; Chapter 8, Verse 6

Anxiety over death has a negative feedback effect on the dying process, creating more fear. We can break that cycle of fear by moving into the next phase with light hearts. Death is literally a transformative experience. Attitude is all that distinguishes dread and foreboding from a sense of adventure and curiosity as to what comes next. The broken, worn out, or exhausted body is about to be left behind along with its physical pain and disease as the soul breaks free of the Earth.

> The Self is master
> and enters and leaves the body
> like the wind carries scents from their source.
>
> —*Bhagavad Gita*; Chapter 15, Verse 8

You can and should prepare for your own death. A Teacher sees death as nothing to fear—no eternal damnation and no heavenly reward for turning the other cheek. The astral is a world where we can have whatever we want, whatever we put our minds to. If we die with a load of guilt and regrets on our plates, we may continue to express that darkness in a place we create for ourselves. If our souls are light and happy, then light and happiness will be our world.

We may consciously tune ourselves to a chosen state, instead of reacting to life with old, unhealthy patterns. The less pain or mental anguish associated with the dying process, the more composed and centered a spirit will be as it moves into this new phase of existence.

Guilt, the fear that we are mortal, and the ego's belief that we are separate from other sentient beings interfere with a gentle transition at death. Kriyananda suggests: "Don't let your mind punish you. God is not vengeful. Everything is working towards your spiritual evolution."

No evolved spiritual being out there wants to see another punished. We must transcend in order to serve as a beacon for those still wandering in the dark. Our ability to help others is nil if we keep punishing ourselves for what we think we have done wrong in this life. Instead, we may look forward and become a being that can help lift someone else up.

Besides working towards our own contentedness, elimination of guilt, and dissolving the ego-based feeling of separateness, my Teacher suggests placing our single-pointed attention on some grand task or *dharma* so that we are drawn back to it. "Feed, emphasize, and commit to your path so it will carry over into your next life."

In retreats on death and dying, my Teacher has spoken in detail of the Kriya view of the transition. The Teacher agrees with the *Gita* that our state of being at the time of death dictates the quality of our next stage. When the curtain falls for people that expect their awareness to end after death, there is a tendency to lose one's ego self as the role that they have been playing comes to an abrupt end. After that last scene they have no direction, no lines to recite, no tape on the stage floor anchoring them to reality. Skeptics of consciousness after death may black out "for 3-1/2 days" as their ego grapples with the "impossibility" of continuity after the death. Confused spirits may sink into a dreamlike semi-conscious state of unfocused awareness, creating implausible scenarios; reenactments of life like the incoherent and scattered scenes of a fever dream. Eventually, consciousness resumes on an astral plane (the "Bardo" of Tibetan Buddhism).

We assume that the astral is a place of higher spiritual awareness, but the astral worlds are not, according to my Teacher, to be thought of as higher states of being. They are *subtler*—more malleable to the creative abilities of consciousness (group or individual)—but not necessarily more evolved environments. This is particularly true in the lower astral.

Somewhere between the dreamers and the seekers of

Prepare for Death

knowledge, are the souls still very much interested in the lives of the loved ones left behind on earth. Astral beings may cross the divide between our world and theirs. Some disembodied spirits go to great lengths to communicate with relatives and friends still experiencing physical incarnations. Some of these spirits are pulled back by the great remorse they feel for harm inflicted on those left behind. Souls, prepared in advance for the transition after death, may leave the dreamy lower astral and the earth plane behind and move on to the higher knowledge planes, and beyond.

My Teacher says that all souls, even those locked in a dream, experience a "life review" before they are born again into the physical world. A life review is a guided trip down the memory track of life, focused on how the soul helped and hurt other sentient beings in the course of the previous lifetime. These life reviews on the astral plane are said to show, in painful detail, how our decisions and behavior have affected others.

If we die with peace and contentment in a life well lived, we may "drastically improve this next incarnation" according to the Teacher. The ancient mystical texts of Hinduism and modern past life hypnotic regressions suggest that a great sage with purpose may reincarnate in just a few months. Aimless souls may enjoy a respite of 4,000 or more years before returning to life on Earth. Either way, they may not notice a difference—in the upper worlds earth time is meaningless.

The souls of the lower astral jump at the chance to come back to the physical world in a physical body, though facing all the aches and pains and heartache that go along with the human experience. Attachment, *karma*, and opportunities on the physical plane for spiritual growth all motivate souls to leave the instant wish-fulfillment environment of the astral. Before being reborn, my Teacher says that souls experience a future life preview so that the soul moves on fully informed as to what they have to expect and what the goals of the next life are to be.

According to the Teachings, certain character qualities increase our chances of a positive, "well born" incarnation, but those that haven't grown spiritually in their previous earth life may find that that they are right back in the same troubled situations that they had left behind. The hermit of the shack meditated on his attachments and greed for one woman so successfully in the Pig Life that my inheritance in this new life was the chance to recreate this Thornapple tree. On a deep level of consciousness I was searching for her long before I saw that sporty cherry red coupe parked outside the Pine Ridge Boys & Girls Club that hot and dusty august afternoon.

My unhealthy obsession for Roxanne bridged the gap between lives. Across time and death, the brown-eyed woman was once again at the hermit's door.

FORTY-ONE

The Third Way

"Rivers meander, but they still get to their destination."

—A Teacher

The good news: We keep reincarnating into the physical until we are ready to move on. The bad news: We will keep reincarnating into the physical until we are ready to move on.

Most of us spend life after life after life slowly gaining in Self-awareness in a creep towards enlightenment. Mystical practices such as Kriya Yoga have been developed simply to give us better odds of reaching our final goal. We don't have to wade through another 800,000 lifetimes.

The everyday mystic seeks the spiritual awareness to move off the karmic wheel of life and death. This is a process that can take 800,000 lifetimes or it can happen as it did to Buddha while sitting in meditation under the *bodhi* tree. Our goal, as everyday mystics, is to rise up out of this prison planet we have checked ourselves in to, helping our sisters and brothers to rise up with us.

To "rise up" is to advance spiritually from lifetime to lifetime rather than reincarnating as an unconscious consequence of *karma* and *samskara*. The *Bhagavad Gita* points to attachments (BG9.03 & 13.21) and a lack of faith in *dharma* (BG9.03) among the reasons that we keep reincarnating. Chapter 16 of the *Gita* identifies characteristics that imply a positive reincarnation experience (moving in the direction of transcendence). These are primarily inner attitudes (qualities that we can actively practice even while sitting in meditation): Bravery, honesty, humility, innocence, peacefulness, perseverance, self-control, self-possession, sincerity, and vigor. These qualities include the outer expressions of austerity, compassion for all beings, generosity, non-attachment, tenderness, and tolerance.

The list of qualities that lead to a negative reincarnation experience is a long one. The inner qualities to be avoided include anger, anxiety, arrogance, attachment, corruption, dishonesty, gullibility, hatefulness, ignorance, incomprehension, lustfulness, pride, the pursuit of power and violence, lack of spiritual substance, opposition to the spiritual, and a baseless spirituality. The outer qualities to avoid or overcome include boasting, insensitivity, claiming god-like qualities, cruelty, destructiveness, dishonesty, greed, indulgence, inflexibility, self-importance, self-punishment, and snobbery.

The man of the Pig Life actively cultivated many of these negative personality traits. He was mean-spirited, unforgiving, cruel, lustful, spiritually baseless, and very, very angry. And yet, I remember a happier scene that seems to be from a life between the Pig Life and my current life:

> An electric light shines outside a small, white church with horizontal wood siding. The church stands in a hollow of tall grass, a dirt road winding around the natural bowl above the building. It feels like the land of the Pig Life, but the electric light would have been out of place there—outdoor lighting only came to some places towards the end of that life and in this memory I am young.
>
> I am gloriously happy and alive and filled with love in the dark, in the tall grass on the slope above the church. The focus of my love is here with me. I remember her long brown hair and longer skirt, but I can't picture her face.

The Third Way

> We embrace and drop to the ground, rolling together down the slope through the grass, the dry stalks casting long shadows, brown hair cascading around us, laughing and happy to be alive and together.

That's all that I remember, but I also have the sense that war claimed the young man soon afterwards. He died with the memory of that night in the tall grass softening his heart and so began the process of dreaming a new dream—a dream with room for love.

Why remember this stuff? What good does it do to remember bits and pieces of past lives that we can't do anything about? Sometimes I feel helpless and trapped in an epic drama with a fixed script playing out over hundreds of years. When Roxanne and I approached romance, I forecast how things would go: We would have a difficult relationship plagued by my insecurities and her need for someone more exciting than an older man who wanted all of her attention. I would seek the quiet country life. She would be drawn to the city. We would quarrel and break apart over and over again. I would finally turn my back on her and retreat into my little shack of a heart.

That is *exactly* what happened.

When Roxanne was diagnosed with breast cancer she wanted the stable, dependable Norman back as an anchor to see her through the surgeries, the chemotherapy, and the long dark nights alone. I read the wish in her words as she expressed regret for our failed past, heard the need for my support in her gentle voice, and felt across the distance her hope for a shared future, if only for my soothing voice on the phone and gentle words in emails.

I couldn't do it. I couldn't let her back in the door. I feared that life would devolve again into endless cycles of need and rejection, of frustrated desires encouraged by ecstatic fleeting moments of rolling together down through the tall grass of a warm fall night. Instead, I turned away, grateful for the stability of my relationship with Gail, determined to move forward spiritually, and with conscious awareness of what I was doing and why.

There is a bigger prize than allowing *karma*, enduring attachments and strong aversions, the *samskaras* of old habits, and our personal ego demons to keep us returning over and over to re-play the same stories hidden within a change of scene and costume—we may rise up.

At a certain point in my spiritual studies I realized that I was hearing and reading hints that we were not faced with just two equally unsettling options: The choice of ego death at rebirth or the alternative of *nirvana*, individual absorption in a sea of unchanging consciousness (not dissolution, but *solution* or soul-union with God or spirit once the ego has been left behind). There runs through the Teachings an intriguing third option of attaining conscious awareness—forever. A spirited debate grew inside of me as my wise Observer Self tried to fend off the haggling of my insecure ego self as I heard more hints of the third way:

"Conscious awareness... forever? Wait a minute! You mean there is a way out of the ego death that comes with birth?" my ego asked.

The Observer demurred, *No, no—forget about conscious awareness forever. There isn't any reasonable chance that we can sidestep ego death.*

"But... we know that once in a while people are born with complete memories of a past life. Sometimes these people even have the same personality as they did in the past life and they insist on being addressed by their old names. Isn't that survival of the personality?"

Okay, yes, there is the very slightest chance that your precious ego may endure to the next life. Remember Shelley and his seven lifetimes of continuous consciousness? But why would we want to hang onto our sad old personalities? Have they been all that good to us? I'm glad to be rid of that old guy in the shack.

"Tell me what you know."

I don't know anything. You might as well ask the dog sleeping on the futon downstairs...

"Tell me!"

The Third Way

Okay, already! I will remind you of what little we have heard in the Teachings. The first reminder—as Kriya Yogis, we are resolved to release attachments and what bigger attachment is there than attachment to the ego? Someday we will all flow back into the creative source, with nothing lost, everything gained. Only great determination or wisdom can preserve the ego mind through incarnations. The odds are so against us pulling this off, why die striving for a hopeless cause?

"Tell me."

You asked three times, so I am bound to remind you of what we know about Self-realization. Remember the causal body? We like to think of it as the causing *body. The causal body contains the higher intellectual and spiritual identities along with the memory track of all of our lives. The causal body exists outside of time and does not perish with birth or death. It is immortal and the home of the Self.*

As Kriyananda has said, through samadhi *there is the potential to link the ego self with the spiritual Self. It is possible for the occasional persistent and stubborn sage to shift their center of* karma-bound *awareness from the temporary physical and astral bodies into the big "S" Self of the causal body. This is the miracle of Self-realization that Yogananda Paramahansa woke us to. You may understand Self-realization better if you call it "Self-attainment" or "Self-awareness." This immortal awareness isn't based in the little "s" self of our current ego personality. Yet this is not the death of ego—the basic qualities of our earthly personalities remain accessible. But it is a change in the ego state, with absorption into expanded consciousness.*

"How can we do this?"

We already know how to maintain conscious awareness across the veils: Through meditation, realized mystical knowledge, selfless devotion to a higher reality, and focused concentration on the spiritual worlds at death.

"What kind of a New Age, crystal-sniffing answer is that?"

The Monk Who Howled Like a Wolf

That internal conversation was an interesting exercise, but I would like to offer some support from more reliable sources. The *Gita* describes just what circumstances at death may be effective in escaping the cycle of birth and death through this union (yoga) with our own souls. Those whose thoughts are absorbed in yoga at death, who have understood the Self as the essence that animates the spiritual and material worlds, and who know that the Self is the foundation of offerings, will know the Self after death (BG7.30). One reaches the divine with a calm mind at death, while absorbed in the power of yoga, offering love to God, and focusing the breath between the eyebrows (BG8.10). To reach the supreme destination, sound "*aum*" as a single syllable at death while continuously thinking of the Self (BG8.13).

Waiting until the death bed to start humming "*aum*' may be too late a start. If we are truly motivated to sidestep the cycle of birth and death and to remain fully conscious and aware into eternity, we must seek absorption in yoga, peace at the contemplation of death, love of the divine, and spiritual knowledge in this life now.

I believe Shelliji's oft-repeated advice for the three most important practices to advance towards this goal of Self-realization is still the best advice: "Meditate. Meditate. Meditate." Remember, this direction came from a man who claimed to have experienced continuous consciousness for seven consecutive lifetimes.

> "These are reruns we are doing.
> All we have are leftovers.
> You are like a groove on a record.
> You are trying to shift and get out of the groove."
>
> —A Teacher

What would it mean to shift our consciousness to the causal?
One thing we can deduce about our divine soul is reflected in our basic nature: The soul is of love. We may make a mess of it,

The Third Way

but with very few exceptions we all yearn to love and be loved. We bicker with those closest to us, but woe to anyone who wants to harm those we quarrel with. The body of evidence from penetrations of the veil between life and death (such as past life recall and near death experiences) suggests that we have two primary goals in our lives—to love and to learn. These two drives animate our core being and reveal something of the nature of the soul.

Resonating within mainstream religions, another quality of the spirit as revealed in Kriya Yoga teachings is that of our own divinity. The *Bhagavad Gita*, in Chapter 13, verses 22 through 32, addresses the divine nature of the supreme or omnipotent Self, dwelling within all of us. For the mystic yogi, there is a holiness (even within other mammals according to BG5.18) that is to be carefully observed, nurtured, sought, and respected.

> "Spirit has no personality.
> Spirit has no *karma*."
>
> —A Teacher

Our spirits are beyond the influence of personality and ego. Our egos are byproducts of spirit's forays into the physical and astral planes, but ego is not an inherent quality of pure spirit in its timeless home. Lacking an ego/personality, spirit is also immune to the twin forces of attraction and aversion that brings *karma* to those of us striving in the world. The *Gita* explains in Chapter 13, verse 31 that the omnipotent Self does not act and is not tainted by the actions of its physical incarnations.

The nature of soul/spirit is all that we yearn to be. We have a beginning. We die. We take up this space beneath our feet and no more. We are constantly changing and evolving. We are "consciousness entombed" in time and space. Our bodies are ever vulnerable to destruction. Our level of consciousness is insignificant compared to the potential each of us contains.

We *can* leave this murky shack that we imprison ourselves in—with our memories and identity intact—and walk out into the sun, joining those who have gone before.

The Monk Who Howled Like a Wolf

> "You are Life.
> You are Life itself—all that ever is and all that ever will be."
>
> —A Teacher

The Kriya Yogis allude to evolving further yet, even beyond this shift of consciousness into the causal body, and getting off this rock for good, transcending the physical, astral, and someday even the causal planes—final absorption into the divine that rules all.

Why on Earth would anyone want to dissolve into a sea of pure being? Kriya Yoga gives us tools to experience peace and contentment on Earth, to become increasingly skillful at manipulating our physical reality, and to recognize and manifest the optimum circumstances for ourselves. Why not be happy with those fine accomplishments and our ever-evolving ability to be content and peaceful, life after life?

These are not bad goals and, surely, far ahead of playing the victim in an unloving, nihilistic universe. What does transcendence and absorption into the divine have to offer us that makes good lives on Earth seem like second prize? What do we have to gain through union with the divine?

That's a question for the saints, but my suspicion is that union with the divine gains us absolutely everything.

And, absolutely nothing.

Absolutely.

FORTY-TWO

The Programming of Karma

Gail and I felt our friend's death as a deep wound. A drunk driver struck Astrid as she bicycled to work early one chill morning on a side street in our little town. To many of us, her sudden loss felt senseless and cruel.

Hundreds of mourners pressed into the high ceilinged meeting room of the Community Center for Astrid's memorial service, many standing to the sides and behind the rows of hard plastic chairs in the back of the gymnasium-sized space. Many loved her and her easy smile and warm greetings would be missed. The youngest of Astrid's four sons was barely a teenager, but he greeted the mourners at a side door. One son had come from overseas, as had Astrid's brother and her mother. Her ex-husband—still her friend years after their divorce—was there too.

While feeling personal devastation at her sudden and unexpected death, and great empathy for her sons, this event was a celebration of her remarkable life of traveling the world and the remote corners of Alaska. The high-ceilinged room was decorated with whole spruce and birch trees cut from the woods and accented with colorful wild flowers gathered from the weedy fields behind the community center. The once sterile and open space now had something of the feel of the boreal forest that Astrid loved so much.

Gail and I sat close to the front, facing a row of tables spread with pictures of Astrid and mementos from her life. We told stories of her adventures and the lasting impact she had on her family and friends. We sang. Her brother broke down in tears reading a poem in his Danish-accented English. He said he knew that she was doing fine on this next journey—Astrid's strong spirituality would have smoothed her transition to the incorporeal—it was the rest of us who were in trouble without her.

I wondered if she was in the room. Many cultures believe the newly dead remain with their loved ones for a few days or return when they feel the attention of those still in the physical. I looked around, up into the corners of the high ceiling and to the space around her family. I unfocused my vision, as a hunter might, waiting for movement out of the corners of my eyes, or for the wandering path of a mysterious orb of light; a shimmer of violet; the hazy outline of a form.

My feeble senses noted nothing mysterious. I had more luck when I quieted my mind. I sent out a silent call that I was open to hearing from Astrid. I concentrated on the essence of Astrid—her smile and bubbling spring of continuous warmth and enthusiasm. In a few moments I felt a rush of joy wash through me, much like the electric charge of *kundalini*, but sourced from outside of me.

She was fine. Still Astrid. She wasn't mourning—she had new adventures ahead of her. She brought no message for me, she just said hello through the sense of her strong presence and then moved on.

I'm not the only one that felt her there that day. I confided my experience to a close friend of Astrid's a few days later. She had also felt Astrid's joy-filled spirit at the service and we knew—as her brother said—that she was fine and happy as always. Her time with us seemed swift and short, but Astrid, bubbly ego and all, smiles still in the astral.

The soul animates thousands of fallible, vulnerable, mortal lives for some indefinable reason. Somehow these "swift and

The Programming of Karma

short" physical incarnations are a necessary expression of the immortal soul.

Karma on the physical planes is both our bondage and a part of our growth. The mystics tell us that *karma* is why the soul sends us back to Earth over and over again. The Denver Teacher points out that, "*Karma* is inseparably linked to reincarnation..." Why is this "Law of Cause and Effect" so important to the soul?

Karma is the expression, effect, and potential of actions in the physical world. The circumstances of our next birth are Self-determined as our soul finds the future life with just the right "fit" for the karmic baggage dragged along by the memory track. We aren't here because we're being punished or because we're victims of some cosmic cruelty. My Teacher insists, "What you are doing to life, you do to yourself. Everything in your life has been caused by you."

We come into life with karmic impressions to process and experience. More *karma* is generated in the new life as our ego interacts with sensual environments, but *karma* may also be avoided or erased in the course of a lifetime by those with some understanding, conscious or intuitive, of how the Law of Cause and Effect works. In my Teacher's terms, the *sadhu's* goals while in the physical body are to soften, balance, neutralize, burn, or transcend *karma* so that our spirits may ever evolve.

Even if we experience pain and heartache in this lifetime, or if we don't meet our own expectations, we should not mistake this life history as an expression of the intrinsic quality of our spirits. Spirit manifesting in body experiences all of what it is to be human—good and bad. Past egos have created our *karma*. Our spirit looks to purge through us some of the *karma* accrued by many egos. We may struggle with issues in this present lifetime that have little to do with our actions this time around. Even if our spirits are very much advanced, our ego expressions may still have some basic lessons to learn.

When a young child is taken to the dentist it may be a horrible experience for her. She doesn't have the language or logical ability to put into context the vaguely menacing strangers, being forced to sit in an unfamiliar chair for so long, the pain, the discomfort, and the humiliation of the process. She doesn't understand that what she is experiencing is designed to help her. To her young mind, the visit may be equivalent to torture, forced upon her by those that she thought were her protectors.

We face many of the same "little picture" barriers to understanding the spiritual context of *karma*. *Karma* is part of our trip to the spiritual growth dentist. It is an appointment that we make for our own benefit, but we struggle to understand the process, tempted to blame the world for its cruelty. Without understanding its spiritual context, *karma* is a horror of being held down against our will.

Part of this context is what gives *karma* one of its pseudonyms: The Law of Cause & Effect. We, and the incarnations before us, are the cause. *Karma* is the effect. *Karma* may be created by our outer actions in the world or simply created by activities of the mind. *Karma* is created both consciously and unconsciously. We have created and continue to create our *karma* through thought, word, and deed—even as we sleep.

Almost all the events in our lives—our relationships, our bodies, our health, our unique qualities, where we live, our careers, our personalities, our talents, and our weaknesses—are expressions of *karma*. My Teacher says that we are 97% preprogrammed by *karma*. He believes the remaining 3%, for most of us, is free will.

The Kriya yogi believes that this Law of Cause and Effect is put into motion through the ego, which mistakenly believes itself to be alone in a harsh universe, attacked by forces beyond its control. Believing this, the ego strives constantly for the illusion of control, generating the "actions" which create *karma*.

The memory track of the causal body is the recording place of all the experiences, emotions, patterns, perceptions, and actions (*karma*) of all the many egos generated by the spirit. The memory track is the accumulated unconscious of all egos, the causal body acting as the intermediary between this lifetime's ego and the spirit.

In terms of *karma*, the spirit or soul is that timeless consciousness which is aware of all egos (*simultaneously*, since it exists outside of time) and has access to the entire memory track. The spirit sees the big "picture."

I have mentioned before that the Teacher says, "Spirit has no personality. Spirit has no *karma*." Although our shoulders may sag from the weight of all this *karma*, the spirit is apparently unsullied by the actions of her many earthly children. The spirit is free, while the personality is 97% constrained by the past.

I wrote earlier about the difference between self with a small "s" and Self with a capital "S." I think of the four-year old in the dentist chair as the ego self. The dentist and the dental assistant together represent the Self (spirit or soul). All three of these actors are parts of the same being. The ego is the physical manifestation of the divine spirit and the Self is the spiritual manifestation. When I say that the procedures of the dental appointment are self-imposed I am alluding to the process in which the Self uses dental records (the memory track in the causal body) to determine what needs to be done in this particular appointment (incarnation) to get the immature ego back on the right track and as healthy as possible despite the patient's dental issues (*karma*).

That four-year old believes that something is being *done* to her. However, the whole process of Cause and Effect is Self-imposed and for the ultimate good, based on the best information and records available.

The four-year old doesn't have the wisdom and perspective to realize that past actions of *karma* are what got her to this point of needing an area of decay removed and something solid put back in its place. But, in fact, the state of her teeth and the discomfort of the dental appointment is the direct result of her accumulated *karma*.

Since "The mind has its origin in the past," we must have awareness and information about that past and its unhealthy patterns in order to guide the mind into a state of balance and peace in the future. It is through this awareness that we begin to leave pre-programming behind and take control of our lives.

Astrid has moved beyond the child at the dentist. I believe Astrid in the astral is continuing where she left off in life: Learning all she can and exploring out to the very edges of her world. Only now she doesn't have to pull a sled loaded with survival gear, trudging across bitter cold plains of northern spruce forest on frozen dogsled trails. Though knowing Astrid, she still pulls that sled down winter trails simply because she enjoys it.

CHAPTER FORTY-THREE

Nothing is Good Nor Bad Lest We Make It So

A week into that first trip to Pine Ridge, Roxanne told me that she felt called to tackle the poverty and hopelessness she saw overwhelming the Lakota people. I volunteered to have a word about her goals with Chick. I thought that Chick, as Executive Director of the first Boys and Girls Club on a reservation might know how Roxanne could help.

Chick welcomed me into her crowded office, desk and chairs stacked with manuals, paperwork, and memorabilia from her many trips and visitors. I stood awkwardly near the door and relayed Roxanne's wish to stay on Pine Ridge and somehow work with the Lakota.

Chick was receptive and immediately said that she was looking for help at the Boys and Girls Club—a staff member to plan and carry out after school activities with the kids. Then this woman that I so much admired and respected cracked me wide open with a few words.

"What about you? Would you like to stay?"

Of course I wanted to stay—the desire tormented me. But that longing did not outweigh my family responsibilities. I shook my head "no," trying to hold back unexpected tears as baffling sensations pierced my body and I mumbled, "I have to get back to my wife and kids."

I fled from the office and sought refuge first in a bathroom and then stripped for a shower as I sobbed with a rush of tears that I had not experienced in decades. The impromptu shower in the middle of the day was to hide those tears while I tried to figure out what had happened to me in the office and why I was crying.

When Chick asked me if I would like to stay at Pine Ridge I had felt an explosion in the center of my chest, under my breastbone—as if a hollow globe of ice had shattered, hurling shards through my flesh, melting quickly in my body's heat. The tears that followed as I fled the office dumbfounded me. I didn't feel sad, but I cried for fifteen minutes. How could my chest explode like that? What was happening?

> "The *karma* finds a home that resonates with the energy of a particular *chakra*. There it waits until such time as it can manifest with the energy of that *chakra*."
>
> —A Teacher

The *chakras* are energy centers in the human body—gateways between the physical and the spiritual. In their simplest Western conception, there are thought to be seven *chakras* in all, located along the spine and symbolized by the seven colors of the rainbow, starting with red at the bottom of the spine and progressing through to violet above the top of the head. The heart *chakra* is located at the center of the chest.

On the more esoteric side of *chakra* lore is the belief, according to Hindu tradition, that *karma* may have physical and energetic expressions in the human body. *Chakras* are the doorway or the conduit between the physical being and the spiritual being. Through these doorways the *karma* of past experiences, memories, personality tendencies, and patterns squeeze through before manifesting in the physical. In Kriya Yoga, *karma* is also thought of as a *thing* that finds its home in the human body before birth, awaiting the opportunity for the correct circumstances in which to manifest into reality; or, alternately, to be softened, balanced, neutralized, burned, or transcended before it can do any mischief.

The quality of this *karma*, or of the *chakra* home it becomes lodged in, is not necessarily "bad." *Karma* may compel us to help the sick or to make wonderful inventions that improve lives.

One day in meditation it finally sunk in for me that *I am responsible for the quality of my thoughts*. I wondered, *How can I keep my thoughts to what is kind, true, and necessary?* I still find myself having uncharitable, cruel, and even violent thoughts, but I stop myself when I catch these feelings intruding into my consciousness—not just out of abhorrence at the idea of committing spiritual violence (though that is reason enough), but also out of a selfish desire to create a better future for myself.

A better life is possible for us all, but ego may blind us to truth as it seeks to externalize blame for the pain of karmic lessons. We sometimes react to the fruits of our *karma* by working even harder to deny the truth of our responsibility.

Karma is an ongoing process. We are making withdrawals and deposits to our karmic "bank" all the time. *Karma* has immense relevance to our future. The effects of the *karma* we create now may hit our lives tomorrow or next week, thirty years from now, or 300 years from now. We *will* experience the results of our *karma*.

The concept of *karma* has penetrated even into popular Western culture, but in this version too high a value is placed on "good" *karma*. If the ultimate goal of our spiritual journeys is to free ourselves from the earthly plane, then all *karma*, "good" or "bad," is a tie that binds us. Good *karma* is like having a rich farm filled with healthy crops, sweet water, chickens, goats, hay to mow and put-up for winter, cows to milk, etcetera. The farm provides a comfortable, honorable living, doing good work, but we are still tied to the fertile land and the animals, unable to quit our chores, buy a sailboat, and spend a year traveling to foreign ports. That good *karma* keeps us imprisoned just as effectively as the unpleasant things that we want to avoid. Good *karma* may keep us on this rock even more efficiently than bad *karma*.

The Monk Who Howled Like a Wolf

The second and ninth chapters of the *Bhagavad Gita* (BG2.48, 2.50, 9.27-28) reference these concepts: "One absorbed in the yoga of discernment rejects both good and bad acts." "Acts" in this context are the thoughts, words, and deeds which contribute to the *karma* binding us to earth. The *Gita* warns us to avoid both the good and the bad. Good *karma* is just another gilded cage to keep us distracted.

The Denver Teacher says, "Your most difficult *karma* usually ends up being your best *karma*." As humans on the physical plane, we tend to assign short-sided values to things, based on our physical environment rather than on the perspectives of the spiritual worlds. Remember the dentist chair metaphor? What seems pointlessly cruel on this side may make perfect sense on the other side. In fact, "bad" *karma* may be a very important forward step in the evolution of a soul.

Kriyananda once massaged a line out of Shakespeare when he said, "There is nothing good nor bad lest we *make* it so."

Good versus bad depends on where one is sitting. What was tragedy may later morph into advantage. A life characterized by bad *karma* may be cover for a noble soul making great strides in Self-realization, while an easy life may do little to transcend a vast storehouse of karmic debt. Whether it is good or bad, *karma* anchors us to earth with layers of attachment. My attachment to a loving family stopped me from serving the Lakota *oyate kin* I was so urgently drawn to. It was a great blessing when the cold encasing my frozen heart shattered that day, yet I realize now that this compulsion to serve was yet another layer of karmic attachment calling to me from the past and I was fortunate to avoid the serious *karma* of leaving my beautiful children behind in my need to recreate what was long gone.

I bear this tender heart of mine towards the mystic's goal—enlightenment.

CHAPTER FORTY-FOUR

The Yogi, the Stag, & the Hunter

*O*n the edge of a clearing deep in the woods, the yogi's meditation is broken as a branch snaps in the dense forest. The birds stop singing as change surges in the still and warm noonday air.

A magnificent stag slips through the brush at the clearing's edge. It stops in the sunlight for a moment, nostrils flaring to catch scent, its flanks heaving from exertion. From where she sits, the yogi can hear the deep breath. For a moment she feels herself in union with the animal. She experiences his fear.

The stag hesitates, his velvet antlers pivoting as he looks left and then right. His eyes lock with hers for an instant, then, in a flash, the stag is off again, changing course, his golden flanks disappearing into the trackless woods.

The birds remain silent for several cycles of the yogi's measured breath as another disturbance approaches. The brush trembles where the stag had burst into her awareness and out jogs a hunter all in brown, carrying a battered rifle, its barrel tarnished with age. The man looks as tired as the stag and as worn with time as his rifle. He sweeps into the clearing on noiseless bare feet, moving closer in his patched and frayed clothes. He is dark from the sun, and moves with an energy and *agility beyond his years, as much a part of the forest as the stag.*

The hunter scans the ground, looking for tracks, broken brush, disturbed grass, anything his practiced eyes can find to tell him which way the stag has gone. But he has lost the trail.

He senses the yogi and turns in one motion to face her as if he had known that she was there all along. His eyes meet hers and he jogs to her and stops, panting, directing his rifle carefully at the ground with one weathered hand.

"Ah! I have heard of the yogini with the red hair. Namaste. *Please, which way did the deer go?" he asks urgently.*

The narrator asks, *"If you were the yogi... what would you do?"*

The Yogi, the Stag, and the Hunter is one of my favorite stories. Like all the traditional stories (this one of many that was introduced by my Teacher), this tale has deeper meanings, layered symbolism, and above all is designed to make us think and grow in spiritual understanding. Of course, the Teacher refuses to supply the "correct" answer. He directs us to think about the story and our studies and to decide for ourselves.

When asked what we would do, we instinctively consider the morality behind our options. The stag obviously wants to live—should we be accomplices in the death of a sentient being? Is it right to tell the hunter which way the deer went? Is it right *not* to tell him? The story forces us to evaluate the morality of our actions or inaction when faced with a choice that affects the wellbeing of others...as many of our life choices do.

Our Kriya teachers tell us that the consequences of *karma* are in proportion to intent and effect, operating on a sliding fee scale. If we steal five dollars from a rich man, the effect on that rich man is negligible. If we steal five dollars out of the cup of a homeless blind woman, our theft may have a huge impact. Our karmic debt in the first instance would be much, much less than the debt incurred in the second example.

With the help of *samskaras*, *karma's* power and influence is stamped on almost every important aspect of our lives. My Teacher has joked about having bumper stickers made that read, "*Karma* Rules!"

The Yogi, the Stag, & the Hunter

Karma rules most of the time. We don't shake responsibility for our actions in past lives just because we have died a couple of times since then. If we wielded the sword then, sooner or later the effects of our choices will catch up to us.

As personally uncomfortable as it is to accept and despite how arbitrary and cruel the world sometimes appears to be, there is a reason for everything. *Karma* operates in the context of certain universal rules. There is justice. Everything we do to another, good and bad, is in turn experienced personally. If we hurt another, we hurt ourselves. If it doesn't boomerang back on us in this life, it will happen soon enough, with *karma* acting as the instrument of our self-inflicted violence. The Teacher told his Satsang once that simply *disappointing* another person might add to *karma*.

Karma is characterized by forgetfulness, ignorance, and unawareness as we blindly follow in the old grooves of our *samskaras*. Yet *karma* also has an important role. As my Teacher says, "*Karma* is designed to show you where you are stuck and a way to get out." *Karma* is how spirits learn.

Our karmic nature magnetizes our birthing soul towards the life that provides the best environment for spiritual growth. Accumulated character at birth leaves its mark in the emotional and physical traits of the new body and literally determines destiny.

Our *dharma* may be to enrich our soul by working our way out of trying circumstances or by facing the challenges of material excess. We all have a responsibility to care for and nurture each other no matter what the circumstances of birth, but to blame anyone or anything for our "bad luck" is signing away our potential to take control of our lives and flourish as powerful spiritual beings. We are doing hard time on Planet Earth, but we got ourselves here and we can get ourselves out.

> "Think about all the things you've done in your life.
> At some point you have to walk back through it.
> That's why we have all these lives to balance this *karma*."
>
> —A Teacher

The Monk Who Howled Like a Wolf

What does it mean to walk back through all the things we've done in our many lives? My Teacher's *guru* gave us the mind-boggling number of 800,000 lifetimes of *karma*-building experiences and entrenched *samskaras*. I have major regrets about this one present life, such as neglecting my wife and kids when I was fixated on Pine Ridge, my affair with a married woman, and my lack of support for Roxanne when she had cancer.

It is an enormous challenge just to understand our individual *karma* on a deep level, let alone to begin to soften, balance, neutralize, burn, and transcend it. We have forgotten our past and so we are ignorant of the karmic forces that have shaped us and which continue to form and inform our experiences. We normally live blind to *karma*, but as developing mystics we inevitably ask, "What can we do about it?"

When I multiply the karmic experience I've accumulated in this checkered lifetime by 800,000 lifetimes, I realize my karmic "bank" may have an *inconceivable* balance. Yet I must return the balance to zero before my debt is cleared and I may leave this rock.

The *samskaras* are without beginning because desire is eternal.

—*The Yoga Sutras of Patanjali*; Book Four, Sutra 10

The accumulation of *karma* and *samskara* can only exist in worlds bound by time. Existing outside of time, karmic imbalances are immediately self-correcting for the spirit, but for us egos, *karma* hops from one incarnation to the next, much as we hang onto a hurt overnight and into the next day. The danger here is that these *samskaras* magnetize us to similar unpleasant or unnecessary circumstances and they limit our ability to see with an unprejudiced perspective.

Adding to the persistence of *samskaras*, we find ourselves reinforcing old *samskaras* and creating new patterns. To confront our karmic legacy, we must root-out existing *samskaras* and stop the germination of new shoots.

The Yogi, the Stag, & the Hunter

> "We are on this wheel and all we are doing is repeating things.
> We are trying to break this wheel.
> Karmically, we are pre-programmed to become something.
> In other words, we're not free."
>
> —A Teacher

If the Teacher is right, we are automatons. Bio-psychological clichés. My Teacher likens this force of *karma* to gravity. "Breaking free of *karma* is like breaking the gravitational pull of the earth. It takes a great deal of energy."

As our knowledge of spiritual principals grows so does the energy available to liberate ourselves from the effects of *karma*. The Denver Teacher says, "The cause and effect of *karma* is revealed more rapidly as we ascend up the ladder." More and more, we see the relationship between cause and effect.

Karma and *samskaras* lodged in our causal bodies slip out of the memory track, living again in our lives as new events, but there may be forewarnings. Before *karma* arrives in the physical world from the causal, it manifests in the astral planes. Consciousness in the astral conceives of a desire prompted by *samskara*. In the astral, this manifestation is straightforward and immediate (such as in our dreams), but *karma* takes more time to precipitate "down" into the sluggish physical plane. Much like a vaguely remembered dream colors one's mood throughout the next day, *karma* precipitating in the astral dribbles through into the mental plane (between the astral and physical realities), then manifests into the physical plane as a thought to color our reality. At this point, the adept may derail the *karma* by not indulging the thought with attention, but, typically, we tend to voice the thought and from there it is a short step to action.

If we can catch the gathering swell of *karma* as it is birthed into the material world, we may purposefully turn the gathering tide of centuries of cause and effect, and transmute the breaking wave of *karma*. Although the everyday mystic has more ground to cover before the ultimate goal, understanding how *karma* works is an important landmark on the spiritual path.

Karma may be mastered.

The Monk Who Howled Like a Wolf

The narrator asks, *"If you were the yogi, what would you do?"*

FORTY-FIVE

The General & the Monk

*D*uring *a long and successful campaign, thousands of soldiers led by a relentless General advanced on a peaceful mountain district. Villagers whispered chilling stories about this army and the General's efficient ruthlessness.*

In this same district, an ancient monastery perched in the rocks high above a green valley of fields and clusters of small rock homes. The farmers were so frightened of the invading General and his army that they abandoned their ripening crops and fled long before the soldiers marched into the river drainage. Soon, the monastery monks were fleeing for safety deeper into the mountains—all except for one senior monk. The younger brothers begged him to leave, but he gestured for them to go on without him.

"All is well. Do what you must do. I shall do nothing right here."

So they and the monk's red-haired maidservant fled, expecting that they would not see the older man again.

After the army had secured the valley, baffled soldiers brought the General to the monastery to see the crazy monk who would not rise from his meditation cushion to beg for mercy.

The General rushed into the temple sanctuary, his armored

The Monk Who Howled Like a Wolf

breastplate shining in the shafts of sunlight piercing through the narrow window openings. He unsheathed his sword as he raced across the cold floor to the monk.

The General yelled, "Don't you know that I am the man that can kill without blinking?"

The monk, one brown eye and one blue eye still focused on the altar, whispered back, "And don't you know that I am the man that can let you?"

A shudder went through the large frame of the General. Fierce as he was, he was also a very, very thoughtful man. Here he had found someone that knew something he did not. The soldier sheathed his sword and bowed low to the monk.

"My humblest apologies for interrupting your meditations, Master."

Meeting his astonished soldiers at the door, the General instructed them to spare the monastery and to cooperate with the old man and the other monks in any way that they could.

News traveled quickly of the day an old monk bested the General in battle.

The Denver Teacher uses *The General and the Monk* as an example of men delivering and receiving *karma* without blinking. Both men leave the exchange with minimal new *karma*: The monk meets the General's anger without reflecting it back to him, and the General drops his violent impulses as soon as he sees that the monk has already defeated death. Both men are aware of the potential of *karma* between them, transcend that *karma*, and move skillfully forward, finding peace in their encounter.

> "One transcends good and bad acts alike when occupied in the yoga of discernment."
>
> —*Bhagavad Gita*; Chapter 2, Verse 50

The story of *The General and the Monk* demonstrates one way we can move past a particular piece of *karma*: Don't play the expected role as *karma* manifests. The monk did not succumb to karmic impulse when his *karma*, in the form of the raging General, entered onto the scene. He recognized the *karma*, but he did not latch onto the bait.

The Teacher tells the cautionary tale of one of his students who got married without first seriously evaluating the relationship. After it became clear that the relationship had serious problems, the man came to my Teacher for counseling and explained that he had married because, "I was bored with my life." Now a bad marriage made boring look good.

Our actions and *karma* continually bump up against other people. If we hurt someone in the here and now with consciousness and intent, it will come back to us, sooner or later. If we treat others with love and respect, that also will come back to us.

Eventually.

When dealing with the individual, Kriyananda says, "Do unto others as *they* would have you do unto them." This twist on the old golden rule is both a nudge in the direction of moral behavior and informed self-interest. If we leave others satisfied with the outcome of their interactions with us, we are much less likely to pick up *karma* that we must resolve later. Treat people well and we are more likely to get good treatment down the road.

People in our lives are a part of our *karma* and we are the porters of other people's *karma*. The General was a part of the monk's *karma*. Conveying teaching lessons with the blade of a sword or in a few careful words is a noble role, but bearers of *karma* are rarely congratulated and may pick-up *karma* themselves.

Another karmic sand pit is group *karma* (which even attaches itself to nations). The Teacher says, "Stay away from groups. Group *karma* is always negative." He suggests keeping our heads low when group *karma* mobs the streets. If we resist the call of the herd, group *karma* may lose its personal relevance and pass on by.

My Teacher, and other explorers of the spiritual worlds, speak even of food as a bringer of *karma*. When we ingest, we are also ingesting traces of the food source's *karma*, the psychic state of plants or animals, and the measure of love with which the food was prepared. He advises fasting to lessen the impact of astrologically heavy karmic cycles (when the changing interrelationships between the planets in a chart suggest caution); avoiding heavy proteins that may transfer energetic impressions of an unhappy life (particularly from the flesh of mammals); steering clear of the foods of youth if we wish to avoid re-enacting that *karma*; and awareness that the cook's state of mind and spiritual energy infuses the meals we consume.

If we don't understand *karma* we are much more likely to get sucked in to the dramas that come with it. Understanding how and when *karma* may materialize gives us the potential to soften it as it triggers.

Examination of individual *karma* may help identify problems with old attitudes. This conscious awareness of a challenging karmic heritage may point to modifications in behavior that bring real improvements in our lives. Rough spots on the ego must be revealed before we can begin to polish the jewel.

We can also work on an energetic level to neutralize *karma*. Although *karma* carries many important lessons and opportunities to move forward on the spiritual path, the *sadhu* may choose to remain shielded from certain effects of *karma* through the processes of softening, balancing, or neutralizing.

The Denver Teacher says, "If you have the *karma* to drown, go live in the desert. If you have the *karma* to fall off a mountain, live by the ocean."

According to my Teacher, "*Karma* reveals what ought to be done," but how are we to know our *karma*? The stories of our lives convey clues. Individual *karma* is reflected in environment, in relationships, and in major life events. The problems we battle now are echoes from the past. The Teacher says, "Whatever your limitations or obstacles are—that's your *karma*."

These patterns or habitual manners of living and relating to others are hints into karmic background. Are you tidy? Do you have an addictive personality? Do you resent authority? Do you make friends quickly? These are patterns that are not easily explained by genetics and often not explained through the environment of our birth and early upbringing.

Identifying our *samskaras* and consciously re-programming ourselves is an important way to sidestep the *karma* of old patterns. This study of personal *samskaras* requires challenging our ego to uncover what it would rather keep buried. One way we can uncover the buried is by being alert to behaviors in other people we find irritating or unacceptable. The character flaws we take note of in others is *relative* to our own natures or we would not pause for a second look. On the bright side, what we see as good and admirable in others is also a part of us.

Lacking direct memories, we may practice spiritual forensics by looking at the trends in our lives. For example, if we have never lacked for any material goods without any particular effort of our own, that is a relevant fact that we would consider in describing our individual *karma*. If we are persistently plagued with ankle problems, that also is relevant. We might postulate that in our single most recent, or several most recent past lives, we were generous to others with our resources, but that at some point we somehow hobbled another.

We need to look at big patterns—not transitory issues. One bad relationship does not mean we are fated to be alone. One lucky lottery ticket does not mean we will always have money.

Circumstances, characteristics, or trends driven by attitude are all likely rooted in *samskara*, such as a tendency to disagree with bosses leading to being overlooked for promotions. On the other hand, circumstances, characteristics, or trends driven by *events* are more likely a result of past actions (*karma*). Ill health due to poor diet and lack of exercise is driven by attitude towards food and exertion, while a broken leg springs from an event.

Once my Teacher initiated an exercise for his students when he asked us to consider the major themes in our lives. He said that these themes would reveal some of our karmic influences. I quickly wrote down my major life themes—abandonment, adventures, anger, creativity, injuries and dental problems, exotic loves, intelligent friends, isolation, many homes, traumatized women, wild places, and wonderful children.

I then divided up these themes into attitude-driven or event-driven tendencies. My attitudinal themes (past life *samskaras*) included anger, isolation, wild places, exotic loves, intelligent friends, and creativity. My "events" (results of past life actions) were abandonment, abused women, injuries, dental problems, adventures, and wonderful children. Of course, some of these items can and do overlap. For instance, does my attitude toward exotic loves bring them into my life, or do events arrange these meetings?

To determine what the list meant from the point-of-view of *karma* I conceived a story line:

> In my last life, or in my last few lifetimes, I was accustomed to spending a lot of time alone and away from cities, using my hands and creativity to craft what I needed. The few friends that I had were entertaining and unusual. The oddness of the people I spent time with extended into my romances. I also had a dark side and used my sense of being taken advantage of as an excuse to hurt people. Although I cherished and treated children well, I injured someone, and bullied or hurt women. I either abandoned someone that was important to me or I hung onto the emotional effects of an incidence of abandonment.

Divining the nature of past lives, based on the circumstances of the current life, may be an emotionally difficult process. Even now, I would prefer not to think about the patterns I discovered in my own life. But by performing this mental exercise I find a framework from which to understand and have compassion for who I am.

Perhaps you would like to try this exercise?

> 1) Write down the major recurring factors, circumstances, and feelings in your life.
> 2) Divide your initial list into two lists: One of event-driven factors, another of items that can be explained as caused by your own attitude towards life.
> 3) Make up a story (in meditation or just while sitting at the table with pen and paper) to describe the history and the person revealed by the events and attitudes in your list. That

story may describe some of your karmic background.

My Teacher suggests additional techniques for uncovering karmic history such as examining the natal horoscope, reflection and meditation, the study of personal aversions and attractions, using the intuition, noting personal values, and identifying major life cycles.

Karma may be recognized as it first comes to life. The Teacher suggests, "If you are meditating enough, maybe you can feel the urge. It usually manifests as a thought. You don't have to respond to it." Insight may intercept sprouting *karma* while it is still in the manageable thought stage, before we find ourselves with problems and strife as we speak and act out our old dramas.

Although not all Kriyabans use astrology, my Teacher and Kriyananda put a strong emphasis on this study of the planets. The Teacher says, "The natal astrological chart is past life *karma*. Where the planets are is where the *karma* is." The accomplished and intuitive astrologer may see past life *karma* in the natal chart (describing the relative positions of the planets at the date, time, and place of birth). This natal chart may also reveal when, or under what conditions, some types of *karma* might trigger or "fire".

We need coping skills better than habitual reaction when the Generals rush us, brandishing the blades of our own hidden histories. The wisdom of Kriya Yoga transmits powerful tools to effectively manage *karma*. We may not always best the General in battle, but by applying these tools we may limp away from the next encounter. With determination, we find inaction within action.

Do we flee from the General into the barren mountains? Or do we chart a fresh path beyond the wraiths of the past?

The Monk Who Howled Like a Wolf

FORTY-SIX

Inaction Within Action

Just as the yogi in the clearing found the world coming to her in the form of a hunter, *karma* has a way of finding us. Sometimes we have to make choices. Sometimes we must *act* in this world, but how do we act without creating *karma*?

The answer is hinted at in sacred texts such as the *Bhagavad Gita* and in the teachings of yogis like the Denver Teacher. We act without creating *karma* when we practice *inaction within action*. If we act with the guidance of the immortal and divine Self that resides within us all—without attraction or aversion to taint our motives—the hold of the ego begins to loosen.

> "Abandoning attachment to the fruits of one's action,
> content, and without need.
> Even while occupied in action—
> one enacts nothing."

—*Bhagavad Gita*; Chapter 4, Verse 20

Non-attachment is an ally in avoiding old and new *karma*. From the Kriya Yoga point-of-view, "action" is synonymous with experiences that express or generate *karma*. Action moves towards karmic inaction as our attachment to outcome approaches zero. Ironically, action is the creator of *karma*, but discerning action is *karma's* master.

> "Kriya is the action, the energy to balance the *karma*."
>
> —A Teacher

"*Kriya*," derived from a root word meaning, "to act," is a reference to addressing the actions that create *karma*. On another level, the word *kriya* is also a reference to acts of service that eliminate *karma* and speed the initiate on their way to enlightenment. An exemplary life is one in which the spiritual lessons of love and compassion are gained through insight rather than through forceful *karma*. My Teacher gives the example of a woman who has accumulated the *karma* for a foot injury. Her practice of good works may mean the difference between a broken foot or a stubbed toe—an example of softened *karma*. The toe is still stubbed, but the *karma*, and the gravity of the injury, has been blunted and softened.

In the manner in which the past action was "bad," we may provide a "good" action that helps repair the damage. For instance, a logging baron responsible for denuding Vermont of trees two hundred years ago might volunteer in this life to plant trees in the inner city. Or a woman retired from the state prison system with vague feelings of guilt, might found a program to bring regular visitors to inmates. A man remembering a crying woman at a locked door in a past life may offer nothing more to another woman in this life than to hold her in the dark during a night of crisis.

Kriya Yoga does not teach that God or Big Brother will reward us for selfless service, but the Law of Cause and Effect will create an inevitable reaction to our acts as surely and as impersonally as gravity pulls us down after we jump up. Effect follows, when there is sufficient cause.

Even when we are no longer adding to *karma*, we may still have lifetimes of *karma* to transcend before moving towards the

Inaction Within Action

final goal of *kaivalya*. Neutralizing *karma* through the dedication of our actions to something higher than the individual self is alluded to in the *Bhagavad Gita* as Krishna the charioteer speaks to Arjuna:

> Arjuna of the *Kurus*,
> your actions,
> whatever you consume,
> and whatever your offerings or gifts of service—
> these actions of devotion should be consecrated to *this* king
> [Krishna, the king, here a metaphor for the inner Self].
>
> This consecration of action produces illumination
> and freedom from the bonds of *karma*.
> Devoted friend,
> with the self absorbed in renunciation
> and striving for yoga,
> you are then freed to join the Supreme Lord above
> [the "Supreme Lord" here the Self].
>
> —*Bhagavad Gita*; Chapter 9, Verses 27-28

In the Teacher's words, "Dedicate your activities to your *Ishta*, your *guru*, to God." Dedicating our actions to something higher than ourselves helps us attain the goal of inaction within action. Our actions are no longer on behalf of egos or even on behalf of Self. We act with innocence on behalf of a higher power.

In another example from the *Bhagavad Gita*, Lord Krishna exhorts a reluctant Arjuna, the Mighty Armed, to take up his bow and fight in the impending battle.

> Fight without anguish,
> surrendering every action to me,
> with thoughts on your enduring nature,
> without desire,
> and without ego.

> Others who follow my teachings,
> faithful and envying none,
> are also liberated from the effects of action.

—Bhagavad Gita; Chapter 3, Verses 30-31

Arjuna's anguish comes from being forced to fight a just war against relatives and teachers. But Krishna instructs Arjuna to devote his battle actions to Krishna, thus avoiding the karmic consequences Arjuna dreads. This is not an easy out from responsibility for our actions. Krishna is *not* saying that we may senselessly indulge our attractions and aversions and remain free of the Law of Cause and Effect. Krishna says instead that for Arjuna to transcend *karma* in this imminent battle he must transcend the ego that both desires victory and fears harm to his loved ones. He must act in deep connection with and awareness of his inner Self, and he must abandon thoughts of personal gain or loss.

An advanced way to neutralize *karma* is through the dream state or during travel in the astral plane. Kriyananda and my Teacher both warn that neutralizing *karma* takes 900 times the effort in the physical world as it does in the astral. This practice is extremely effective for those rare birds that can remain consciously aware on the higher planes.

Burning *karma* is an advanced approach in which the mystic roots out *karma* as it lays dormant in the *chakra* system, before it germinates into the astral and penetrates our thoughts. Traditionally, extreme body disciplines such as fasting and celibacy are used to burn *karma*. The grueling Lakota sun dance is an indigenous North American example of this process.

From Chapter 4, verse 18 of the *Bhagavad Gita*:

> *The one that sees inaction within action,*
> *and action within inaction,*
> *is wise,*
> *immersed in yoga,*
> *and accomplishes all action.*

—Bhagavad Gita; Chapter 4, Verse 18

Inaction Within Action

It is easy to latch onto the words "inaction within action" and feel that the best course for the yogi is to hole-up in a shack or cave and pass our years in secluded contemplation. But this quote not only implies that there is a way to approach action without generating *karma*, but that sometimes shrinking back and not acting may land us in the *karma* we have been trying to avoid. There are times on this earth that our *dharma*, like Arjuna's, is to fight with the ferocity of the General. It is the way of the Kriya yogi to seek the peaceful path, but if we must fight, we seek inaction within action and fight with spiritual awareness and compassion.

The Monk Who Howled Like a Wolf

CHAPTER FORTY-SEVEN

Loving Kindness

Every day of those first two weeks on Pine Ridge in August 1999 approached 100 degrees. In the hot afternoons we often found shelter with indoor jobs. On this day, Roxanne and I were about to start painting the Boys and Girls Club bathrooms when Chick suggested that we lunch with her. The Club ran a 50's-style diner as vocational training for Lakota teens, but it was crowded indoors, so we settled under the umbrella shade of an outdoor table on the deck.

We chatted with Chick until it came time to order. Though one of the Lakota words for Europeans, *washichus*, translates literally as "fat eaters," Roxanne and I both ate a near vegetarian diet. We searched the traditional American fast food menu and Roxanne chose a grilled cheese sandwich with fries. I picked a toasted sandwich, but asked the earnest young waitress if I could have it without the meat. I returned to the conversation with my new Chicago friend and the Lakota Director.

A few minutes later, lunch almost forgotten in our enthusiasm with this private conversation, the young waitress interrupted us again. She leaned over to whisper something into Chick's upturned ear.

Chick turned to us and said, "I have to run to Sioux Nation

The Monk Who Howled Like a Wolf

[the grocery store in Pine Ridge village]. The kitchen is out of something for a lunch order."

"Oh, no!" we both protested, "Let us go while you sit here and relax."

Although Chick took some convincing, she gave us five dollars and our very short shopping list—one item. We hopped into my van to begin our important trip to the store in service to Chick and the mission of her Boys & Girls Club. I swelled with the importance of the role we had for the children of the oppressed Lakota people. We were indeed doing something special. Chick had trusted us with this errand. We would not fail her!

As I pulled out of the parking lot, Roxanne knotted her brow. She asked me, "What did you order?"

Surprised at the timing of the question, but still buoyed by the game-changing significance of our errand, I began, "A bacon, lettuce, and..."

Oh.

Chick had asked us to get a head of lettuce for my own lunch.

> "Loving kindness.
> Two different things smashed together."
>
> —Kriyananda

Compassion (or loving kindness) is the sympathetic, perceptive, and deep interest in the physical conditions, emotional environment, and happiness of other beings. Sincere compassion leads to an inclination to serve when the opportunity presents itself. The Denver Teacher and Kriyananda stress the importance of both compassion and service, considering these virtues as naturally evolving attributes of anyone on the path of expanding consciousness.

My Teacher says, "Compassion becomes a natural response to your own unfolding." This unfolding is the movement towards *moksha*, enlightenment. Compassion isn't just a happy side effect of spiritual growth. Compassion is *necessary* for spiritual growth. All of the positive attributes of a balanced

Loving Kindness

Kriyaban personality (such as happiness, compassion, service, peacefulness, and contentment) are part of the process that leads to expanded consciousness. This is part of the "eternal core of *dharma*" referred to in the conclusion of Chapter 12 of the *Bhagavad Gita*. Those fated to attain union with Krishna (here, a manifestation of God) revel in the happiness of all beings (BG12.04). Those favored few have no contempt for any life (BG12.13).

True compassion, as Book 1, *sutra* 33 of *The Yoga Sutras of Patanjali* tells us, is a means to relieve the volatility and blundering of the ego. I spent years wanting to go to Pine Ridge and "help" the struggling Indians, as I saw them then. Then I met Chick Big Crow and I focused all of my years of immature white savior fantasies on her. My selfish desire to have an important role on Pine Ridge through Chick was comically exposed when I was confronted with the fact that my service in the run to the grocery store served only my needs.

Once focused on the spiritual life, compassion naturally picks up speed. In chapter 16 of the *Gita*, compassion for all life (BG16.02) and deeds of service (BG16.01) are among the 25 attributes that move one towards *moksha*. Compassion's core lies in acceptance of the concept of We Are One. When the illusory boundary that separates physical beings wears thin, spiritual students begin to accept that our sisters and brothers are in fact just another divine manifestation of ourselves and it becomes increasingly natural to experience their pain as our pain. We cannot be whole or truly content until each of us is at peace. We cannot, as individual egos, be healthy until all are healthy. Compassion for the plight of others and thus a move towards service to lighten the loads of fellow souls is a natural development in the Kriyaban's practice.

The Teacher points out, "We all know what pain is like, so why would we want anyone to be in pain?"

The mystic develops a growing self-awareness and empathy for the challenges of the earth experience, extending that awareness then to others. Time may bring compassion to the most hard-hearted of us all.

The Monk Who Howled Like a Wolf

"If you want to be happy, practice compassion."

—A Teacher

Happiness is an interesting and perhaps unexpected side effect of compassion towards others. If unhappy, help others towards happiness. Doing a good deed, preferably anonymously and without expectation of reward (unlike leaping up from lunch to get a head of lettuce), tends to be rewarded with feelings of increased self-worth and confirmation that we occupy a useful role in the community.

"How can you make any progress unless you love yourself? How can you walk the path and how can you love anyone else? Yoga is rooted in compassion for yourself. "

—A Teacher

In order to have compassion for others we begin with compassion for ourselves; that's the foundation. If we can't generate self-love and understanding we can't produce untainted works of service for others. Kriyananda, a perceptive student of human psychology, has pointed out how our inability to love the world around us creates an internal programming trap:

> People are bad.
> Bad people don't deserve good things.
> I'm a people.
> Therefore, I am bad.
> I don't deserve good things.

In order to successfully serve, we must love our neighbors as ourselves and we must forgive and accept our own faults. For the Kriyaban with an awareness of the imprint of past lives (some lived virtuously and others lived less so), self-love may present a challenge. Somewhere in me there is an old *samskara* telling me that I'm a bad person. And perhaps I do share a common root with ego personalities that were once "bad" in the

Loving Kindness

conventional sense, or who were bad a million times. But that does not mean that I have to be a bad person now. We need to love ourselves in order to express healthy love for others. This movement towards understanding and acceptance may take action on our part (a type of *kriya*) such as uncovering and addressing our dark material in meditation or in therapy.

> "Imagine everyone around you is your child.
> If a child makes a mistake... you correct them gently.
> Practice compassion as if you were a mother."
>
> —A Teacher

A less judgmental, more feminine approach nurtures forgiveness, loyalty, and love. Life becomes easier when we accept people as they are. We must practice non-attachment to other people's choices or lifestyles while practicing loving kindness towards them. As Kriyananda says, "They are people, peopling."

If we wish to serve, we can't judge, but must instead cultivate a sense of kinship for others. We must focus on getting to the place where we can, as Kriyananda often says, "Help with skillful means."

> "You cut a person with nasty words and
> sometimes it takes three or four lifetimes to heal.
> Try to make all your actions, actions of love."
>
> —Kriyananda

Compassion of thoughts, words, and deeds are linked together. A critical perspective, even at the thought level, is in direct opposition to the expression of compassion. We must become non-violent in all our interactions with the world in order to prepare ourselves to serve.

> "Meditation is the flower, compassion is the fragrance."
>
> —A Teacher

The Monk Who Howled Like a Wolf

Osho says, "Without meditation, energy remains passion; with meditation, the same energy becomes compassion." Meditation is an ally in this goal of greater compassion towards all sentient beings. In fact, *The Yoga Sutras* direct that we can develop strength in compassion through a practice of *samyama* in which the *sadhu* simultaneously experiences *dharana* (concentration), *dhyana* (meditation), and *samadhi* (meditative absorption). (YS3.23)

As we develop and refine our sense of compassion, we begin to approach a state of being in which we may serve without discovering that we have run off on an errand to fetch our own lettuce.

FORTY-EIGHT

The Work of the Indwelling Sun

By early 2000, Roxanne and her boyfriend were living in school district housing in Kyle Village on the Pine Ridge Reservation when she mentioned that their pre-manufactured home didn't come with a washer or dryer.

A few days later, the owner of a hardware store in Gunnison asked if I wanted a used washer/dryer set that a customer had replaced. I didn't wait for him to change his mind and immediately loaded the awkward and heavy cubes into the back of my service van.

The Lakota Partnership for Housing in Pine Ridge had told me that they would interview me for a job the next time I was on the Rez, so I was already eager to head for South Dakota. I figured I might as well bring the washer and dryer to earn floor space for my sleeping bag. I wrapped-up loose ends in my repair and remodel business and began another ten-hour drive to Pine Ridge.

At Roxanne and Joe's place in Kyle we unloaded the van and muscled the appliances down the hallway to the laundry hook-ups. It didn't take long to get the washer and dryer working. Roxanne thanked me so many times I felt embarrassed—it wasn't a big deal. The units were free and the install was one of many familiar ways in which I made my handyman's lower middle class income. Sometimes service happens this way—a simple thing for one, an important lightening of the load for another.

However, my upcoming job interview seemed like a big deal to me. In those days I wanted very much to find a way to live at Pine Ridge and somehow contribute to the lives of the people there. Since six months earlier when Chick had asked me if I wanted to stay on at Pine Ridge I had thought of little else. I was good at fixing things and from my limited perspective there seemed so much to "fix" at Pine Ridge.

Mostly, I just felt a deep and primal tug towards the people and the place and I was looking for a way to satisfy that yearning to be on Pine Ridge. But another part of me wouldn't forget my responsibilities to my wife and two children. I lived with this continuing dilemma: How to reconcile these two opposing demands on the heart that was cracked wide open in Chick's office?

Fate was kind to me—I would have no morally ambiguous choices to make. I was not offered a job building affordable housing in South Dakota and I would not burden my limping marriage with yet another challenge. But as I was dropping down from a high ridge near the KILI radio station at Porcupine Bluff, driving to the unsuccessful interview, I caught the movement of a red-tailed hawk. The hawk emerged from the ponderosa pines to my right, flapping a course to intersect my van. I braked as we locked eyes. The raptor swooped within inches of my windshield and then veered forward, leading me for a few seconds, only ten to twenty feet in front of my van.

I coasted on down the hill into the haunted valley of Wounded Knee spreading below me and my hawk friend, where on the sub-zero morning of December 29, 1890 the Seventh Cavalry led by Colonel James Forsyth left two to three hundred Lakota children, women, and men dead in the windswept snow.

Service to other beings is complicated. My attempts at service haven't always turned out as I imagined. I felt that day of the interview that the hawk was honoring my efforts to give of my knowledge and experience to the *Lakota oyate kin*, but below me

The Work of the Indwelling Sun

the restless ghosts were a reminder of what may happen when someone thinks they know how others should live.

One charity that supports young children in undeveloped countries, Plan International, recently stopped accepting gifts for individual children from donors. Now gifts come in the form of general donations that will contribute, for example, to a latrine or a new well for a village. Plan International learned that giving a gift to one child while the rest of the children go without might create animosity and jealousy in the social structure. The lucky child may end up regretting the gift. It's often better for a dozen children in a community to each get a box of colored pencils than it is for only one child to get a new pack for her schoolbooks.

Ideally, service expresses a higher calling. Kriyananda explains, "At some point we have to put down the dreams of humankind and pick up the dream of the Divine. The dream of the Divine is to serve."

To the Kriyaban, service is an assumed part of *dharma*, albeit with countless possible manifestations from the overt to the esoteric. The *Gita* reinforces the importance of service when it says, "...the needs of the world compel you to act" (BG3.20) and "...with non-attachment, the knowledgeable should act for the benefit of the world." (BG3.25) The undeniably knowledgeable The Denver Teacher says, "I am here to serve. That's part of my vow."

Studies of transcendental meditation have indicated that the greater the percentage of meditators in a community the lower the crime rates. People sitting alone in a room may literally change the activities of entire towns, lowering aggression and harmful acts. Cave yogis, though isolated and eschewing the company of others, may be doing more than anyone to keep this world afloat and humming along peacefully. So don't feel bad if the best you can do is radiate contentment. It seems to be catching!

From the traditional Hindu perspective some are born to serve in supporting roles. The *Gita* (Chapter 18, verse 44) refers to the skilled worker caste of old India, the *Shudras*—those who kept society afloat by completing menial, tedious work, with little notice or reward. I spent much of my life doing small home repairs and carpentry. This work gets little attention, but without the people in the aprons and the coveralls we would find ourselves in the dark and cold, distracted by the search to supply basic necessities, without energy or focus for our own enlightenment.

> "If you cannot build harmony with your family, you cannot build harmony with your community and world."
>
> —Kriyananda

When I first got the urge to service it came with a stubborn attachment to Pine Ridge although I had a wife and young children and very little money in the bank. It was not in harmony with my *dharma* to give up paying jobs and travel 500 miles away from home to satisfy the attachments of my ego when I already shared a roof with people who needed my attention.

Healthy relationships become even better when we shift our perspective to one of service to the divine in our partners. Not only is our first *dharma* to serve those whose lives and *karma* we have been born into or gravitated towards, but our ability to serve our loved ones harmoniously is a true litmus test of our ability to serve others in the greater community.

> "If they ask for help, you are obligated.
> If someone comes to you, serve them.
> But don't go looking for service."
>
> —A Teacher

In the past I actively sought outlets for service, on Pine Ridge, and closer to home. Now, I have planted the intention to help when asked and keep an eye out for situations and circumstances in which I can be of assistance. I find opportunities to serve through my work, everyday life, and in my neighborhood, rather than through traveling hundreds of

The Work of the Indwelling Sun

miles to help in other communities (though that phase left me with some great stories). There are sentient beings where I am that appreciate "help with skillful means."

> "If you're serious about enlightenment in this life and service is not helping you towards that goal, maybe you should not be doing service."
>
> —A Teacher

Overt service may not be our path to illumination. My decision to throttle down and re-focus my service work was partly a recognition that I needed to gain wisdom before I could effectively discern where my efforts would be most helpful. Now I am more willing to let the consciousness that informs the workings of the universe do the picking and choosing for me.

Acts of service at their best are not acts of kindness towards the less fortunate. Instead, they are sacred offerings to *Ishvara*, the God within us all. The old woman that the Boy Scout helps across the street is also the Goddess. The restless boy that you tutor *is* Krishna. If We Are One and all is divine, then service becomes a prayer.

> "To be able to do the work of the indwelling sun you have to serve without the attachments of the ego."
>
> —A Teacher

Attachments to outcome get in the way of our ability to serve and remain flexible in that service. When I first went to Pine Ridge, I had preconceived ideas about how I was going to serve, but I found a broken water heater at the Boys and Girls Club. The other volunteers wanted to take showers after a day's work on the hot playground outside. So I fixed the water heater. Instead of my immature fantasy of rescuing a noble and abused minority, my first act of service at Pine Ridge was to make the lives of middle class white liberals more comfortable. My reward for this action was to be able to take a hot shower myself.

The Monk Who Howled Like a Wolf

And that shower felt good.

Another approach to service work—to serve with wisdom—deserves a closer look. Sometimes our subconscious and conscious motivations guide why and how we serve, rather than being guided by the needs and desires of those whom we serve. We must have the wisdom to recognize our own inspiration for service before we can serve with clear vision. The Teacher's perspective:

> "Be extremely careful of what you think you are doing for the benefit of others. Seva (unselfish service) is the heart of Kriya, but as we develop we realize that it is extremely difficult to serve unselfishly."

The goal is to give what will be appreciated rather than what we imagine ourselves giving. Maybe our investment knowledge is less useful than watching kids for a few hours while a harried mother gets a break.

We give what we are capable of giving with wisdom. Writing a check may be the best option and not just an easy cop-out: Dollars given represent the time and effort it took to earn that money.

> "People with bigger egos on the path tend to channel it into service."
>
> —A Teacher

The strong will power and determination of a big ego doesn't necessarily make for a bad ego just like a big horse isn't necessarily a bad horse. If that big ego is balanced, controlled, and softened it becomes a powerful tool in service work. A big ego can overcome much, including spiritual obstacles.

> "*Karma Yoga*:
> This is probably the easiest way

The Work of the Indwelling Sun

> for most Westerners to burn off *karma*.
> That is doing service consciously on behalf of all beings;
> service without imposing;
> focused from wisdom and love."
>
> —A Teacher

Besides neutralizing past *karma*, an attitude of service may also function to avoid accruing new *karma* in this lifetime. The Denver Teacher is a great proponent of offsetting thoughts, words, and deeds in this lifetime with conscious service (*kriyas*) to balance missteps in the here and now. This proactive approach to *karma* is one of the fundamental concerns of *Kriya Yoga*.

My Teacher says, "Once you realize you should have done something there has to be some movement, some action, some *kriya*. It's only balanced if something is done."

Give what you lack. "If you are lonely, go help the lonely." This is a powerful message of generosity to the universe and a potent way in which to transcend *karma*.

My efforts to "help" at Pine Ridge began with ridiculous fantasies of being the white savior and evolved towards gratefulness for the chance to watch Chick's granddaughter for a few hours. I eventually found some humility and deepened my spiritual awareness on the magical western plains. I gave what I was capable of giving at the time and was rewarded in unforeseen and splendid ways.

> "There is no faster way to unfold
> than to help people."
>
> —Kriyananda

The Monk Who Howled Like a Wolf

FORTY-NINE

The Dreams of Others

> "The hard truth is,
> mystically,
> everybody is where they need to be.
> But you still need to help them.
> If you see someone in pain, you need to help.
> If they don't want your help,
> you're helping in the wrong way."
>
> —A Teacher

My compulsion to return to Pine Ridge was driven by the attachments of *karma* and *samskara* and was not in service to the needs or the goals of my spirit. Nor was I sufficiently self-aware then to provide selfless service to others. Eventually I had to ask if I was at the Boys and Girls Club in a sincere, non-attached sense of service to others, or was I a moth to the flame of past patterns? Service for the wrong reasons may be worse than no service at all.

Kriyananda warns us not to "disturb the dreams of others." Although Kriyananda is a strong advocate of service, he warns that ill-informed service may trigger *karma* both in the server and the served.

In a world operating according to the Law of Cause and Effect, the hardship and heartache we perceive around us is the product of old, old *karma* that must find an outlet or somehow be transcended. Service not completed with skillful means may disrupt lives that appear dysfunctional from the outside, but may instead be a complicated and ingenious balancing act of people doing the best that they can with what they have. We have to be careful not to disturb functioning dynamics if we leave nothing in their place.

A merit-bringer is someone who improves the world around them through their thoughts, words, and deeds. This is a person that others enjoy being around and who seems to lift the mood and awareness of everyone that they come in contact with. But before you determine to be this person, consider how your efforts to lift those around you will interact with the karmic patterns that surround you.

In a Retreat, Kriyananda was asked, "How do you become a merit-bringer without disturbing the dreams of others?"

He answered, "Don't be a merit-bringer. Don't be the trigger of *karma*."

The Teacher confirms, "Mystically, it's not necessarily good to help people."

Not everyone is suited for a path of service. It takes a certain amount of self-esteem to believe that one has something useful to offer. I find myself becoming less convinced with each year that I have the wisdom to help anyone. Yet, we still have an obligation to assist all sentient beings to the best of our ability when we are asked for help. The trick is to perform service that successfully addresses the needs and desires of those served. To help in a way that is meaningful and effective, we need to spend more time listening and less time talking.

My twelve-year-old son and I once arrived a few days before the opening of the brand new Boys and Girls Club on rural property on the eastern outskirts of Pine Ridge Village. Chick always seemed glad to see me and always had things for me to do. When we pulled up in my white Toyota station wagon, Chick stood in a field ringed by a couple of her staff and several

The Dreams of Others

Lakota men next to a small skid steer loader. The group was hesitating, debating what to do next. We walked over and let her know that my son and I wanted to help out with getting ready for the grand opening. Within twenty minutes of pulling to a stop I was on that skid steer loader, turning a bumpy field into a level ceremonial dance ground. The night before the opening ceremony my son and I slept in a teepee to watch over the Club and the dance grounds. These were the jobs that needed to be done, but ten minutes before we got out of our car we could not have imagined that we would be asked to help make a dance grounds and act as overnight security by sleeping in a teepee.

First Responder medical training supplies an important rule for service work: Don't endanger yourself. If an Emergency Medical Technician is injured on scene while attempting a risky rescue it creates even more strain on scarce resources and results in less attention for the original victims. We must be safe and fed (physically and spiritually) if we want to be of use to others. If we are suffering, our service will suffer as well.

My Teacher has found in his years of service to his *sangha* that, "Most people who ask for help really don't want help." People often ask the Teacher for advice in transcending the unhealthy patterns in their lives, but are unable to apply his insights and soon slip back into the dreams that they are dreaming. Until we are ready to wake we will continue to sleep.

There are outlets for service everywhere. It's not necessary to drive to Pine Ridge. Why not help the wasp struggling in the dog's water dish or the bird stunned on the lawn below the picture window? If we can't help the wasp then how prepared are we to help the neighbor with the flat tire or the child care gap? How could I hit the moving target of selfless service when my struggling marriage was tugging at one arm and my teetering finances were pulling on the other? Kriyananda tells his students, "Get your earth life in order." It may be enough of a challenge for now to establish a stable, drama-free life from which we can be prepared some day to serve others.

While you may think that you see something that you can "fix," the people involved may like their lives the way they are. Cultural bias may lead us to see a need for our help where there is acceptance or even contentment.

If we see men walking about with no possessions, begging for one meal a day, and constantly on the move from town to town, we may feel compelled to help. We might want to find them a place to live or even an entry-level job. But there are dreadlocked wanderers in tropical India who have renounced possessions and other attachments in their unceasing quest for enlightenment. These men (and a few women) are *sannyasins* in the Hindu world. Some live their days "sky clad"—nude. The *sannyasins* practice their rituals, meditate and chant, and travel frequently so that they do not even become attached to a familiar place. Though they seem to live in desperate poverty, these holy men and women have always been highly respected in India, released even from the stubbornly persisting caste system as part of their renunciation of worldly things.

Of course, trying to push possessions and jobs on the *sannyasins* would be an appalling intrusion. We must understand the dynamics of complex realities before we can be of help in the larger world.

> "It is not easy to give something
> to a person who doesn't deserve it."
>
> —Kriyananda

It may also be challenging to serve those with heavy loads of *karma*. Kriyananda tells a story about working against a palpable repulsive force when he wanted to offer money to a homeless person. On approaching the man to give him a dollar, Kriyananda found himself veering away and passing by, feeling a visceral repulsion that interfered with his generosity. Recalling the spirit of his own words, "It is the people with karmic debt that need to be helped," Kriyananda turned around and reached into his pocket. This time a folded twenty-dollar bill was successfully transferred to the unsettling man.

> You should not cause self-doubt in in those that are,
> through ignorance, gathering *karma*.

The Dreams of Others

> The wise one,
> who acts while fully absorbed in yoga,
> should allow the uninformed
> to pursue their attachment to action.
>
> Those attached to the illusions of the physical world
> are creating *karma*.
> One who is informed should be gentle
> and not disturb those others.
>
> —*Bhagavad Gita*; Chapter 3, Verses 26 & 29

Once the water heater was working it became obvious that the showers were draining too slowly—murky wastewater backed up and pooled around our naked feet. The sound of flushing toilets filled us with anxiety as we looked down, willing ourselves the power of levitation.

I was so determined to get the "real" project done (clearing weeds from a field for a playground) that I ignored the complaints about the slow shower drains for a couple of days even though I was no stranger to sewer repairs. But when team moral plummeted I offered to see what I could do about the clogged drains.

Chick was happy for the help and together we went on a scavenger hunt for the necessary labor, tools, and supplies. A couple men from our group of middle and upper middle class service workers volunteered to help. One was a dentist. Chick arranged with the Oglala Housing Authority to borrow a sewer tape (a long and narrow metal strip coiled up tightly like a roll of tape when stored, the free end terminating in a small ball).

In the middle of a cluster of queasy but fascinated Unitarians, I slowly pushed the uncoiling rusted tape down the sewer line through an opening called a clean-out. The terminus ball moved haltingly around the twists and turns of the underground piping. It wasn't long before the sewer tape encountered a dense obstruction.

After pulling the dripping tape out and laying its length out on the ground, I had a good idea of where the problem must

The Monk Who Howled Like a Wolf

be—just outside of the exterior walls of the building.

We began to dig. My respect for the dentist and the other volunteer grew as I saw how cheerfully they applied themselves to shovels and picks, digging carefully to find the pipe. A couple hours later, as the day heated up, we were clearing dirt and rock away from the tops and sides of the black plastic sewer line. We excavated another five or six feet in either direction from the suspected pipe clog so that we would have plenty of room to work in. The dirt around the pipe was only slightly moist and fresh smelling and the pipe was free of breaks so we inferred that the problem was on the inside of the line. The guys took a break while I went on an errand to the hardware store at the back of the nearby Sioux Nation grocery store where I found more of the black plastic pipe known in the trades by the chemical abbreviation "ABS" and a couple repair clamps.

Once all of the crew was back at the job site, Chick and three other Unitarian volunteers came out of the Club to watch. Chick had asked the people still inside not to use the drains. I cut through the pipe a few feet on either side of the suspected clog with a handsaw. On my second and last cut I could tell that I was cutting through a semi-solid. I was relieved that my measurements and guesswork had gotten me to the trouble spot. Chick was watching us from above with folded arms. Dark, rank sewage water leaked from the cut, forming a thick pool in the bottom of the trench.

What was the clog? I mentally ran through the list of some of the culprits that I had encountered in the past—tree roots, cleaning rags, tampons, sand and silt dribbling into pipes from breaks.

The moment of truth finally came with the cut completed. I slid my gloved hands under the freed section of pipe and began to lift. My digging colleagues, Chick, and the curious Unitarians leaned closer. As I raised the pipe, it tilted and the barricading contents rushed out, plopping back into the trench.

In confused silence we grappled with the sight of hundreds of two-inch long pale white plastic doll arms, their tiny fingers waving back at us from the raw sewage.

Chick broke the silence. "You're probably wondering what

The Dreams of Others

kind of Club I run here."

There was a titter of nervous laughter. Chick explained that the Club building used to be a doll factory—yet another failed effort to bring jobs to the Rez. I remembered the heavy grates over the long troughs in the concrete floor inside. I had pulled off the grates and checked the floor drains below for clogs when I was first trying to uncover the problem with the shower drains. It was clear now how the main sewer line had clogged: Rather than pick up tiny doll arms dropped to the floor, employees had swept doll parts into the grated troughs. Eventually the accumulating white arms washed down the drains and collected in the level section of sewer line outside. The gathering mass allowed water through slowly, but eventually stopped solids from getting by. The increased load from our large service group had made the problem obvious.

Our crew of college-educated plumbers cleaned out the doll arms and made sure the rest of the piping was open and clear. We didn't talk as much as when we were digging down to the line. Instead, we chewed on the puzzle we had uncovered. Our digging had exhumed the story of a business opening a factory on the reservation. The company might have seen the tribal environment, with few industrial regulations and stunningly high unemployment, as a source of cheap labor and profit. Armed with the hype of economic opportunity, they hired a native labor force to produce white dolls for white children.

Unfortunately for the investors, the people of the plains are not suited to work a forty-hour week making white dolls in a windowless metal building. Doll arms and money were swept down the drain. Income projections were not met and the entrepreneurs walked away in disgust from the small factory.

The abandoned building reverted to the Tribe. A Lakota woman asked for the former factory site to start a Boys & Girls Club on the Rez. The tribe gave her the building for a dollar and she opened a sanctuary for the children of Pine Ridge with no budget and no income projections. Idealistic and enthusiastic volunteers from all over the country came to serve. The drains couldn't take the load. The volunteers had to dig.

Down in the muck and stink of the trench, I felt something

The Monk Who Howled Like a Wolf

inside me shift as I watched those doll arms pour out of the pipe.

CHAPTER FIFTY

Path Opens

When I was a boy I dreamed of being two things when I grew up—a writer and a forest ranger. Those two vocations cohabitated in the same life story; stubbornly linked in my young heart.

I have had many adventures and loves since. I spent my first winter of many in the north country of Alaska when I was still a young man, living with Kellie. That first cold, long, dark winter in Alaska gave me the luxurious gift of time, and I wrote a novel at the table of a chilly fifth-wheel trailer, pecking away at an old hand-me-down electric typewriter. I received one polite rejection letter from a publisher and I tucked the manuscript away in a drawer. I told myself that I didn't have much to say and that I should put more life behind me before I bothered any more editors. I filed my writing ambitions away with the manuscript.

I married the woman who had waited patiently while I typed that first winter and I focused on my seasonal job landscaping summer resorts and building a home in the north on five acres. It was a good job and good land. I became better at what I did for a living and soon I was leading other workers. Word spread that I was a reasonable man to work with, though still young. People left other jobs to be in my happy work group and worked with me for many seasons. Gail was one woman that landscaped with me for years. We became accustomed to each other, like old acquaintances, though our lives rarely intersected outside of work.

With crucial hands-on help from my generous father (a retired union carpenter), Kellie and I finished our little cabin with the million-dollar view of the mountains of the Alaska Range. Two welcomed souls eventually joined us, newborn in this world. The old *dharma* to be a writer was left behind, as life demanded my full and practical attention.

Eventually we made the fateful decision to move south to the "Lower Forty-Eight" to be closer to the grandparents, away from the wild northern mountains. The high desert of the new home also sang with a unique wild spirit, but this place was dry, dusty, and sparsely grown with twisted sagebrush and juniper. The green southern mountains were close, but the demands of building a new home and a new business pushed away the target of writing and working in wild places. I wandered down this path for many years.

"You are exactly where you want to be."

—A Teacher

"Conscious manifestation" is a phrase and concept that has wormed its way into the periphery of western culture. I used to think of manifestation as something that the focused and skillful might achieve with work, but Kriya Yoga overturned my view of reality and my role in my own life with this simple teaching: We already manifest with the commission of every thought, word, and deed.

The Buddha said, "With our thoughts, we create the world." The Teacher expands on the concept when he says: "We are the creative principle."

It is natural that we feel resistance, even outrage, at this central element of Kriya Yoga cosmology. Kriya Yoga asks us to take personal responsibility for every horrendous event or twist of fate. But it also asks us to take credit for every moment of redemption and beauty.

Any philosophical or mystical life path must be able to prove itself of value or wait to become just another curiosity of the history books. Kriya Yoga is no exception. The ancient knowledge, philosophies, and practices—when applied—must leave a unique, observable, and beneficial stamp on the everyday mystic. After a few weeks, months, or even years, the Kriyaban should be consciously focused in their pursuit of a minimum of worldly or spiritual goals; should find that the misleading influences of attraction and aversion are receding; should experience life as a natural and comfortable flow from day-to-day; should not labor under imbalances or dis-eases placed on them by group *karma*; and the Kriyaban should be increasingly effective at neutralizing or side-stepping past and present *karma*.

In other words, the Kriya Yogi's life should be as orderly as their mind.

This is the final test of our practice, whatever the practice may be: Does this path improve our life?

When the old monk checked on the initiate on the island, he found the young man howling an unorthodox new chant. But that howling *worked*. That's all the evidence that the old monk needed. The proof was standing, un-sinking, on the water in front of his rowboat. The old man took up the howl himself.

We too may become a monk that howls like a wolf. If our path is effective, life begins to smooth and settle (as the muddy pond hiding the jewel) and our focused intentions become reality.

Creation, manifestation, or "Path Opens" happen when our focused, conscious attention gradually creates a reflection of our internal landscape on our external reality.

> "Why aren't we happy with being where we want to be? You worked really hard to get yourself to where you're at."
>
> —A Teacher

There was an ache in my heart when I thought of the land and the cabin that I had left behind in the north, but I worked hard at my new repair and remodel business in the sagebrush country. As it turned out, I worked too hard. My long hours and the trips to South Dakota kept me away from home far too much. Kellie let me know she didn't like this path that I was on, but I kept working my long hours, without reason.

Though I loved my children very much, the love Kellie and I shared in our new little house far from the northern mountains began to falter and shift. For the third and final time, she said she wanted to move without me out of those southern mountains to Denver, to dream her own dreams. Together we decided the children would be better off with her during the school years. She had the fierce mother bear love that would keep the young ones safe and cared for. I would send money each month and see the children on long weekends and holidays.

This arrangement worked for a long time—I stayed in the high desert valley surrounded by mountains and Kellie lived down in the rolling country where the Great Plains met the Rockies. But after a few years I decided that I wanted to live closer to my children. I didn't know how this shift in my life could happen, but I didn't try to imagine the how, I just felt the what.

Path opened for me when I listened to the patient voice of my Self, reminding me that this was the time to be a father. One day I told a new acquaintance at a workshop about the move I wanted to make to Denver and the other man said, "I know of a job for you."

I interviewed for this job and I wasn't surprised when I was offered the position. The job paid well and I found just the right house where the three of us could live together when my children (now teenagers) weren't with their mother. It was good to be near my children again and to be a part of their day-to-day lives as they grew towards adulthood. I grew vegetables in the warm rich earth of the large yard and I could see the far off mountains from an upstairs window.

Obstacles fall away when Path Opens. We ease gently and naturally into a job, romance, creative endeavor, living situation, sunset, or chance meeting. The idea of "Path Opens" offers a contrast to the active striving and struggle that seems required by

Path Opens

so much of our lives. When Path Opens, major life changes happen as if they were planned.

We all know people for whom barriers seem to fall aside and the elements of success drop into their laps, while the rest of us scramble and flounder, never seeming to get *it* right. Why them and not us?

> "If each of us are part of the divine flame.
> We need to manifest that divinity.
> We need to stand on our own two feet."
>
> —A Teacher

Those were good years in Denver with my children and close to the Teacher's Denver Kriya Yoga Center. I spent much more time with my kids, but the job was stressful and not a good match for my personality or *dharma*. I was happy with what the job had let me do, but I wasn't content within the job. My basement office window faced a blank concrete wall. No view of the mountains, just a ribbon of sky above if I tipped my head towards the glass and looked up and out. My lifestyle and interests were far from the norm of my co-workers and colleagues.

Then my life began to shift and the seeds were planted for change once again. My youngest turned another year older, releasing me from any legal obligation to help my ex-wife with child support. I no longer needed the high paying job.

Two months later I was called to the boss' office.

The economic downturn, you know? Thank you for your service. Here's a plaque and some money so that you won't sue us. Can you please turn in your keys by 3:30?

I had had hints that this day was coming—I wasn't the first well-paid middle manager to be bottom-lined out of that place. Although it was a shock to lose my job, there was also a part of me that felt the peace of the Master accused of fathering a child in the village.

"Is that so?"

I filled a cardboard box with my things from the office with the window looking into a concrete hole. I left the brick building for the open air under a blue sky and I didn't look back as I walked away.

I had no plan for what to do next. My Kriya studies with the Teacher at the Center were going well and my spiritual life showed promise, but my earthly life had no focus and no income. I started two businesses, but I didn't make much money at one of them and I lost a lot of retirement savings through the other. I didn't care much. I smiled passively and said, "Is that so?"

One day my son (soon to graduate from college) said to me, "Dad, let me take that old paper novel manuscript of yours and see if I can digitize it so you don't just have that one old hard copy."

By and by he handed me a thumb drive. I scanned a couple of pages and saw that some of the letters came out wrong. Some of the t's had turned into j's and some of the n's had become m's. I would have to read through the whole old story and set everything right.

So I started at the beginning, fixing all the letters, and I soon discovered something very surprising in all those pages and pages of words: "Hey! This novel isn't all that bad!" I decided to polish it up, edit a couple scenes here and there. "You never know," I thought. "Someone might want to read this."

And that is how I became a writer again. And it is also how I began the journey to the land of knowing what I wanted.

> "If you don't know who you are and what you want, you will end up doing what everybody else is doing."
>
> —A Teacher

We are where we want to be—I overlooked that truth most of my life, looking outside myself for someone to blame or someone to credit for where I was. I imagined an external locus of control when control was within.

Out of that transition time at the foot of the Rocky Mountains, I learned to take control of my life. But first I had to understand where I wanted to go and make a plan for how to get there. As the Teacher says, "We are the creative principle."

Perhaps, like me, you don't spend much time or energy envisioning where you would like to be in a year, five, or even ten years from now. For most of us, life is something that happens rather than something we master and direct, but the Kriya yogi can be the queen of her castle, master of her domain, the architect of her reality. If we indeed are the creative principle in our lives, we must harness and contain this force for our own purposes or it will become like a flowing fire hose, whipping about without direction, perhaps doing more harm than good.

Examining our dreams—our sleeping dreams—may reveal hidden aspects of our creative force. Dreams, like much of our existence, seem like they are happening to us, but we create almost everything in almost every dream we have—every nightmare, every sexual encounter, every confused, nonsensical disturbing image. We also create almost everything in our waking life—good, bad, or indifferent, conscious or unconscious—at some level at some time (in past lives, if not in this one). Imagine our subconscious as the untended fire hose, whipping about, knocking us down with cold water.

After a few more misadventures and false starts, I called Gail one Father's Day in June and on November 11, 2011 I was pulling my car into the gravel driveway of my new Alaskan home during the first real snowstorm of that winter.

As winter gave way to spring, the semi-wild woman and I settled comfortably into Interior Alaska dating rituals: Grocery trips to town (100 miles one way to Fairbanks); movies on a DVD player; ski runs down icy dogsled trails; nights keeping each other warm in her carefully crafted cabin nestled on six acres.

I applied for summer work with a couple of the larger local employers: A private hotel and tour business (the source of my paycheck years before) and also with the National Park Service at Denali National Park & Preserve.

The hotel company hired me early in the spring and I found myself swinging a hammer for pay again, but when the National Park Service offered me a job for much more pay, I accepted the new position with only twinges of guilt.

The new job had me living and working deep in the National Park, forty miles from the nearest pavement in a magnificent wide glacial river valley, just below the tree line that soon gave way to alpine tundra and scree slopes stretching up the mountain sides. My schedule was "eight and six." Eight ten-hour days in a row and six full days off to go back to my semi-wild woman and my writing. It was easy and natural to move in with Gail now as I was gone most of the time and the transition to a shared household on my weekends went smoothly.

One day I shoveled snow from the walks of a visitor center on a bright blue day, white mountains ringed about me. As I stopped for breath and looked out over the glacial river bar far below with the northern sun reflecting off the slowly melting snow, I realized, "This is exactly what that boy meant when he wished that he could be a Forest Ranger and a writer."

Somehow I had stumbled into that future I had imagined all those decades before.

Path had opened.

FIFTY-ONE

Twenty Tools of Manifestation

"To a yogi, all life is divine.
There is nothing wrong with sex, fine food, good clothes..."

—A Teacher

I have reached goals in my life slowly and without much help from myself. I have never shown an aptitude at uniting my conscious and subconscious to do my bidding. I have never been good at learning through insight, as Kriyananda suggests, but have excelled at learning through mistakes. There were a lot of bumps in the road before I found myself back in the mountains, writing seriously, living in a wild place, with the love of a down-to-earth woman.

For those of us with better listening skills than I have, my Teacher and the Kriya Teachings tell us how to go about "creating in focused and effective ways." There are many manifestation techniques and practices.

"Only you can evaluate your own mind
and admit to yourself what you really want."

—A Teacher

Kriyananda suggests that the first step in harnessing our creative energies is "know thyself." That self-knowledge can come by looking back to one's early life and recalling our passions (such as a dream to be a ranger and a writer) before life with all its demands clouded our perceptions and forced us to submit to what was expedient and practical.

It is a journey in itself to get in touch with what we really want. Remember the definition of *dharma*: A life plan, in harmony with spiritual laws. Path is more likely to open for us if we set goals in accord with our unique *dharma*.

> "It is about changing your world internally first. But people want to change things on the outside first."
>
> —Kriyananda

Goal setting may come naturally or we may only uncover our enduring motivations after deep reflection or years. Attitude also determines our ability to forge content lives for ourselves. Kriyananda is a great proponent and living example of how attitude can mold our reality rather than allowing reality to mold us. In his words:

> Are you willing to work for what you want to obtain? Your attitude can change the past. The past can change the future. You can make choices... It is in this moment that you can change the future. As I change my attitude, the event *does* change.

Not surprisingly, the ability to simplify is key to conscious manifestation. Stuff, mental and physical—packed into an overloaded Subaru or cluttering our minds—reduces our ability to zero in on the things that are truly important and valuable.

The Denver Teacher says, "Make the space for something new to come in. You need to start eliminating the excess energy and the extra activities to achieve your goals. You have to simplify your life if you want to accomplish anything."

The need for simplification extends even into our internal

worlds. We must tune our thoughts to screen out the background noise and focus in on what is truly important.

> "Be inspired by something or you are already dead...
> What do you want in life?
> Not many people can be focused on one thing."
>
> —A Teacher

One of Kriyananda's core teachings for an effective life guided with conscious creation is that of focus. "Our problem is that we are fragmented, creating conflict and confusion." If your thoughts and activities are all over the place, the creative results will also be scattered and disorganized. Recall the equation: Force = Intensity x Duration? As we increase the Intensity (focus), the Force (creation) increases. Life may require restructuring, as mine did, to make this increased focus possible.

> "If you are an immortal being,
> you have an eternity to become what you want."
>
> —A Teacher

It may be a slow process harnessing consciousness and reality to manifest the conditions in which we wish to live, limited by the laws of *karma* and the physical world. We may never be able to reach into beach sand and extract a cup or a piece of jewelry, like a rare Indian adept such as Sai Baba. The patience (*titiksha*) of the six *Shat Sanpatis* (qualities of self-control and discipline) is necessary for the Kriyaban seeking to manifest their inner vision in the outer world.

If all else fails, we must try something new to harness our creative consciousness. As the Teacher says, "If I want a different outcome, I've got to do something else." It doesn't make sense to keep applying the same old techniques that haven't worked in the past. We must experiment with something that we haven't done before and then release our hold on this new labor, allowing it to complete its work.

The Monk Who Howled Like a Wolf

> "God is within you.
> You can ask for anything you want...
> but we treat God like an ATM."
>
> —A Teacher

One of the more accessible ways to seek manifestation is through *supplication*: If all else fails, ask for help. We may ask for help from our cousin, our dead relatives, our college instructor, our *guru*, from Jesus, or from Babaji. We can do this in the privacy of our own home, or in a church, or in a secluded grove of trees. It doesn't matter so much what or whom or where we ask for help as does the asking itself. If we let the world know that we are sincerely and deeply ready for a change, the world tends to step in and give a hand. I believe speaking out loud helps. Sometimes supplication to God (or whatever you would prefer to call your *Ishta Devata*) is an effective way to see manifestation come into life. However, sometimes the answer to our prayers is exactly what we needed, but not exactly what we wanted.

Years ago, when I supervised construction in Colorado, the groundbreaking for an affordable housing community was fast approaching. As the construction supervisor of the project and as someone with a soft spot for animals I had one big concern: The vacant meadow site on the edge of the small mountain town was home to a prairie dog colony with dozens of burrows. I felt terrible about the bulldozers and excavators headed their way, as were many of the homeowners-to-be. We discussed ideas for getting the prairie dogs out of harm's way, such as live trapping, but nothing seemed likely to work on the scale we needed.

With nothing better to try, I turned towards my shamanic training. Late one night on the last full moon before groundbreaking, I walked through the dry grasses into the middle of the planned development. I had some tobacco with me. I calmed and deepened my breathing, faced south and recited the Four Winds Prayer in Lakota, offering tobacco to each of the directions and asking the spirit beings for help. I explained aloud to the four-legged ones that big machines were coming. I asked the prairie dogs to please move to the other end of the field where no construction was planned and I apologized profusely for this disruption to their families. I ended with "*Wopila tanka, mitakuye oyasin.*" (Thank you very much, all my relatives.)

In the days leading up to the equipment work, it seemed like there were fewer prairie dogs around, but I was so busy that I didn't have much time for watching the fields. And then the big day had arrived and after a short ground breaking ceremony with county officials, a reporter from the local newspaper, and shovels spray-painted gold, the real digging began. I couldn't watch and took refuge in my office a few blocks away. I imagined little bodies ripped from the earth and collapsed burrows.

The next day I stopped by the job site to see how the work was going and I checked in with the owner of the excavation company, a large man in Carhartt overalls. He was no nonsense by day, but occasionally I would run into him and his wife at plays and concerts in our small town.

He had a question for me, "How did you do it?"

"Do what?"

"How did you get rid of the prairie dogs? Did you gas them or did you drown them?"

"The prairie dogs are gone?" It wasn't hard for me to act surprised.

"We didn't find one prairie dog here."

Manifestation obeys the principles of the birth of *karma*, with its thought/word/deed progression. Think about what you want, unite your subconscious and conscious in purpose, and voice your carefully phrased request out loud. Then you may be two-thirds of the way towards controlled manifestation.

Another gem of esoteric knowledge: We give what we want to have. Kriyananda says, "If you want to be happy then you strive for all the people to be happy." When the tide comes up the boat rises for us all, metaphysically speaking. When we give freely, the gift tends to come back to us. The Teacher warned me once when I hit on hard financial times, "Don't be tight with your money!" In proportion to your ability to give, share what you have. When we cut off the outward flow of physical world *prana*, we risk cutting off the flow of resources towards us as well. The same goes for love, friendship, or knowledge. Give what you have if only so that *you* may have.

> "Everything has a cause and effect.
> Once you realize that you are responsible,
> you realize you can change your world."
>
> —Kriyananda

    One quality that enhances awareness also comes in handy towards the goal of manifesting—imitation of the masters. Sages live the way that they do because it is in alignment with their inner being. Imitating their approach to life will increasingly align our spiritual side with their perspective.

    We also exercise our ability to manifest through the conscious application of the powers of the mind. The Denver Teacher says, "You want to stay healthy. You want to stay strong. You want to stay sane. The masters would say, 'Self-knowledge. Self-realization. Self-discipline.'" The Teachings address three categories of mind stuff relating to manifestation: Mind control, resonating thoughts to the creation, and visualization.

    The Teacher pinpoints the crucial importance of mind control when he says, "For most people, they become what they think. Change the thought—change the life." If we can consciously attune our thoughts to the "form" we wish to manifest (whether that "form" is something physical or an idea or a circumstance) then the plot line of our life will seek out and resonate with the fresh mental note that we have struck.

    We may bring about this sympathetic resonation by visualizing the creation. As Kriyananda says, "To visualize it is to manifest it." Creative visualization is an old tactic, but its longevity doesn't make the approach stale; rather, it is proof of visualization's effectiveness in manifestation.

Hai Ram.

Twenty Tools of Manifestation

Jai Ram.
Jai, Jai, Ram.

—*Mantra* for dissolving fear

Surprisingly perhaps, sound, such as this chanted *mantra*, can be used as an ally in achieving conscious manifestation. Kriyananda points out:

> Sages believed that if you pronounce the *mantra* long enough that you will manifest the meaning of the *mantra*. The process will produce a change in your consciousness. That change in your consciousness will eventually create a change in the external world.

For thousands of years chanted *mantra* has been used for manifestation. The word "*mantra*" itself reveals the creative purpose of the act. The Teacher explains, "*Man* equals 'human.' *Tra* equals 'to think,' and it translates as 'manifestation' when used as a suffix. So *mantra* means 'human thinking,' or 'human manifesting.'" This dovetails well with the ancient Asian Indian and South American indigenous beliefs that sounds may be a creative force.

And of course, no discussion of manifestation would be complete without mentioning meditation. One of the many goals of meditation is that of conscious manifestation. From finding lost objects, to Paramahansa Yogananda sitting in a train station waiting for a spontaneous benefactor, the ability to attain what one wants through meditation has attracted much interest and concrete results for thousands of years.

My Teacher's *guru*, Kriyananda, links manifestation with *pranayama*, "Exhaling and holding manifests into events and people." When we focus on the breath we can use this technique to enhance our spiritual resonance with the one thing that we have identified as desirable in our life.

Manifesting rests on the cooperation of the subconscious. Returning to the iceberg metaphor: We are the penguins sitting on top of the iceberg. We think that we understand why we move in the direction that we move, but nine tenths of the mass of our perch lies beneath the surface and is moved by forces we do not understand. One of the focal tasks of the Kriyaban, particularly if we want conscious control of our continual manifestations into the physical world, is to understand and make allies with what lies below the surface—the subconscious.

The Yoga Sutras teach that our awareness of reality is subject to distortion due to our faulty interpretations. Typically, we first perceive reality through the senses of perception (*grahana*) of these physical bodies—incomplete and superficial. This is the first layer of distortion. The ego and the intellect then interpret these sensual stimuli. Their own limitations add on two more layers of distortion.

Further distortion of reality follows by our own emotional interaction with what we perceive. Objects of the senses, in terms of Kriya metaphysics, can be grouped into two classes. The first class of objects are those that carry the potential to influence us to advance in enlightenment. The second class of objects must be treated carefully—these are the objects with the potential to further entangle us with the sensual, physical world.

Some of the obvious examples of this second class are sex, food, and technology, but we also should include heartbreak, pain, and social isolation. This potential for further attachment to the "real" world (through pleasure and pain) is yet another distorting filter placed on our perceptions.

How do we consciously manifest despite the hurdles of sense perception, interpretation, and emotional entanglement? We increase the odds by understanding how reality is created. The *Sutras* teach that everything in this Universe is composed of primordial matter—*prakriti*. While *prakriti* has the familiar characteristics of sound, touch, sight, taste, and smell and the less familiar physical aspects of ether, air, fire, water, and earth, all *prakriti* is at its most basic a blend of one or more of the three creative qualities or *gunas* ("the binding rope"):

> *Sattva*—the essence of intellect, illumination, and knowledge
> *Rajas*—the essence of activity, movement

Twenty Tools of Manifestation

Tamas—inertia, ignorance, sloth

All three of these essential building blocks of the universe are aspects of creative consciousness. Yoga cosmology assumes that the Universe is made of mind stuff! Everything required to create the world is contained within consciousness itself.

> *Nimittam aprayojakaṁ prakṛtīnāṁ*
> *varaṇa-bhedastu tataḥ kṣetrikavat*
>
> *Prakriti* is not the cause of creation.
> Instead, creation is like making gaps in the berms
> between a farmer's fields.
>
> —*The Yoga Sutras*, Book 4, Sutra 3

Implied in that *sutra* is the "farmer," controlling and directing the flow of primordial matter through the fields in a process of deliberate creation. In order to manifest, the farmer or *purusha* makes gaps between "fields," allowing the irrigation of *prakriti* to fill the rows and make them productive—*consciously manipulating primordial matter.*

According to the *Yoga Sutras*, we know that we do not live in an illusory universe of our own making simply because objects do not disappear when we remove our attention from those objects. We can forget about a box of miscellaneous memorabilia in a shed for ten years, but everything we originally packed in that box will still be there when we (or anyone else) finally opens it again (see *The Yoga Sutras*, Book 4, Verse 16). Contrastingly, in a dream, having once manifested a box of possessions, we may never see that box of stuff again. Normally in dreams we create a transitory personal reality based purely on awareness. The contents of our dreams are entirely subjective and vanish as soon as our attention goes elsewhere. But our waking life is different. Physical objects endure beyond our attention and are perceived by others in an objective reality (*The Yoga Sutras*, Book 4, Verse 15).

What do dreams have to do with manifestation? In the subjective reality of dreams, manifestation is easy. We create a fantasy and there it is—in the comfort of our own mind. But in objective reality we are dealing with a much, much bigger universe and our creations need to endure within the awareness of the outer world.

Obviously there is huge difference between creating an illusion in the instant gratification of the dream state and manifesting real changes in the physical, but this brief survey of yogic esoteric knowledge hints that consciousness may be able to manipulate the building blocks of creation (the three *gunas* of primordial matter). Manifesting in the physical takes a great deal more force than manifestation in the dream state. This difference in energy inputs can be thought of as the difference between melting ice into water and boiling water into steam. The first change of state takes much less effort than the second transition.

So how do we deal with the difficult demands of manifesting into the physical? Well, we can apply a great deal more intensity or duration or both.

$$\text{Force} = \text{Intensity} \times \text{Duration}$$

Or, we can take the shortcut... my Teacher says,

> It is easier to change things on the astral plane than in the physical plane. Yoga dreaming is about changing your dream symbols before they manifest down. On the astral plane it is easier to change your projections. You can enter the astral plane and change your life right now. Creation happens in the subtle world.

Conscious dreaming, in which we have conscious control of events and environment, is an important goal for yogis. If we can apply conscious effort in the astral we have the potential to leverage that effort into manifestation on the physical plane. We may not move mountains, but perhaps we may move a prairie dog colony.

CHAPTER FIFTY-TWO

Hang Onto the Paddle & Pull the Red Cord

"Baby, it's all illusion, no matter how groovy it gets."

—Ram Dass; *Be Here Now*

I suggested earlier that a successful Kriyaban has a well-ordered life, consistently sidesteps group *karma*, isn't influenced by either attraction or aversion, and lives in a world of serendipitous opportunity. If a focused Kriya Yoga practice doesn't improve life, we need to try something new. In the last chapter we looked at the means to consciously manifest opportunity in our lives. Now it is time to consider some of the stubborn forces acting against our determination to create the lives we want.

First of all, there is the age-old tendency to be trapped by the illusions of the physical world. We are taught from birth that we are victims—unwitting passengers on a cruel journey with only one tragic fate waiting for us at the end of our short lives. Our understandable desire for pleasure and our fear of pain further train us to perceive the world with either the rosy lenses of attraction or the dark filters of aversion. Mystically speaking, these perspectives are both illusions of our own making.

The Monk Who Howled Like a Wolf

The Teacher says, "We are like the rabbit staring transfixed at the advancing cobra. Only this cobra is a creation of our own undisciplined thoughts and unresolved *karma*. We get mesmerized by the creation..."

Getting trapped in illusion only happens with the assistance of heavy daily doses of self-deception. You have no doubt witnessed people in your own life falling into the same destructive behaviors over and over again, surprised when they get the same chaotic results with each doomed effort. This endless rewind is only possible with self-deception.

When we are looking for things to blame for botched and misdirected attempts at conscious creation in our lives, we have to tip our hats in respect to lack of self-esteem. In the 1970's an English professor told me that he expected to hear of me as a professional writer. I plunged into several days of depression. *Depression*! A part of me could not accept the possibility that I might get something that I wanted. On a deep level I did not feel that I deserved that satisfaction in my life. Instead, I expected strife and struggle. So what would a person with that basic expectation get out of their efforts to consciously create? Yes, strife and struggle, of course.

"The bewildered self believes it is the creator of action."

—*Bhagavad Gita*, Chapter 3, Verse 27

An immortal soul has played out every possible moral scenario in their lifetimes. Some of these story lines are achingly beautiful and some sub plots are horrifically bad. We learn from these experiences, we take *kriyas* (actions) to make amends for the bad stuff, and we rejoice in the times that we acted on behalf of all beings. The Law of Cause and Effect will tie up any loose ends we mistakenly believe we, or others, might have avoided. There is no need for us to seek or inflict punishment.

Unnecessary guilt or negativity hurts *everybody*. Every sentient being benefits when we live in joy and the clear light of illumination and it is the responsibility of each of us to seek our own enlightenment because that is the only way that we will all

Hang Onto the Paddle & Pull the Red Cord

get off this rock.

> "Very few people know what they want anyway.
> So I don't know what they are expecting."
>
> —A Teacher

Lack of self-esteem thrives where there is a lack of self-knowledge. On the outside we may be insisting that we want to know God, but all the while on the inside we are bellowing, "Safety! Safety! Safety!" while clinging to the shore.

> "I am thinking
> you are afraid to admit to yourself what you want.
> What in heaven's name do you want out of this life
> and why don't you have it already?"
>
> —Kriyananda

On a recent sea-kayaking trip in Alaska's glacier-ringed Prince William Sound, we were warned of the hidden underwater mass of the small icebergs around us. Assumptions as to the size or shape of what was underwater based on what we could see were risky. And at any moment the melting icebergs could shift and overturn, possibly upsetting our little crafts.

This warning reminds me of the next barrier to our ability to consciously manipulate our worlds: That great mass below the surface—the subconscious—controls us far more than we would like to believe. Until we can manifest in harmony with our subconscious, our efforts at creation may produce uneven, even disastrous results. The subconscious is capable of turning our world upside down, revealing what was once hidden and sending a destructive wake surging through our lives.

> "You do not want to focus on the negative
> and get caught up in it.
> You want to focus on enlightenment."
>
> —A Teacher

During a rough bay crossing during a squall on that same kayak trip I found myself repeating a dark *mantra*: "*Hang onto the paddle and pull the red cord. Hang onto the paddle and pull the red cord.*" This is the advice for someone in a kayak that has flipped over—do not lose your paddle (you are going to need it if you can get back into the kayak) and pull on the red strap in front of you to release the waterproof skirt cover that once kept you warm and dry, but which now may trap you underwater, upside down in an overturned kayak. I was rehearsing and reinforcing what I would do when faced with failure, instead of focusing on my important and immediate efforts to make a safe crossing of that stormy, wave-tossed stretch of bitter cold salt water. I had not completed the foundation work of understanding my own motivations and had fallen prey to "negative prayer." I was figuratively and literally focusing on overturning my boat.

Successful manifestation may have a miserable outcome, so we need to be careful how we phrase our requests. For instance, instead of "I will marry Hilda" how about "I ask for a loving, mutually supportive relationship based on spiritual growth"? Instead of "I want to rule in this contract negotiation!" how about "I ask for peace for all parties"?

Despite my gloomy *mantra* that day in Prince William Sound, I managed to stay out of the water, but I discovered that there is still a part of me, normally under the surface, that expects disaster. This self-understanding came when I was forced to look under the surface. Why is it why we do what we do, is of so little interest to so many of us so much of the time? Illusion is strong and our egos are so frightened of admitting weakness that we trick ourselves into believing we know our motivations, but our closest friends and confidants, watching from the outside, may know us better than we do.

> "There is a Saturn delay in manifesting.
> You will get what you are thinking about,
> but it may come later than you were hoping to see it come."
>
> —Kriyananda

Hang Onto the Paddle & Pull the Red Cord

A final barrier to our perception of successful manifestation is what the Kriya world calls a Saturn delay: The wait time between the application of force and the effect of that force. Astrologically, Saturn delays results. We may start out conscientiously applying conscious creation techniques, but grow impatient and give up while that Saturn delay is still ticking off its days and weeks.

After my first time on the reservation I experienced a "spiritual emergency" during which I worked hard for six months to find a right livelihood for myself. I finally gave up on my fruitless striving and took a vacation with my family, letting go of my effort for a couple of weeks. It was during this surrender that my path began to open with no action required—two unsolicited phone calls came in on my answering machine on the same day. One caller asked if I was interested in applying to manage a youth program on a southern Colorado Indian reservation and the other asked if I wanted to supervise construction for the affordable housing program in my own town of Gunnison, Colorado. The Saturn delay had ended while I took a break and enjoyed myself.

The lesson for me was to envision a successful crossing to my goal, speak that intention to the world, and give manifestation its time to do its subtle work under the surface of reality.

The Monk Who Howled Like a Wolf

FIFTY-THREE

Acceptance

*I*n my first life I lived in a land turned upside down by war and bloodshed and all I could think about was, "Food, food, food."

In my second life I wore the orange robes of a celibate monk. There was always enough to eat, but all I could think about was, "Sex, sex, sex."

In my next life I lived in a land warmed with a brilliant yellow sun. I had so much food and sex that I never knew want for those things, but all I could think of was, "Money, money, money."

In my next life money came easily to me in a green countryside where I kept a shop in a small town and traded across the waters for fine things to sell for even more money. But I cared for none and no one cared for me. All I thought of in my elegant home was, "Love, love, love."

In my next life I had a doting husband and many children. I lived in a cottage in the windswept cliffs above a blue sea. I was never without the comfort of family, but I yearned for the talent to create pictures as pleasing as the landscapes around me.

In my next life I was a famous artist in oil and watercolor. I lacked for nothing, but still something was missing. This time my restless quest went inwards. I spent this whole life in a search *for, "Wisdom, wisdom, wisdom."*

In my last life I was an eccentric genius of a woman, living alone and wearing purple. I had had all I wanted of food, sex, money, love, creativity, and wisdom.

All I wanted now was to be with God.

It may sound heavy-handed to describe the subtle process of conscious manifestation as getting what we want, but that is what the practice boils down to. Getting what we want isn't necessarily bad. Even Osho was reportedly chauffeured about in a Rolls Royce, a gift from his devotees. However, we run the risk of binding ourselves to earth if we become attached to the things of this world. If we wish to know God we must liberate ourselves from shiny objects and accept the deeper spiritual truth underlying our world of attachment and aversion.

Acceptance, letting go, and surrender are mystically important stages of personal growth linked together in the Teachings. These are inevitable stretches to be traversed on the sacred road.

Acceptance, in this sense, means grateful submission to the world we have created. Acceptance is living in the now and following the timeless advice of Pema Chodron to "*Start Where You Are*" (as one of her books is entitled) on our journey towards knowledge. Acceptance is being the office worker or the ditch digger or the engineer with grace and enthusiasm. Acceptance is using what we have, every moment, to make the world better for other sentient beings.

Acceptance is not spending idle hours wishing impotently that we were somewhere or someone else. Acceptance is not passive resignation to the overflowing trash bin in our room or to the bad habits that we have accumulated. Acceptance is a dynamic state that recognizes that we are continuously evolving spiritual beings, working every day through our practice to become better souls. The investment banker should apply herself to be the best damn investment banker that she can be. But tomorrow—if the stars are right and Path Opens—she may gratefully accept the opportunity to craft a poem.

Acceptance

> "How are you going to live the rest of your life? How are you going to handle things while you are in this form? Part of it is accepting our humanness and then transcending it."
>
> —A Teacher

Acceptance begins with our human imperfections. There are two significant barriers to accepting our humanity. The first is that we hold ourselves up to an impossible standard of perfection. Though we all have problems and imperfections, every one of us also contains a piece of God. We are all divine beings lingering in the physical to learn more about the universe and about ourselves. As Kriyananda says, "We have to learn to like ourselves. We have to learn to accept ourselves. There is nothing wrong with any of us."

The second barrier to acceptance is that in our squeamishness to embrace our imperfections, we hide our problems and thus remain in thrall to the limitations we refuse to see. What do the addiction counselors tell us? The first step in handling a problem is recognizing there is a problem. Or, as my Teacher says, "It doesn't disappear because you don't acknowledge it."

If we blind ourselves to our rough edges and throw a rug over what we would prefer not to see, we miss opportunities to stretch and to create of our souls something better and grander. We need to accept our mistakes and flaws with grace and clarity of vision unclouded by rationalizations or evasion. Extend acceptance even to ego. As the Teacher says: "A fully-developed ego is comfortable with itself in all its humanness. You must accept the mind/body personality to move beyond it."

The General who could kill without blinking, and the monk who could accept death, tell us something about accepting *karma*. The monk could accept that it may be his *karma* to die, but he was also able to take an action, a *kriya*, to transcend and soften *karma* for himself and the brutal General. As the Denver Teacher puts it, "The movement is to accept the *karma* with full acquiescence and then move through it."

My Teacher says that along with our unique karmic history comes a unique spiritual path, "You must accept the fact that your path is unique to you. No two people will come to enlightenment in the same way."

Kriyananda speaks bluntly and urgently of the need to accept our personal route to enlightenment, saying, "It's not about you, you, you. It's about the path. If you are out for power, it's not the path. If you're out for wealth, it's not the path. You need to know why you are here."

He also warns that acceptance extends beyond the interior into the outer world. We also need to accept what the world has to offer us. "It's an ego problem not to be able to accept gifts. If we cannot accept simple gifts from a human being, how can we accept gifts from a divine being?"

The Teachings suggest that a practice of acceptance works on many levels. I must accept that my spirit yearns for the wild places, but that I harbor an ego that expects my kayak to topple me into the cold sea, and that my karmic past with Roxanne makes friendship between us a challenge we may not overcome in this life. We must learn to accept our human imperfections, our earth lives, our bothersome egos, the *karma* that we come here with, our unique spiritual paths, the gifts that life is prepared to offer us, and the constant change that characterizes the physical world. We must even accept death. Acceptance is a first step in freeing our souls before we learn to let go.

FIFTY-FOUR

Letting Go

> "Non-attachment
> is considered the greatest of all spiritual practices.
> What can you let go of?"
>
> —A Teacher

The next attribute on this final approach to *kaivalya* is letting go. Letting go is releasing the need to be the investment banker. Letting go is abandoning the need to be the hero or the rescuer or the even the monk. Letting go is dropping the need to be in control, releasing the frightened ego, and heeding the guidance welling-up from deep inside.

A yogi might see worry as focus on the inconsequential. Like the child in the dentist's chair, we mistake the transitory pains of our earth life as meaningful. Worry is negative prayer—passive and harmful—a trap set by the illusions of the physical plane.

"Stay away from right and wrong," says Kriyananda. We should not accept the authority of those who would tell us how to live and what to believe. Test limits. Find out what resonates with our *dharma*. We must move "with skillful means" into uncharted territory. We can't be satisfied with letting someone else's rules mark the boundaries of our spiritual expression. My Teacher has often said that those with no early religious training are the lucky ones—they have no bad spiritual habits to overcome and no misleading ingrained beliefs to shake.

Mistaking *yoga siddhis* for progress on the path is a tempting but unfortunate detour. The Teacher says, "You can have all the power you want, but it is not enlightenment. If you are looking for power, you are not looking for the divine." Power is merely the ability to occupy the stage and accumulate *karma* in the *maya* of this physical world. Instead, we need to focus our efforts on bringing merit to our world rather than seeking what merit the world can bring to us.

As the Denver Teacher points out, "Most people try to control the uncontrollable." Control is an illusion. Just how much are we controlling the outside world when we ourselves are controlled by lifetimes of deeply ingrained emotional patterns and karmic cause and effect? How can we aspire to control when our knowledge of this universe we seek to control is pitifully incomplete and shallow? We have a limited understanding of what is going on from one moment to the next and little ability to judge what is good or bad. Bad may masquerade as good and good disguise itself as bad.

This is the story of *The Farmer's Son*:

The two old friends, a farmer and a carpenter, were sitting in a sunny courtyard drinking tea, when the farmer began to tell the tale of his son.

"One day a wild stallion began coming to our paddock late at night, bothering our mares. My son became obsessed with this stallion and despite my instructions, he left his work in the fields and spent days looking for this outlaw horse."

"Oh, that's bad," commiserated the farmer's old friend.

"No, that's good, because finally my son was able to capture this horse and it turns out that the stallion is very valuable and an excellent racer and breeder."

"Oh, that's good!" cried the friend.

"No, that's bad, because my son took up horse racing with this fast stallion, despite my forbidding it."

Letting Go

"Oh... That's bad?"

"Not really, no, because this stallion was very fast and my son made a lot of money doing this."

"I see now. That is good."

"No, because one day while racing the horse, my son was thrown from the wild beast and broke his leg. He couldn't race or work in the fields. He just lay in the cottage all day!"

"That's bad?" ventured the friend.

"No! That's good! The general had heard about my son and his fast horse so the army came to take my son away to war but found him here unable to walk and they had to leave my son with me. Plus, they took that darn stallion away with them!"

"Well then, that is undeniably good. You kept your son and got rid of the bad luck stallion at the same time."

The farmer shook his head sadly, "No that's bad. Don't you see? The mares followed that stallion first chance they got and then I had no horses to plow the fields!"

The friend said nothing at all.

The farmer continued, "But that turned out to be good because the stallion escaped the soldiers and brought back all my mares, plus six more. Suddenly I was rich with horses!"

"That is good then."

"Oh, no, that's bad because..."

Ultimately, no event is good or bad unless a sentient being assigns that meaning. Through our interpretation and the intent of our controlling actions, we create good and bad where there was no moral value to begin with. The Teacher says, "Get away from all your loyalties and your prejudices."

I used to attempt to assign meaning to my rocky relationship with Roxanne. The two of us obviously have a deep connection on a spirit level and I feel we are locked in a dynamic that has transcended lifetimes. But now we are spirits trapped in the physical.

Roxanne is cancer free after her confrontation with breast cancer, and is doing well. We trade the occasional email or phone call, messages tinged with defeat—a reminder of a road not traveled. I am happy and grateful for my life with Gail in the little house in the big mountains of Alaska, but sometimes I struggle still with letting go of Roxanne and wish we had seized the opportunity to transmute the heavy *karma* between us.

In the *Bhagavad Gita,* letting go of the "fruits of action" identifies another form of letting go. In this tradition, action in the world is the birthplace of *karma.* Chapter 4, verse 5 suggests that we can avoid the consequences of action when we act with contentment and peacefulness, relinquishing, or letting go of attachment to the potential rewards of that action.

> "Relax and open.
> With resistance comes aversion.
> Enlightenment is offering no resistance."
>
> —A Teacher

My Teacher also stresses letting go of resistance to the way things are, letting go of resistance to our place in the world, and letting go of resistance to the nature of our friends and family. These types of resistance are ineffective and ignore the learning our unique environments have to offer. Resistance has its roots in attraction and aversion and needing to change the way things are. As the Teacher says, "The world is a training ground for souls. We need the world as it is." Who are we to say what should be resisted and what serves a purpose beyond our superficial understanding?

Finally, we are asked to release even our hard-earned knowledge. Many of us on the path, myself included, work hard to push ourselves towards enlightenment through "head stuff," such as this book. I spend far more time writing about meditating than I do actually meditating. Were I truly letting go of my resistance to enlightenment, I would spend more time on the mat and less time hunched over my keyboard, staring at a glowing screen.

My Teacher suggests that we "take all this head stuff I see people doing on the spiritual path and make it heart stuff." The head is where the ego lives. All the knowledge of the Kriya lineage does nothing for us if we don't swallow the Teachings and allow them to pervade the center of our being. The ego dwells in the shallow surface waters of consciousness, forever rationalizing the irrational. Placing our consciousness under the direction of ego means that we perceive and act through *samskara*, attraction, and aversion rather than through the insight and wisdom of the spirit. Instead of awareness through ego, we must cultivate Observer awareness through the third eye of the *ajna chakra*. As an observer we are able to surrender our actions to the divine and transcend *karma*.

The Monk Who Howled Like a Wolf

CHAPTER FIFTY-FIVE

Surrender

"Surrender is a key concept spiritually. Surrender of attachment, ego, and the need to control. To endure and do what needs to be done in your life."

—A Teacher

Now we have entered the pivotal quality of surrender in our quest for *kaivalya*.

Surrender is abandoning the need to understand or the instinct to seek security. Surrender is the acceptance of all that is. Surrender, the Teacher tells us, is at once accepting our world and transcending it. Surrender is bowing in humility and respect before the incomprehensible spiritual fabric that weaves past, present, and future together in one tightly woven tapestry of creation.

There are five principal areas of surrender for the spiritual aspirant. The first element of surrender is surrender to the Teachings. The Denver Teacher says, "The danger is that we hear a thought and we think, 'I get it.' But it's not about that. It's about absorbing the Teaching. *Becoming* the Teaching." The

Teachings must be absorbed to work their mystical magic. They need to become a part of us and of our way of perceiving the world. The Teachings need to become our own personal cultural background—the filter through which we view everything of this world and beyond. Another area of surrender is surrender to direct experience of the mystical. Watch what happens to your consciousness in meditation. Suspend the limitations of logic in shamanic trance or in the ecstasy of dance. Be open to bolts of intuitive knowledge that may change your life in a flash.

> "You have to adjust to the world.
> Don't fight the world—it's too powerful."
>
> —Kriyananda

And then we must surrender to the world. How many saints have been able to resist the group *karma* of this dense physical reality? Think of the role models that valiantly resisted the world in fighting the good fight. How did they end up? Yes, we may be able to think of a couple notables, like Babaji, that seem to have escaped the need to look both ways before crossing the street, but there are precious few that truly have succeeded at being "in this world, but not of this world."

If we stand on railroad tracks a train will hit us. If we neglect our earth life we will find ourselves distracted from the spiritual life by crises in health, wealth, and family. Surrender to the world. As my Teacher points out, we asked to be here—why should we act surprised at what we find?

> "There is a balance between the mind and the heart force."
>
> —A Teacher

The wisdom of the heart has been one of the great teachers for me in this lifetime. Sometimes the heart is a coward, and sometimes it's a lion. At times it sees clearly, and at times the heart hides under the bed for fear of seeing what is outside the

Surrender

door. The heart and its ways mystify me and yet I know that there is something powerful in this heart of mine. I have come to accept that we are in this universe for three stunningly important accomplishments: To love, to learn, and to serve. I can't truly love unless I surrender to the heart. If we harness the wild love of the heart and the persistent intelligence of the intellect, then we may develop the careful wisdom to serve.

The Teacher says, "I don't think it's a non-controlled mind or a controlled mind. I think it is no mind. In mysticism there is continual subtraction until attaining the void: *Sunyata*—that which we are—cosmic consciousness." The next thing we must leave behind is our mind-body complex (the identification of self with the ego and the physical form). As long as we cling to the belief that the mind-body complex is what we *are* then we separate ourselves from the rest of all that *is* and turn our backs on the mystical principal of We Are One. We must find that place in pure meditation in which we no longer exist, in which the self has dissolved into the void of pure awareness—timeless and dimensionless.

> When thought is directed,
> when one dwells only in the Self,
> and when there are no selfish hungers,
> one is engaged in yoga.
>
> —*Bhagavad Gita*; Chapter Six, Verse 18

"I know surrender to the will of the wind." Finally, as my Teacher quotes, we seek surrender to the divine. *The Yoga Sutras* direct us to devote ourselves to *Ishvara* (Book 2, *sutra* 1) and tell us in Book 2, *sutra* 45 that this allegiance will bring us the perfection of *samadhi*—union with the object of meditation and, ultimately, union with everything...

Enlightenment.

The Monk Who Howled Like a Wolf

CHAPTER FIFTY-SIX

Samadhi

"According to the Teachings,
the goal of *samadhi* must come before all others."

—A Teacher

Samadhi is the eighth and final limb of yoga (enlightenment itself is beyond even the practices of yoga). According to *The Yoga Sutras of Patanjali* (the best traditional source of information on *samadhi* from the yoga traditions), *samadhi* is a mental state in which the meditator merges with the object of meditation and loses self-awareness (YS3.03).

Samadhi should not be confused with enlightenment. Even *samadhi* is yet another step on our journey to *kaivalya*, but *samadhi* is the gateway to enlightenment.

Samadhi may be thought of not as a specific state but as a spectrum of expanded consciousness, moving increasingly towards Self-realization. The elaborate classification systems that various esoteric disciplines assign to expanded states of consciousness are well-meaning efforts to describe what is indefinable and ineffable. *The Yoga Sutras* describe nine levels of *samadhi*, each deeper and more ethereal than the last.

We may slip into one of the nine stages of *samadhi* spontaneously for a few seconds and then not re-experience that state of mind for months, or ever. Or we may move quickly and easily through four levels of *samadhi* in one session on the mat and then have these higher states of consciousness disappear completely on rising and find ourselves right back in our everyday lives again.

The first level of *samadhi*, *vitarka samadhi*, is easy to imagine—it is the state in which we are absorbed in physical awareness. Yoga *asanas* may help us attain this state in which our chattering monkey mind grows quiet and our awareness focuses on what our bodies are experiencing. *Vitarka samadhi* is also accessible to us in childbirth, long distance running, mountain climbing, shamanic drumming, ecstatic dance, bicycling, First Nations' sweat lodge ceremonies, or even walking—any physical activity that captures our full attention.

The second level of *samadhi* is *vicara samadhi*—subtle or insightful awareness. This is meditative absorption in rarefied thought itself. This is the nutty professor lost in equations or an hour passing quickly while we puzzle with a crossword. This *vicara samadhi* is melding with the deeper "subtle" reality of the object of meditation.

Ananda samadhi is absorption in the bliss of a sunrise or in the eyes of a newborn baby. In *ananda samadhi* ecstatic joy fills the meditator without source or reason.

Last in this *Samprajnata* group of the first four, relatively accessible levels of *samadhi*, is *asmita samadhi*—"absorption with the Self." In this *samadhi* the meditator becomes transfixed in awareness of the spirit or soul.

The Yoga Sutras, in their sparing explanations, prescribe intense application to the goal of *samadhi* and devotion to *Ishvara* as routes to these first four levels of *samadhi*. To attain the fifth level of *samadhi* (*asamprajnata samadhi*—non-mind *samadhi*) *The Yoga Sutras* suggest that we will be aided by faith, energetic focus, past experience, immersion in the lower levels of *samadhi*, and the ability to discriminate between phenomena of the physical world and those sourced from the spiritual

Samadhi

(YS1.20).

The sixth level of *samadhi* is *nirvitarka samadhi*—complete absorption of the mind in the object of meditation and freedom from the fluctuations or distractions of consciousness.

The seventh level is *nirvicara samadhi* in which the inner Self reveals the truths and wisdom of the physical and spiritual worlds in instant intuitive flashes and the yogi can manipulate *karma* to render triggering *samskaras* harmless (YS1.47-50).

In the eight level, *nirbija samadhi*, even wisdom and discernment are left behind as consciousness is absorbed into the *purusha*—the soul—and the physical world recedes. There is now no activity in the mind whatsoever and hours may have passed in an instant to the meditator regaining conscious awareness after *nirbija samadhi*.

The final, rarefied ninth state of *samadhi* is *dharma-megha samadhi*—otherwise known as "Cloud of Virtue" *samadhi*. It is said that at this point the living yogi has already been liberated, although still in the body, and is impervious to the five *kleshas* or obstacles to union (ignorance, ego, attachment, aversion, and clinging to life). This is *kaivalya* while in the flesh though there is nothing of the flesh left to hold the yogi here (YS4.29-31). As the Teacher says, "In the final ninth level of *samadhi* there is no going back."

We have probably all experienced levels of *samadhi*, but the higher states are harder to wrap our minds around. The Denver Teacher believes that the Kriyaban may already be awakened when experiencing the lower levels of *samadhi* (in the sense of "awake" used in the title of the movie about Paramahansa Yogananda, *Awake: The Life of Yogananda*) and yet still have more levels of *samadhi* to explore before attaining complete *kaivalya*.

What the masters do agree on is that there are levels of consciousness higher than the human norm, presaging the threshold to illumination. How do we attain these higher states of consciousness? Kriyananda suggests specific preparations that we can make for *samadhi*. Some of his advice may be surprising. First, he says that we must accept all our pain, anguish, suffering, and the way that we are right now. We are not to use what we perceive as our limitations as an excuse to shrink back from the challenge of attaining *samadhi*. He says we should accept that money is the *prana* of this western world of ours, but that we can use this *prana* to feed our experience, intelligence, and bodies, encouraging conditions in our lives that give us the luxury of fostering *samadhi*. He says that we should have more fun and embrace life, love, and the divine. Eat better, healthier food, but eat less of it. Avoid chlorinated and fluoridated water. Stabilize our moods.

Before *samadhi* visits, we may have to replace our fear of death with a deep acceptance of immortality. Trust our mystical experiences. Change our attitudes towards life in order to change the limiting stories we tell about our pasts and futures. Forgive the transgressions of the past so that we may move without baggage into the present. Don't let events in the physical world control us with stress. Deal positively with our relationship problems. Accept that good and bad fortunes are the consequence of personal *karma*. Accept and control the creative power of our thoughts.

Kriyananda says that we should cultivate deep meditation and use it to improve our lives while within the astral. Balance our *chakras*. And finally, we can dissolve *karma* and improve our lives from within the causal planes to create the focus that allows a pursuit of *samadhi* and *kaivalya*.

> "The goal of *samadhi* is to link the ego self with the spiritual Self."
>
> —Kriyananda

Linking the ego self with the spiritual Self is *Self*-realization. The state of *samadhi* may heal the unnatural rift between the physical and the spiritual and allow us to become simultaneously aware of the existence, on all levels, of a spiritual being—*our* spiritual being—of which this physical plane and what we think of as "I" are one very small part. *Samadhi* is the gateway to this expanding awareness that leads to enlightenment.

CHAPTER FIFTY-SEVEN

The Nature of Enlightenment

"If you see life as the way for souls to attain their enlightenment, then you should always be smiling, no matter what happens to you."

—A Teacher

This book is a guide for the journey towards enlightenment or *kaivalya*. The personal irony contained within these pages is that I write this book because this process of organizing my notes from years at the master's feet is the best way for me to swallow the Teachings. This book is my personal guide to enlightenment.

I don't have adequate words to describe union with the divine, nor do I have any conscious memory of a fully enlightened state, though my Teacher has said, "We have all been enlightened, that's why you are seeking it." Once again—as so often in these pages—it is my task to describe something that I do not fully understand. I am guided in this overly-ambitious task by the words of my mentors in the Kriya Yoga lineage: The masters who point the way for all us who have the ears to hear.

The *Metta* Prayer

May all beings be peaceful.
May all beings be happy.
May all beings be safe.
May all beings awaken to the light of their true nature.
May all beings be free.

Clues regarding the nature of enlightenment are contained in the last two lines of the Metta Prayer—"true nature" and "free." Enlightenment is regaining our true nature, *Self*-realization, as a divine, *free* being—and simultaneously a part of the core awareness that permeates all of reality.

Kriyananda has defined *nirvana* (the state of enlightenment) as "extinguishing your mind's desire." This is yet another clue into one of the qualities of enlightenment—a sustained place of non-attachment—a state of pure understanding or discriminative discernment.

So is this state of discriminative discernment or pure understanding our final enlightenment? No! Book 2, *sutra* 26 of *The Yoga Sutras* states that even this stage of pure understanding (attainable while in body) is just a *means* to liberation. That liberation only comes when we have transcended the reach of *karma* itself.

What is a yogi to do? It is tempting to assume that enlightenment is too ambitious and rarefied a state for mortal aspirations. Sometimes I wonder if just practicing the Eight Limbs is enough self-improvement for this life. A healthy practice of the Eight Limbs certainly would be a life well spent, but the robed lineage still whispers to us that more is possible. A life well spent still separates us from ultimate awareness and returns us to this baleful playground once again. The masters tell us that we can do better. We may join them in a place beyond even the astral. Enlightenment is why we are here.

Nityananda writes, "We have to practice union with our source through our body and in life only." Not only is the search

The Nature of Enlightenment

for enlightenment the purpose of our life here on earth, but Nityananda and Kriya Yoga teach that the movement towards enlightenment is the purpose of reincarnation. Corporeal life doesn't hamper Self-realization—it is *necessary* for Self-realization. Something about the indulgent environment of the astral planes hampers or even freezes spiritual evolution. We require the rigors and hardships of the physical to coax us towards greater perseverance, self-discipline, and accomplishment, preparing us for ultimate union with the divine.

> "The spirit in perfection knows not itself fully.
> They come down into time to experience conflict,
> to know themselves."
>
> —Kriyananda

The Denver Teacher says that every justification we use to hang onto our lives here on Earth is a rationalization. "Your birth was a glorious moment because it gave you a chance at enlightenment. In Kriya, the only *dharma* is to seek your enlightenment, period. It is the reason, according to the Teachings, that you have reincarnated again."

Our *dharma* is to become enlightened and our various life paths are to move us forward on this journey. In the final Chapter 18 of the *Gita*, verse 45, it says, "Being accomplished in one's own *dharma*, one attains perfection." We seek our *dharma* and find that balanced state of Path Opens in order to bring ourselves closer to enlightenment—*dharma* is the spiritual map towards our final destination.

When I feel overwhelmed at the challenge of achieving enlightenment in this troubled and brief lifetime, I remind myself that I have as much time as I need—a dozen lives, or a thousand, or 800,000!

Time doesn't matter.

The Universe will wait.

> "Enlightenment is not of the mind."
>
> —A Teacher

Kaivalya is, due to its own nature, indescribable. How do I use my mind to describe something that is beyond mind? And where will I get my information? To my Teacher and to his *guru*, Kriyananda, this ascension is a rediscovery. Within this perspective, we are all enlightened beings that have lost their way.

The second Book of the *Sutras* describes a spiritual journey intended to dissolve ignorance and gain true insight, allowing discriminative discernment, or pure understanding, to permeate the yogi until finally our *samskaras* (the unconscious assumptions and preconceptions created by our karmic heritage) fall away. It is this state of pure understanding beyond the reach of *karma* that is enlightenment.

History is filled with well-known individuals that would appear to have had some measure of enlightenment. We have stories of Buddhist monks transfiguring into rainbow bodies, leaving only their empty robes behind, and we also have the Buddhas and Sri Yukteswars (Yogananda's *guru*) that live and teach among us for decades. The *jivanmuktas* (those living on earth while liberated) may have their own ripening to complete before the physical plane holds no further purpose for them. We tend to think of Self-realization as an all or nothing accomplishment, but in reality it is an infinite process, not an endpoint. *Turiya* (the transcendental state) may be defined as "Recognition of the Self as all that is." This realization may come in a flash or it may come gradually, in the course of years of meditation. There are no shortcuts, but there is a clear sequence to the journey. As the Teacher says, "You have to go through the basement to get to the penthouse."

There is a tendency to move back and forth on the spectrum of illumination. During one lifetime we may be at the helm of a relatively evolved ego, but in the next lifetime we experience a more base reality to round out our experience. A soul may backslide from enlightenment in the course of one lifetime, in one decade, or even in the span of a day.

The process of enlightenment can start, stop, slow, and speed up. Consider the old metaphor of the trail up the mountain. A hiker may walk fast or slowly. They may stop for a break then

The Nature of Enlightenment

remember they left their walking stick behind and retrace their path down the slope for many miles before they start back uphill again. We may pass people on their way down who can tell us about the journey ahead. We reach false summits we thought would be the top of the mountain only to find a beautiful lake glittering in a sheltered sub-alpine bowl where we stop and rest for hours. Or, after a long and difficult climb, we are frustrated to find that the trail ahead leads us downhill for a long, long ways, losing much of that painfully gained elevation. We are ready to scream with frustration! But this is the trail. This is the path.

> "Many people feel that if they gain enlightenment
> they will always be happy.
> Why should you think you should always be happy?"
>
> —A Teacher

Even after we have gained some measure of illumination (as you certainly have already), there are still going to be bad days. Even the Buddha could get grouchy over a fly in his soup. It's not all rainbows and unicorns for the everyday mystic and we may spend years on the path looking in the wrong places. Remember the yogi that went to the pizza parlor? He asked, "Make me one with everything."

> "The whole idea
> is to wash out of your consciousness
> the idea of perfection.
> There is no one walking on this world—
> including Jesus—
> who is perfect.
> I am here, comfortably, because I am imperfect."
>
> —Kriyananda

Even experiencing *kaivalya* while on this physical plane or in the lower astrals, we still have to do the work of dealing with our ego and our *samskaras* and we still have to play nicely with others. My Teacher cautions us not to expect liberation from who we are at our core. "A person enlightened will still keep their basic personality traits. Enlightened, you still will be doing what you are doing, just with a different viewpoint."

> "If you want to be happy
> then you strive for all the people to be happy.
> We are not separate islands unto ourselves.
> If we want to be enlightened
> we must work towards the *world* being enlightened."
>
> —Kriyananda

We must *all* be enlightened. To the extent that any of us are enlightened that enlightenment must be applied towards the enlightenment of others.

Now that we have these enlightenment disclaimers out of the way, we can move on to the interesting stuff: What we know about enlightenment from the Teachings and the teachers that have gone before us.

> "It is better to sit and do nothing
> and let your enlightenment come."
>
> —A Teacher

Enlightenment is non-striving both in the pursuit and in the practice. While on the path it is best to enjoy the journey and not focus on the destination. That is what *kaivalya* is all about—a process, not an end. Illumination is revealed in a way of life rather than attainment of a goal. As Yogananda is quoted as saying, "The citadel can not be taken by force."

> "Relax and open.
> With resistance comes aversion.
> Enlightenment is offering no resistance."
>
> —A Teacher

The Nature of Enlightenment

Kaivalya is a state of non-resistance. There is nothing to fight because all our imagined adversaries are a reflection of ourselves and of the divine. That's not to say that goals are not set and pursued. It's not to say that we are passive doormats or that we don't work to end misery, violence, poverty, or oppression in our world. But we do not externalize these problems and imagine dualism where there is none. The tyrant and the saint are both a part of us. Both deserve loving compassion.

Enlightenment is characterized as a nurturing state. The Teacher says, "We must all turn back to the feminine principle.... more receptive, more nurturing, soft, non-resisting."

The enlightened are content. Remember *santosha*, the second *niyama*? *Santosha* means inner contentment. My Teacher stresses that everything that comes into our lives, no matter how unpleasant to the ego, is an opportunity for enlightenment. In that context, what is there to oppose? It is all another chance to flourish spiritually.

Wisdom is an undeniable attribute of increasing Self-realization. The sages are often living examples of astonishing intuition and even detailed scientific knowledge. When we read the works of Krishnamurti, Osho, or Rumi we sense a brilliance shining from within the words. Kriyananda describes enlightenment as coinciding with omniscience and omnipotence though in grasping at these qualities *kaivalya* slips through our fingers like water.

"What's wrong with giving up emotion?"

—Kriyananda

Enlightenment is at the reigns of a bridled and controlled ego. In Chapters 5 and 18 of the *Bhagavad Gita* there are references to the disciplined selves of the enlightened (BG 5.25 & 18.51). Verse 52 of Chapter 18 describes those who have attained enlightenment as controlling deeds, words, and even thoughts and the Teacher says, "You must die to your ego to live."

Not only do the enlightened control their ego, they also ultimately transcend the ego. The ego/self is tied to this personality of the physical world and the lower astrals. To move into the causal planes and beyond, the ego has to be left behind. The ego is born of this life, not of the eternal state that the Self resides in. Nothing is lost when we leave our egos behind, but a great deal is gained.

Interestingly, the *Gita* also lists living apart from others as a characteristic of those that are enlightened. Solitude isn't a prerequisite for enlightenment, but those who have reached a certain level of *kaivalya* are more likely to live alone, as does my Teacher. The world with all its clamoring voices may be an unwelcome distraction and temptation to the single-pointed mind. Don't expect to find saints and sages surrounded by admirers. They are more likely to be the hermit, content in the woods.

Not surprisingly, the *Gita* warns us away from attachments if we ever wish to become enlightened. Unhealthy attachments specifically mentioned by the *Gita* include approval from others (BG 14.24), the need for possessions (BG 2.71, 5.21, 14.24, 18.53), attachment to sense objects (BG 2.58, 18.51-52), passion (BG 5.26, 14.23, 16.22, 18.52), desire (BG 2.56, 2.55, 2.70-71, 18.53), special relationships (BG 2.57, 14.22-26), attachment to misery (BG 6.22), and identification with one's actions (BG 2.51, 3.19, 5.12, 14.24-25, 18.53).

The higher states of Self-realization only come with freedom from the dual pitfalls of "reality"—attraction (*raga*) and aversion (*dvesha*). Chapter 18, verse 51 of the *Bhagavad Gita*, in the summation of the abilities necessary to reach *siddhim* (complete attainment within the Supreme Spirit), includes the requirement of discarding attraction and aversion. As I've written, these two natural impulses lead us towards decisions, mundane and spiritual, that effectively bind us into the repeating cycle of birth and death.

Kriyananda illustrates the struggle of an enlightened being continuing to operate in the everyday world: "There was really only one time my *guru* truly became angry at me. I made a bad comment about Yogananda. Shelliji said to me. 'You are talking about someone that transcended humanity and then came back down and had to act like you.'"

The Nature of Enlightenment

> "Breaking tunnel vision is transcending your culture.
> It is to transcend your gender.
> It is to transcend your economic class.
> You must transcend, ultimately, your humanness,
> if you are here to be enlightened."
>
> —A Teacher

One of the qualities of those who have attained some measure of enlightenment is to be "In the world, but not *of* the world," as the old saying goes. This quality of not being of the world includes distance from culture, gender identification, loyalty to the group, and even loyalty to humanity itself. Instead, one's identification lies with the higher Self.

In describing those that have transcended the three primordial qualities that define and confine consciousness in the physical world (the *gunas*—*sattva*/intellect, *rajas*/activity, and *tamas*/inertia), Krishna says that the sage is "seated as if seated apart." (BG14.23) They are here and yet they are not here.

The Denver Teacher says, "A real seeker of truth has no family. The whole point of yoga is to transcend your humanness. The teaching is that you are an immortal spirit." The Teacher warns that our loyalties effectively imprison us. We must be loyal only to the search for illumination.

If we are to leave behind culture, gender, and even family, what do we have left? We have the enduring happiness and constant contentment within the sublime higher Self (BG5.21, 6.18-20). *Kaivalya* is a *prana*-based state of uncorrupted bliss—*ananda*. Kri*yananda* says that, "To get happy and stay happy is to be enlightened. You are happy first, and then comes enlightenment."

> "*Ananda* is a better word than happy
> because happy allows unhappy.
> *Ananda* has no negation.
> Bliss is like the Mount Everest of happiness."
>
> —A Teacher

The Monk Who Howled Like a Wolf

There is no hangover from this high, no regrets lingering after the pleasures of the night before, nobody that we can't look in the eye the next day, no dark cloud behind the silver lining. This happy of *ananda* comes from the inside and may well-up during meditation or during our morning jog or while sitting on the front porch in the evening. It has little to do with how our workaday life is going—this joy abides—a sublime and pleasant mystery from within our souls. Call it grace or call it foolish—it is real and unmistakable when it happens. Let it wash over you. Rest unquestioning as the bliss flows through your flesh and bones and don't wonder or grasp. This incredible sensation (a brief taste of enlightenment) is to be savored.

As Graham M. Schweig points out in his excellent commentary on the *Bhagavad Gita*, one of the meanings of *nirvana* is the extinguishing of worldly existence and experience and replacing it with tranquility and peacefulness. This is bliss/*ananda*. There are no struggles for a minute or two—even an hour, if we are fortunate.

Self-realization has been characterized as a state of expanded consciousness. The Teacher says, "That's what enlightenment is—becoming fully conscious. Not just a little conscious." Kriyananda has described enlightenment as a noetic experience: Absorption of mystical information without ego attachment. According to *The Yoga Sutras*, expanded consciousness is literally liberating for the *sadhu* and omniscient in character, with awareness of all things simultaneously (YS3.54).

This expanded consciousness is not based in the brain or even in the heart. Consciousness has expanded out of physical space. From the *Bhagavad Gita* again:

> *sarvabhūtastham ātmānaṃ sarvabhūtāni cātmani*
> *īkṣate yogayuktātmā sarvatra samadarśanaḥ*

> If you see your Self present in everything
> and everything present in your Self,
> You are absorbed in the highest yoga teaching,
> observing spirit in all.

> —Bhagavad Gita; Chapter 6, Verse 29

The Nature of Enlightenment

Even approaching enlightenment, the *samskaras* of *karma* and a stubborn sense of individual identity may still influence the advanced *sadhu* as cautioned in Book 4, *sutra* 27 of *The Yoga Sutras*. *Kaivalya* is a process, not an endpoint. The further we get, the more there is to do. Who can say where this journey ends? Eventually, the Self-realized become the embodiment of We Are One because they are indeed one with everything—in a non-pizza sense. The *Chandogya Upanishad* says, "It is spiritual wisdom that all life is one." (VI.1.6)

> "Collapse the dualities."
>
> —A Teacher

Like a Big Bang for the soul, eventually all the pieces of our fragmented universe collapse down into themselves and we achieve a singularity. We are but a single point of reality and yet we contain the Universe. As *The Sutras* tell us, the power of consciousness rests in its own essential nature, the ego dissolves back into the void, and the cycle of birth and death is left behind along with the physical realms.

> "That divinity exists within you.
> As soon as you give it a form, you limit it.
> The form is already limiting.
> We have to transcend the form.
> We can use the form to get to the formless."
>
> —A Teacher

Kaivalya is a transcendent state. Beyond humanity; beyond the limits and boundaries that once gave form to ego; even beyond the realms of time according to Kriyananda who goads us to, "Stop being human."

> *idaṃ jñānam upāśritya mama sādharmyam āgatāḥ*
> *sargepi nopajāyante pralaye na vyathanti ca*

The Monk Who Howled Like a Wolf

Approaching this higher knowledge and becoming as I,
Overcoming birth,
and no longer fighting the end of ego awareness.

—*The Bhagavad Gita;* Chapter 14, Verse 2

CHAPTER FIFTY-EIGHT

Techniques for Enlightenment

I think about Kriyananda's statement that the average spiritual seeker has 800,000 lifetimes under her belt. Laboring through 800,000 false starts doesn't sit well with me. Fortunately, the Teachings tell us how we can shorten the route to *kaivalya*.

Since we are unique beings, our paths are unique. No one else can do our work. As my Teacher points out, a *guru* cannot grant us enlightenment. We must enlighten ourselves, but we can get help from those who have gone before.

"Self-study," the fourth *Niyama* (observance) of the Eight Limbs, can be thought of as not only a study of the Teachings done by the self, but also a study *of* the self. It is only through knowledge of the self (the gateway to the big "S" *Self*) that we gain the "pure understanding" that is a means towards enlightenment.

The Denver Teacher says, "Live as if you are enlightened. Because you are a magnet, eventually you become enlightened."

Even if our attempts to look and act enlightened are a complete charade compared to how we feel on the inside, taking on a positive and enlightened role in this "play" will start to steer our consciousness in the desired direction. Change happens in our lives through thought, word, and deed. If we can't think like an enlightened being, reflecting illumination in our words and deeds will still move us slowly in that direction. There is no point in dwelling on what might be a certain amount of insincerity in our actions. Consider that it is more pleasant to be around someone "acting" good than someone *being* bad.

According to my Teacher, our astrology contains clues to our path to enlightenment. Examine the Seventh House of your natal chart for "the form that your enlightenment will manifest itself in." The Seventh House in Western Astrology is at the Descendent—the one section of the twelve sections of the zodiac wheel descending below the western horizon at the exact time of birth. This setting sun House is symbolic of interactions with others and of partnerships. Enlightenment is the ultimate partnership—union with the divine.

In Appendix L I examine my own natal chart for clues to the form of my enlightenment. If you would like to repeat this exercise for yourself, you may go online and find many sources of Astrological natal (birth) charts. Some are free. Be prepared with the date, exact time, and place of your birth. Even better, take this information to a qualified astrologer like the Denver Teacher for a natal reading, and ask what they see in the Seventh House that might give clues to the form of your spiritual growth.

There are many ways to foster spiritual evolution. The greater the focus, the better the results. If we spend our time and effort on our job or on making our yard look good, that is what we will be good at. We'll have a great career. We'll have a great looking yard. The same focus can be brought to the spiritual life. The ascetics of India abandon almost all possessions and spend their time in *mantra* and devotions. Their focus is on their spiritual growth and they get results.

> " Enlightenment is getting rid of everything
> to reveal the perfect being within.
> It's about getting rid of stuff.
> Greed.
> Fear.
> Violence."
>
> —A Teacher

Techniques for Enlightenment

If we want enlightenment we have to make room for it in our lives. Instead, we tend to fill our existence with many distractions from spiritual reality. Geshe Michael Roach did an excellent job of stressing the importance of traveling light in his magnificent book, *"The Diamond Cutter."*

> "...on some level, you are keeping a mental inventory of all the things you own. Which also means that some part of your mind space is taken up with these details; remember that the mind is like the hard drive of a computer—it only has so much space. You know how computers start acting when their hard drives get near to full: programs stop working, everything gets slower, systems crash..."

Prolonged, persistent, and dogged repetition of a practice is key to establishing a pattern and an effective avenue for spiritual progression and revealed truth. My Teacher says, "it doesn't have to be Kriya Yoga." While we may have noticeable results in just a few days, it may also take months before we notice changes in our consciousness or unusual or mystical episodes. Persist and persevere. Every new practice takes many repetitions before it becomes part of the routine. Changing practices after a few weeks when we hear of another fad takes us back to the start of our journey and prevents establishing a habitual pattern.

It doesn't matter so much what the practice is as long as we are doing *something*. The practice could be walking our dog or crocheting. What counts is that we give ourselves daily predictable time to reflect and achieve a level of inner quiet. It is during this inner quiet that muted communications from the higher Self can be perceived by the normally inattentive ego self.

When we adopt a formal practice, it is important to acknowledge the teachings of that discipline or order. If we are sincere Christians, we must operate through the basis of the central teachings such as the Ten Commandments. A Hare Krishna probably won't eat meat or will have a very good reason for doing so. We all make mistakes, but it is important in adopting an approach to be internally consistent within that approach. To say one thing and do another is considered spiritually lethal to the mystic. Thought, word, and deed need to be in alliance in order for our practice to be the most effective.

The ancient spiritual principles and practices described in this book may be a foundation for anyone seeking to be a better person. The Eight Limbs, like the Ten Commandments, may be applied by anyone, in any culture, in any religion. We don't have to be a Hindu to be a Kriyaban. But we may be a Kriyaban and also be a Hindu or a Christian or a Muslim or a traditional Lakota.

> "You have to get all your *chakras* balanced.
> In other words: Balance your life.
> In doing so you will allow yourself to transcend."
>
> —A Teacher

Focus, simplification, and practice are important steps that bring us to the next technique for enlightenment—balancing life. The *chakras* (energetic centers within the human body associated with the nervous system) are thought to govern various concerns of human experience. These can be grouped loosely into survival, relationships, resolve, love, creativity, intuition, and spirituality. To balance life from a *chakra* perspective means that we can't be fixated on sex and expect self-discipline to flourish; or for love to triumph when we are fighting for our survival. If each of these seven areas are rooms in the house of our being, all of these sacred rooms must get loving attention before our house is ready to accept the "guest" of Rumi's mystical writings.

> "I think people need to be more selfish.
> I see people not selfish enough to walk the path.
> I see people neglect the spiritual path because they are married,
> or have kids,
> or have a job."
>
> —A Teacher

The seeker has a mandate to make enlightenment the top

priority. It is hypocrisy to say enlightenment is our focus while filling up our lives with other pressing and time-consuming earthly commitments. Much of my adult life has been spent pouring energy into career, furiously engaged daily in ephemeral blue and white collar battles, going home emotionally and physically drained, unable to sit peacefully in meditation for twenty minutes because the rest of my life replays in my scattered mind. When I lived in Denver, I spent a couple of focused hours on my spiritual welfare at Michel's *Satsang* every Sunday. If you had talked to me on a Sunday afternoon it might have sounded like illumination was a priority in my life, but if you took a look at the way that I lived during the week you would have smiled politely and said nothing, as my Teacher did.

What my Teacher did say was, "To the mystics, it doesn't really matter what we are looking for in this life, but we really need to narrow it down. People seem to think that the more that they do, the more it will improve their lives. But in the spiritual life, it is really about the opposite."

Real progress is being made towards illumination when we simultaneously experience the three levels of contemplation as defined by *"The Yoga Sutras"*—concentration (*dharana*), meditation (*dhyana*), and meditative absorption (*samadhi*)

pūrveṣām-api-guruḥ kālena-anavacchedāt
tasya vācakaḥ praṇavaḥ
taj-japaḥ tad-artha-bhāvanam
tataḥ pratyak-cetana-adhigamo-'py-antarāya-abhavaś-ca

Ishvara was the *guru* of the ancient ones
because he/she is not bounded by time.
His/her name is symbolized by the mystical syllable, '*aum.*'
It should be recited and contemplated.
Through this repetition of '*aum*' the inner Self is realized
and the worldly obstacles to *yoga* [the *kleshas*] are destroyed.

—*The Yoga Sutras*; Book 1, verses 26-29

Chant and *pranayama* are frequently overlooked in the West

as elements of a successful practice geared towards enlightenment. The Teacher points out that chant and sung *mantra* are an indirect means to practice the specialized breath techniques of *pranayama*. There are also few pleasures sweeter than to intone serenely in harmony with a CD of *kirtan* music (call and repeat, singing and chant) by one of the modern masters. If you get the chance, go to a live *kirtan* and enjoy the special feeling of an auditorium filled with spiritually-minded people united in song.

A *pranayama* as taught by my Teacher is "The Large Breath Pranayama," designed for *kundalini* awakening. As always when approaching active *kundalini* awakening, I strongly suggest that you have a trustworthy guide to "verify the scenery."

- ॐ Extend the fingers of your right hand flat (if you are right handed), but touching each other, with the thumb extended to the side (like the profile of a mitten).
- ॐ With mouth gently closed, after an inhalation through your nostrils and with your raised hand in this same position, use your right thumb to plug the side of your right nostril, and then exhale with an "M" sound through your left nostril.
- ॐ Repeat the process 3, 5, 7, or 9 times.

Ritual can be of use in our efforts towards enlightenment, whether it is sweat lodges or Catholic Mass. The Denver Teacher once suggested the *Adhikara Darzana* technique ("Teaching from a *Guru*") as a specific practice for encouraging enlightenment. First, adopt a meditative pose. Then:

- ➢ Quiet the mind.
- ➢ Still the body.
- ➢ Take a couple deep breaths.
- ➢ Visualize yourself entirely within a cocoon of white light 18 to 36 inches away from your body.
- ➢ Hold this visualization for 30 seconds.
- ➢ Change the white light of the cocoon to a vibrant gold and

hold this image for another thirty seconds.
- Change this gold light to a peacock blue and hold for thirty seconds.
- Take the "Death Breath"—inhale into your belly through your nostrils, then turn your head to the left and exhale fully in two quick puffs through your mouth and down towards the left shoulder.
- Return to face center and slowly inhale like sipping through a straw. Feel the cool breath descend your spinal column.
- As you inhale, visualize the peacock blue coloring each of your seven *chakras* in turn, starting at the root chakra and working up the spine.
- Hold this visualization for thirty seconds.

The *Adhikara Darzana* ritual reminds me that when all else fails, ask for help. In my quest for enlightenment, I may call upon the *Adhikara* that have walked this Path before me—the *Kriya Yoga* lineage. If you are like me, you are slow to ask for support when often there are people all around that would be happy to help out. Being stubborn about changing a tire by ourselves is one thing, but we are talking about our souls here! Why not ask for a little help from our friends, even if they are floating about in the astral? In prayer, meditation, through offerings, or in ritual—these are all ways to ask for the help of past masters. Being thoughtful in how we phrase our request and having a clear idea of whom we are asking for help are good approaches. We likely will be heard, but the spiritual aid we get may not always seem helpful or timely from our limited perspectives. Awakening *kaivalya* is not necessarily comfortable or punctual.

We may also take steps to lift our spiritual awareness or vibratory level. Imagine each of us as having a signature tone or note that radiates ceaselessly through the body and being. Imagine now that the clearer or higher the tone, the higher our awareness penetrates into the spiritual worlds. A low vibration means that we are more solidly anchored to the realities of the physical. The higher our vibration, the more we begin to lift from this world with its limitations, compelling attractions, aversions, and ego identifications.

This book is a map for increasing spiritual awareness through lifting vibratory level. Though optimum functioning of *all* the *chakras* is important for a balanced *chakra* system, my Teacher suggests that when we focus our consciousness in the higher *chakras*, we increase our harmony with enlightened states, and speed up the process of *kaivalya*.

The various techniques described above are valuable tools, but a *jivanmukta* or enlightened master should have the last word on this subject. Through *Mejda*, Yogananda points the way to "...the *sadhana* that leads to God—renunciation, *brahmacharya*, *pranayama*, meditation, and God-realization through *samadhi*."

CHAPTER FIFTY-NINE

We Are Here For One Reason

"The desire to evolve is the last nightmare."

—A Teacher

There are pleasurable distractions and painful detours in this dense, physical world that block the route to *kaivalya*. One of these barriers to Self-realization is the attachment to enlightenment itself. Long after a yogi has controlled her vulnerability to virtually all the earthly sense objects of attraction and aversion (*ragah* and *dvesha*), she may still find herself yearning for illumination. However, the Teacher points out "Even the aspiration for enlightenment must be let go of at some point."

Another barrier is thinking too much. Enlightenment cannot be reasoned into being or figured out. Mind has little to do with the spiritual. The mind needs to take a back seat in this journey.

The New Age movement has gone down a dead end in at least one respect—its enthusiasm for passion. Passion is not helpful in *kaivalya*. Passion is unbridled attraction and aversion run amuck. I am reminded of a popular song that croons about how you can't experience highs without experiencing lows. And

The Monk Who Howled Like a Wolf

what's the point there? The point to me is that extreme swings of emotion, good or bad, are not to be encouraged or sought after. Passion is a destabilizer and blinds one to the reality of the present moment. Passion is an amplification of attraction or aversion. Passion is the ego's lack of discipline. The *Gita* says in Chapter 2, verses 54 through 56 that a sage established in *samadhi* has no passion, desire, fear, or anger. This is a good thing.

"Without books you might get to enlightenment faster."

Information and sensual experience provide us with further distractions from illumination. All the books and all the experiences filling our lives may be distractions from the path; helpful up to a point in introducing us to new concepts, but in the end we must offer these earthly pages to the fire of consciousness.

> "To the mystic, the reason we came here is to be enlightened, but we get caught up in all these experiences and forget."
>
> —A Teacher

We get sidetracked. There is so much to do and so much to see here: Pretty sunsets and uplifting music, pretty men and pretty women, puppies, sweet candy, agonizing stomach flus, horrendous terminal illness, and bad break-ups. We fill our lives with all this *stuff*. I apply more focus to doing the dishes than I do to lifting my soul. It's no wonder we take lifetimes to make progress. It's a wonder our thoughts ever turn to *Ishvara*.

One of the more unsettling phrases that I have heard from my Kriya Yoga teachers is, "Let the world drown."

What does that mean? This harsh statement is acknowledgement that we can't save the world. When I catch myself trying to save the world it is usually because I believe I know how to solve someone else's problem and I imagine myself the hero with lots of attention for how smart and kind I am. What about other people's *karmic* evolution? Perhaps they have a reason for being where they are. I do not know another soul's path to progress. Perhaps the people I have "helped"

We Are Here For One Reason

preferred to be where they were, with their own Thornapple trees.

Helping is tricky business and is sometimes used to avoid our own work—the search for enlightenment. We can't enlighten any one beside ourselves. This is our first job. The world is the way that it is for a reason. The ways of the world are not pretty, but they serve a purpose for the souls that call it home.

> "Most of us tend to prefer practices without discomfort.
> No one attains enlightenment without discomfort."
>
> —A Teacher

Discomfort is used to avoid our own enlightenment. Ever watch someone squirm on the meditation mat or when first lying down to sleep? As soon as we are asked to focus on a task a clamoring cacophony of competing aches and pains and itches and tickles begin to bellow for our attention. When we try to quiet the mind in meditation every possible postponed chore and coming appointment struggles for our attention when we would instead have the mind be silent. Discomfort comes with the physical territory. Enlightenment comes when we develop strategies to live with our discomfort while keeping our eyes on the prize.

> "Boredom keeps us from *samadhi*.
> Maybe boredom is the opposite of *entheos*—enthusiasm.
> Some people are walking around, but they are dead.
> We need to come alive."
>
> —Kriyananda

A lack of energy is another barrier along the path to our enlightenment. The Denver Teacher encourages us to "pour forth your energy, your *kriya*, to awaken in this life." My Teacher and Kriyananda stress the need for us to thrive on an individual level to provide that energy for the task of enlightenment. Debilitating fasts and harsh austerities may discipline the mind to concentration, but in the end require so much focus on our bodies that we have no attention left for expanding our minds. We need to feed, water, and exercise this steed that carries us on our journey.

A common pitfall is compartmentalizing spiritual identity. We often live like the Sunday morning churchgoer who leaves the sermon behind at the church door. The search for enlightenment is a 24/7 endeavor.

There is a trap in deciding we know what enlightenment looks like. As the Teacher says, "Let go of your idea of God or spirituality or enlightenment. Get rid of the thought of what holiness is." My Teacher has said more than once that he prefers the company of "fools" to that of sophisticated people because the fools are often closer to the truth.

> "You are trying to move away from this earth plane.
> We spend all our time digging in.
> Death—it is just part of the transition.
> We are not here to gather more experience.
>
> —A Teacher"

Finally, this is the most compelling distraction from the Path—making a home here. If we really believe that the earth plane is an illusion to entertain our souls in our infancy, why do we go to such great lengths to grow comfortable here? There is an ancient saying in the Muslim world, "Life is a bridge. Don't build a dwelling here." Don't make decisions as if this physical reality is the important one.

Remember the Teacher's words, "You are here for one reason—*enlightenment*!"

CONCLUSION

Putting the Practice Into Practice

"The Teachings are to get past the Teachings.
Throw them away if they're not helping."

—A Teacher

What do we do with these Teachings?
First, we may decide what of *karma*, *Shat sanpattis*, *kaivalya*, relationships, and non-attachment resonates with us. The rest of this material we can set aside for another day perhaps, but what now makes sense in our gut or excites our sparkling jewel of awareness when we are tranquil and thinking clearly? What brought epiphany or reminded us of something we once held sacred before the world told us what was real? What makes us feel like we have found ourselves back home after a long journey in an unfamiliar land?

Remember how the Denver Teacher tells us that concepts manifest into the earthly plane? Thought, word, and deed. If we intend for anything to become a part of our life first we must think it; then we must speak it; then we must do it.

We must put our practice into practice. If meditation seems like a good place to start, then follow the advice of Shelliji and

The Monk Who Howled Like a Wolf

"Meditate, meditate, meditate." If you don't know where to start, consider the counsel of Swami Nityananda Giri, "It is always better to practice one technique than knowing many."

If your body won't let you sit still long enough to get peaceful on your cushion, then perhaps physical *asana*, through *Ashtanga* yoga, is your path for now. Find a teacher. Join a class. Get a book.

Look through the appendices in the next pages and see if any of the information feels like it would be handy and **rip** it out of the book. Go ahead—that's why it's there. Print it out. Copy it. Put the Eight Limbs up on your wall if you would like a daily reminder. Then think about it, talk about it, and DO IT!

Put your practice into practice. "Swallow the Teachings." Make them a part of you.

> "It's a completely different language—mysticism.
> A mystic doesn't need the priest
> and he's not afraid of God
> because God is within.
> If you gained anything from the Denver Kriya Yoga Center
> it is because of Kriyananda.
> And he would say you gained because of Shelley,
> and *he* would say you gained because of the lineage.
> And the lineage would say
> your gain was because of the Teachings."
>
> —A Teacher

One last story...

The Master's hair was white and thin now; his face weathered like the braided river bars of the mountain valleys; his once blue eye a faded gray. He sat for hours on the soft meditation mat in the bright room; narrow window shutters flung open to the harsh light of the high mountain slopes.

Nearly covering a small wooden table near the master was a large leather bound book, open to delicate ivory pages of the finest vellum, worn and soft from many turnings. An open pot of black India ink, a fine pen, and a dried brush perched carefully

Putting the Practice Into Practice

on a small bamboo mat on the table next to the book. The manuscript was open to the final pages, revealing freshly inked words—reedy, but carefully drawn. At the bottom of the text was a space and then a final character centered at the lower edge of that page—the swirls and careful brush strokes of the mother sound, aum.

Rasping with a voice hoarse from disuse the Master said, "You may come in."

The plank door to the hall cracked open slightly and a brown eye appeared, low.

"Come," his voice growing stronger.

There was a shuffling sound of sandals being kicked off before a barefoot boy slipped past the gap between door and frame, eyes darting quickly about the room. The Master noted how the boy's eyes fell on the open bottle of ink, the brush drying with its final strokes, how the smooth brown skin of the boy's face revealed a moment of stunned awareness.

The boy stepped carefully around the Master's mat and dropped to his knees in front of the old man, head bent low, showing only a thick forest of closely cropped jet-black hair.

The Master sighed. "You empty the pot by my pallet. I should bow to you."

The boy waited.

"Please relax, young one. I am too old for this foolishness. What is it you would like to say to me?"

The boy lifted his head then, his eyes announcing a question before he spoke, searching carefully for the words.

"Master, the monks say that there are rituals and practices that you must know—being ever wise. She *could* help you. They would keep you..."

There, the boy's words failed him.

"Not old?"

"Yes," the boy whispered gratefully.

The Master leaned towards the boy ever so slightly, as if to share a secret.

"You have been kind and true to me, son." The Master stopped for a moment, closing his eyes and steadied himself with one thin arm against the floor.

"These tricks that the monks speak of take time and would scatter my attention. Yes, she could help me with them. She will make a better master than I, you will see. But we must all find the one thing that makes us happy, yes? I have been focused on something else."

The boy's eyes darted to the table and then back to his master.

"And now you are done?"

"Yes. And this meditation mat is so comfortable I could sit right here until every bit of me has dissolved away like the dew with the coming of the day, but outside the sun will soon slide behind the ridge and I can hear the sounds of preparation for the puja in the courtyard below. I have one last thing to do."

The boy's eyes widened with understanding.

As the Master began to slowly unfold from his lotus, the boy rushed forward to help. Together they lifted his weak and trembling legs and re-positioned them so that he could rise, stiffly, in the cooling room. With the boy holding his arm, the Master shuffled carefully towards the table. With each step his balance grew better as blood and strength of purpose began to flow back into his limbs.

"This is my time for telling secrets: You know she is not really my daughter?"

"No, of course... I mean..."

"The Master ignored the boy's guilty stuttering.

"There are plenty of people in the countryside that believe it still, but I had no children. Monastic orders do not take in women easily so I let the jealous monks believe that she was my daughter and that I needed her to take care of me in my dotage. It was a scandal for the Order, yet she is the one that will save the Order. Slowly she has gained the trust of the rest of the monks, disciples, and novices like you. You will follow her. She is the one now that will howl like a wolf and walk the mystic's path."

He looked down at the boy.

"Then someday perhaps... you."

At the table he bent to gather the heavy book into his arms.

"This book," he told the attentive boy, "Contains everything

Putting the Practice Into Practice

that I know of the mystic path that you will someday walk. No, I don't mean the rules and memorizations that the monks teach you. This book is about freeing the soul from walls of stone and rules. It's about liberating the mind and finding your way in a living universe filled with possibilities.

"It took me seven years to write this book. I became old writing this book, young son, but I will be young again—like you—soon enough.

"I have finished just in time for the ceremony. Let's not be late!"

Outside an assembly was gathered on swept cobblestones, seated on mats around the sacred fire. A middle-aged woman (her reddish-brown hair beginning to streak with gray) waited at the front. The Master took his seat of honor before this woman and the rest of his people, grateful for the warmth of the fire. The ritual began with its chanting and drumming—prayers, and incense. Aromatic propitiatory herbs were sprinkled into the flames.

Then it was time for him to pass on the role of Master to his protégé. She rose. The old Master locked eyes with her for a moment and could see from the tears on her cheeks that she knew he was leaving now that his work was done. A shadow crossed the master's lined face—her display of grief—had she not learned the lessons of the immortal mystic after all?

Two young boys—second born and sent to the Order for good luck—rushed to the Master. Stubbornly, he clung to his book, making it harder for them to pull him to his feet. He hobbled into the flickering firelight with his prize clasped to his chest, joining his special student.

He could feel a strange buzzing at the back of his head. The time was here! When he spoke to the assembly, it was with wonder and gratitude.

"I am deep in my winter now, looking for my rest. But, 'Doing nothing, spring comes.' It is your spring now. You, who have learned the lessons and know the ways of the mystic: It is your turn to give counsel to the young and protection to the old. It is your turn to help the seekers walk their path to the divine."

The buzzing grew louder. The Master could tell that his

special student could hear the strange vibration, but it seemed no one else around the sacred fire was aware of this heavenly call. Tears streamed down her face, but the Master could tell now that these were tears of joy. She knew the release that lay ahead for him! She had swallowed the Teachings—they were a part of her and the mystic path was in her blood.

The Master continued on with the most important part of the ceremony, hurrying now for fear that there might not be enough time.

"You *are* Master now! I give you this book, the work of all my years on the path and the sum of all the years of those that have walked before me. This manuscript contains all that I know of spirit and of the quest for kaivalya."

The old Master, his vision clouding with a haze of white, the buzzing loud in his ears, thrust the book towards his child—his spiritual child—the middle-aged woman before him.

She took the book gratefully, tenderly, caressing the cover and inhaling deeply of its scents of ink, incense, and the sweet smell of the old Master she loved.

"Thank you, Master. You honor me."

Then she turned and threw the book into the hungry fire.

If it had not been for the two boys clinging to his side, the Master would have pitched himself into the roaring blaze after his manuscript. Stunned, he pulled his pale face from the red glare, questioning horror in his eyes as he looked at the woman.

She answered gently, "Have you not listened to all that you have taught me?"

In a flash he remembered the Teachings. And he realized what a precious gift and what an exquisite lesson he had just been given.

With a sudden roar the vibration reached a crescendo and the white haze turned to a swirl of rainbow colors in the air about him. Even as his knees gave out and the two boys lowered him gently to the ground he realized that the new Master had unburdened him in the blink of an eye. He was now in full possession of his spirit.

"Thank you," he whispered.

Putting the Practice Into Practice

APPENDIX A

The Traditional Schools of Yoga

Bhakti Yoga—Bhakti is the path of selfless devotion to God. The Hare Krishnas practice Bhakti Yoga with the Hindu deity Krishna as their focus of devotion.

Hatha Yoga—With a western stress on *asana* (yogic postures), Hatha also employs body cleansings and different techniques for the control of spiritual energy with the goal of *samadhi*.

Jhana Yoga—The yoga of knowledge uses a combination of intellectual pursuit of metaphysics and philosophy coupled with meditation on the breath and the profound question, "Who am I?"

Karma Yoga—This is the yoga of service to others dedicated to a sacred concept or power higher than that of the individual. These acts of service naturally dissolve the bondage of *karma* and bring the practitioner to *samadhi* and union with the Divine.

Kriya Yoga— Along with Hatha and Raja yogas, Kriya Yoga shares the goal of *samadhi* attained through individual efforts. Kriya does this through control of the body and mind with disciplined practice of *asana*, careful diet, breath work, activation of *kundalini* energies, and advanced Kriya techniques.

Raja Yoga—Raja (Royal) Yoga has a stress on meditative practices to achieve *samadhi* and does so through adherence to the *"Eight Limbs of Ashtanga."*

APPENDIX B

The Limbs of the Eight-Fold Path of Yoga

1. **Yamas**—Respect for Others
    Ahimsa—Abstaining From Violence
    Satya—Abstaining From Deceit
    Asteya—Abstaining From Theft
    Brahmacharya—Abstaining From Sensual Indulgence
    Aparigraha—Abstaining From Greed
2. **Niyamas**—Respect for Yourself
    Shaucha—Observance of Purity
    Santosha—Observance of Contentment
    Tapas—Observance of Austere Self-Discipline
    Svadhyaya—Observance of Self-Study
    Ishvara-Pranidhana—Observance of Attunement to the Divine
3. **Asana**—Harmony of the Body
4. **Pranayama**—Harmony of Energy
5. **Pratyahara**—Harmony of the Emotions
6. **Dharana**—Harmony of Thought
7. **Dhyana**—Meditation
8. **Samadhi**—Blissful Consciousness

APPENDIX C

The Four Pillars for the Spiritual Aspirant —The *Sadhana Chatushtaya*

1. *Viveka*—Discerning the enduring and real (from what is temporary and illusory).
2. *Vairagya*—Non-attachment to the physical/sensual world, its temporary objects, and the imagined fruits of our actions here.
3. *Shat Sanpatis*—A grouping of six mental aptitudes that allow the self-control and discipline for self-knowledge, concentration, and meditation.
    Shraddha—Faith in your yogic journey.
    Titiksha—Non-attachment to the good or the bad.
    Shama—Control of your mind to remain peaceful even in adversity.
    Dama—Control of the effects of the senses on your awareness.
    Uparati—Peaceful focus on actions of necessity or to further spiritual growth.
    Samadhana—Consistent perfect meditation.
4. *Mumukshutva*—The intense desire for freedom from the bondage of *karma* and to attain enlightenment.

APPENDIX D

Encouraging Mental Discipline (*Shama*) to Maintain Peacefulness

1. Resist desires and attachments (*vasanas*)
2. Cultivate and encourage activities and surroundings in your life that enhance your *Shama*.
3. Abstain from that which upsets your *Shama*
4. Utilize the conscious physical practices of *Dama* (body and sense control) to remain usefully occupied, such as meditation, prayer, chant, *mantra*, exercise, singing, *asana* (yoga poses), and *pranayama* (breath work)
5. Maintain an inner control rather than allow control by the temporary sensual objects of the physical world and your external senses (*indriyas*)
6. Do not give in to karmic impulses that threaten to pull you back into the past at the expense of the present moment
7. Concentrate your mind on the divine source of your own serenity
8. Dedicate your activities to your divine source, transforming actions into prayer
9. Return to *Shama* each time you are diverted

APPENDIX E

Encouraging Body & Sense Control (*Dama*)

1. Be aware in the moment of the effect your senses are having in drawing you away from helpful and rewarding actions
2. Indulge your senses only to meet needs rather than to satisfy desires
3. Satisfy the senses through uplifting stimuli such as great art, beautiful sunrises, lovingly prepared meals, the fragrance of flowers, or self-less love-making as an expression of deep appreciation for your partner
4. Keep the senses actively engaged in non-harmful pursuits while you continue your spiritual work (through yoga poses, incense, *mantra*, focus on the breath while you meditate, or uplifting movies)
5. Consciously direct your senses to serve higher purposes such as meditation without distraction
6. Give priority to sensual activities that contribute to your ability to bring merit into the world and that keep you on the path of your own *dharma* (calling)

APPENDIX F

Maintaining *Samadhi* (*Samadhana*)

In Chapter 2, verse 54 of the *Bhagavad Gita*, Arjuna asks Krishna how to recognize someone established in perfect meditation. Krishna answers in verses 55-59 with these attributes:

1. Undisturbed by discomfort
2. Free from extreme emotions such as passion, fear, and hate
3. Thoughtful
4. Without sentimentality
5. Does not gloat
6. Does not mourn
7. Free from desire
8. Unattached to worldly objects and pleasures

APPENDIX G

Practices of the Kriya Yogi

1. Preparing the body for concentration (*dharana*) through physical discipline such as *asana*
2. Preparing mind and attitude for spiritual growth such as through the *Yamas* and *Niyamas* of the Eight Limbs or through fasting
3. A daily practice that may include reflections on the day, meditation, *mantras*, *mudras*, and *pranayama*
4. Study of traditional texts such as *The Yoga Sutras of Patanjali, Bhagavad Gita,* the *Upanishads*, and the *Brahma Sūtras*
5. Maintenance of a diet and lifestyle that recognizes the *karma* in bringing harm to sentient beings
6. Performance of service (*Karma* Yoga)
7. Making *kriyas* or acts to balance past misdeeds
8. The practice of advanced Kriya Yoga techniques
9. Working with personal *karma*

APPENDIX H

The Inner & Outer Practices for Attracting Healthy Relationships

The Inner Practices:

- ॐ Self-Acceptance
- ॐ Self-Examination
- ॐ Control of Emotions
- ॐ Resisting Fear
- ॐ Finding the Others in the Room
- ॐ Self-Containing
- ॐ Forbearing
- ॐ Softening the Ego
- ॐ Flexibility

The Outer Practices:

- ॐ Be What You Want to Have
- ॐ Attend to the Quality of Your Thoughts, Words, and Deeds
- ॐ Devote
- ॐ Give
- ॐ Don't Cling
- ॐ Listen
- ॐ See Others Clearly
- ॐ Forgive
- ॐ Do Not Disturb the Dreams of Others

APPENDIX I

Neutralizing Action Karma

Act...

1. Out of need for the maintenance of the body (BG 4.21)
2. With the ego purified, controlled, and free from sense gratification (BG 5.07)
3. In accordance with one's own nature and *dharma* (BG 18.47)
4. Without hate, envy, attachment, or duality (BG 3.31, 4.20, 5.03 & 07)
5. With contentment and focus (BG 4.20, 5.03 & 07)
6. In accordance to Yoga (BG 4.41)
7. With dedication and faithfulness to Krishna (BG 3.30 & 31)

APPENDIX J

The Twenty Tools of Manifestation

1. Know your *dharma*
2. Mold your reality with your attitude
3. Simplify the external
4. Simplify the internal
5. Focus
6. Patience
7. Self-control
8. Discipline
9. Try something new
10. Know what you want
11. Ask for help
12. Work so that others may get what you want
13. Emulate those that have the success that you want
14. Attune your thoughts to the creation and visualize the result
15. *Mantra*
16. Meditation
17. *Pranayama*
18. Union of the conscious with the subconscious
19. Control of the three qualities or *gunas* of primordial matter (*sattva, rajas,* and *tamas*)
20. Conscious dreaming on the astral plane

APPENDIX K

The Seventh House as the Form of Enlightenment

I'll use my own natal chart as an example. Mercury in Libra and Neptune in Scorpio are both in my natal Seventh House. My Mercury is in a medium to weak strength conjunction with Mars in Libra, just above the horizon at my birth in the Sixth House (a conjunction means that planets are within about 8 degrees of each other). My Mercury is in opposition to my Ascendant, which simply means that Mercury was setting in the western sky at my birth nearly exactly opposite the eastern horizon where the sun rises. Mercury weakly sextiles Uranus in my natal chart and Neptune more strongly sextiles Venus. A sextile is when any two planets are approximately 60 degrees apart in the sky and is considered a beneficial "aspect." The closer a sextile is to an exact 60-degree separation between planets, the stronger the beneficial effect.

Next I examined what these astrological positions suggest as potentially relating to my own form or path to enlightenment (Ignoring the underlying personality traits, of which the negative are legion!) starting with Libra in the Seventh House...

Libra in the Seventh House suggests the capacity to deal effectively with a variety of people while Scorpio in the same house suggests an inclination towards the spiritual and a focus on relationships.

Mercury in the Seventh House leads to the ability to analyze, understand how others think, turn enemies into friends, communicate, share information, get people interested in what I have to say. It may also be true that I like having an audience, but I am most comfortable with one-on-one communication.

Neptune in the Seventh House says that I may have an aptitude as a public presenter on occult or mystical subjects.

Mercury in Libra suggests a natural and respectful diplomat and advocate for social change that is good at merging ideas, perhaps in writing or as a speaker.

Neptune in Scorpio means that energy and enthusiasm may provide transformative inspiration.

My Mercury's weak conjunction with Mars means that I *might* teach or write, driven by curiosity and a thirst for knowledge, yet sense that the answers I am getting in my search conceal even deeper mysteries.

Mercury in opposition to the Ascendant means I have the potential to be a good communicator, blending a variety of viewpoints, comfortable in speech and in writing, and independent.

Mercury's weak sextile with Uranus might lead to a willingness to share knowledge as a teacher and openness to new ideas.

My Neptune's stronger sextile with Venus brings attributes such as the ability to communicate, help with other people's problems, work creatively for social harmony, and spiritual, religious, or mystical tendencies.

There are some cautions in my Seventh House features that may interfere with my enlightenment. Among them—my impulsiveness and desire for adventure may put my life in danger; a preference to be alone; a tendency to push understanding of the inner being to the extreme; business partnerships tend to go poorly; a troubled relationship life; a tendency to provoke arguments or even violence; an idealism that could upset the stability of my physical world; a tendency to see things as better than they really are; a failure to take the initiative; poor planning; a carelessness when putting things in writing; a tendency to get sidetracked; losing sight of what matters; too great a need to make people happy; making too many demands on my physical body; too aggressive and sharp tongued; and a resentment of anything that restricts my freedom.

These astrological aspects are a lot to pull together in a brief statement that sums up the form that my enlightenment might take, but here is what I have come up with after hours of research:

My born curiosity, interest in the spiritual, enthusiasm,

and energy—coupled with my ability to analyze, merge ideas, and work for social harmony—may inform my path to enlightenment through mystical subjects, advocacy for social change, and sharing information through writing or speaking (getting better with practice).

Qualities of mine that might push me off the path for a lifetime or two include impulsiveness, risk taking, aggression, turbulent relationships, rigid idealism, misplaced priorities, isolation, procrastination, ineffectiveness, poor planning, sloppy communication, and a need to please that may compromise my values and priorities.

If you would like to repeat this exercise for yourself, you can go on line and find many sources of Astrological natal/birth charts (some are free). Be prepared with the exact date, time, and place of your birth. Even better, take this information to a qualified astrologer, such as my Teacher, for a natal reading, and ask what they see in the Seventh House that might give clues to the form of your own spiritual growth.

Sanskrit Glossary

Adhikara (from above + duty) 1) Authority; 2) Teacher

Ahamkāra (I am + the doer) 1) Ego; 2) The mind-body complex. See also *"asmita"*

Ahimsa (not + violence) 1) Nonviolence; 2) The first of the five Abstentions or *Yamas* of The Eight Limbs of Ashtanga

Ajna chakra (command + wheel) The sixth subtle energy center or *chakra* at the third eye, behind the center of the brows. See also *"chakra."*

Amatrah (boundless + in this place) The no-letter, no-sound that follows in the silence after chanting *aum*

Anahata chakra (untouched + wheel) 1) Heart *chakra*; 2) The fourth subtle energy center or *chakra* located at the center of the chest, near or in the heart. See also *"chakra."*

Ananda (bliss) Bliss, independent of the dualities of attraction and aversion

Ananda samadhi (bliss + deep absorption) 1) Meditative absorption characterized by bliss originating from *sattva*; 2) The third of nine levels of *samadhi.*

Anandamaya kosha (bliss + spiritual form + sheath) 1) The subtle energetic bliss body; 2) The fifth and final of the "bodies" or sheaths encasing the essential core of *Atman*

Annamaya kosha (food + spiritual form + sheath) 1) The physical body; 2) The first of five increasingly subtle "bodies" or sheaths encasing the essential core of *Atman*

Antahkarana (interior + mind) The internal organ of mortal consciousness composed of *buddhi* (intelligence or discriminating intellect), *manas* (mind), *ahamkāra* or *asmita* (the ego), and *avacetana* (the subconscious). See also *chitta* and *prayojakam chittam*.

Antaranga (inner + place) Internal practices—the group of the last three of The Eight Limbs of Ashtanga—*dharana, dhyana,* and *samadhi*

Aparigraha (away from + grasping) 1) Non-covetousness; 2) The last of five Abstentions or *Yamas* of The Eight Limbs of Ashtanga

Asamprajnata samadhi (unconscious + deep absorption) 1) Non-mind *samadhi*; 2) The fifth of nine levels of *samadhi*

Asana (posture) 1) Sitting posture conducive to meditation; 2) Modern: Various yogic poses designed to focus the mind and body on meditation; 3) The third of *The Eight Limbs of Ashtanga*

Asmita (I am + established) 1) Ego; 2) The mind-body complex; 3) When used in "*asmita* samadhi" (the fourth of nine levels of *samadhi*), *asmita* refers to the *chitta's* awareness of *purusha*. See also "*Ahamkāra.*"

Asteya (non + theft) 1) Non-stealing; 2) The third of the five Abstentions or *Yamas* of *The Eight Limbs of Ashtanga*

Atman (higher perception) 1) The divine and immortal non-corporeal consciousness which animates all sentient beings, untouched by the *karma* of its incarnations or the *maya* of the physical, and beyond the capacity of mind or ego to describe; 2) Self; 3) Soul; 4) *Purusha*; 5) Supreme lord; 6) *Vasudeva*; 7) *Ishvara*; 8) Cosmic Self; 9) Indwelling Self; 10) *Brahman* in some philosophical schools

Aum (*aum*) 1) A *mantra* of three uttered syllables (ah, oo, mmm...) followed by a fourth silent measure representing the primordial void (the *amatrah*), thought to induce a resonation of ego self with the inner Self; 2) The mother sound, 3) The primordial sound; 4) The cosmic *mantra*

Avacetana (under + conscious) The subconscious

Sanskrit Glossary

Avatar (away + passing beyond) 1) A physical incarnation of a divine being; 2) An incarnation of Krishna

Bahiranga (outside + assembly place) 1) Of the exterior; 2) The *bahiranga sadhana* are the external practices—the first five of the Eight Limbs of Ashtanga

Brahmacharya (study of the *Vedas* + practice + behave) 1) The student stage of life; 2) The first of four traditional stages of life; 3) The fourth of the five Abstentions or *Yamas* of *The Eight Limbs of Ashtanga*; 4) Sense control; 5) Monogamy; 6) Sexual restraint; 7) Celibacy

Brahman (expand + perception) The Supreme Being or impersonal consciousness of this universe; believed to be the same as *atman* in some philosophical schools

Buddhi (understand + because of) 1) Intellectual capacity; 2) Intelligence

Chakra (wheel) Normally numbered as seven, these centers of spiritual energy are located along the spine and in or near the head and serve as communication hubs between the physical and spiritual worlds

Chitta (mind) The mind, which is further divided into four forms of consciousness: *Buddhi* (intelligence or discriminating intellect), *manas* (mind), *ahamkāra* or *asmita* (the ego), and the *avacetana* or subconscious. See also *antahkaraṇa* and *prayojakam chittam*.

Dama (self-restraint) 1) Control of the effects of the senses on awareness; 2) Fourth of the six *Shat Sanpatis* that form the third pillar of the *Sadhana Chatushtaya*

Dharana (having + joy) 1) Concentration; 2) Harmony with one's thoughts; 3) The sixth limb of *The Eight Limbs of Ashtanga*

Dharma (favored actions) 1) Life's work; 2) Calling; 3) Right conduct; 4) One's natural state of being; 5) Spiritual law; 6) The characteristics of one's nature

Dharma-megha samadhi (right conduct + cloud + deep absorption) "Cloud of virtue *samadhi*"—the ninth and final state of *samadhi* in which the living yogi has left behind all desire for the fruits of her/his actions, is already experiencing *kaivalya*, and is impervious to the five *kleshas* or obstacles to union (ignorance, ego, attachment, aversion, and clinging to life)

Dhyana (thinking + breath) 1) Meditation; 2) Uninterrupted concentration on the object of meditation

Dvesha (dislike) 1) Aversion; 2) Dislike

Garhasthya (family life) 1) Family life; 2) The second of four traditional stages of life

Gunas (ropes) 1) The three creative qualities of primordial matter (*prakriti*): *Sattva*/intellect, *rajas*/activity, and *tamas*/inertia); 2) All *prakriti* and thus everything in physical reality is a blend of one or more of the *gunas*, defining consciousness and material objects

Guru (teacher) A spiritual instructor

Hamsa (swan) 1) A foundational inhalation/exhalation breath practice of Kriya Yoga; 2) Self; 3) Soul; 4) Spiritual teacher; 5) Swan

Indriyas (the symbolic number five) The five external senses (hearing, touch, vision, taste, and smell)

Ishvara (lord + best) 1) The divine and immortal non-corporeal consciousness which animates all sentient beings, untouched by the *karma* of its incarnations or the *maya* of the physical, and beyond the capacity of mind or ego to describe; 2) Self; 3) Soul; 4) *Atman*; 5) Supreme lord; 6) *Vasudeva*; 7) *Purusha*; 8) Cosmic Self, 9) Indwelling Self

Ishvara Pranidhana (supreme lord + devotion + treasure) 1) Devotion to the elemental divinity; 2) Submission to God or

Sanskrit Glossary

Brahman; 3) Union with the Divine; 4) Attuning to "the indwelling reality;" 5) Fifth of the five Observances or *Niyamas* of *The Eight Limbs of Ashtanga*

Iwa (in the same manner of) 1) "As if;" 2) Acting as if it were so

Jivanmukta (acquire + freedom) A person liberated while still in a physical body

Kaivalya (absolute unity) 1) Union with *Atman* and release from *karma* and physical incarnations; 2) Enlightenment; 3) Self-realization; 4) Liberation; 5) Illumination; 6) Transcendence; 7) *Nirvana*, 8) *Turiya*, 9) *Moksha*

Karana sharira (causing + body) 1) The ageless and timeless body of the causal realms which contains the higher intellectual and spiritual identities, the soul memory track, and *samskaras*; 2) Including both the *vijnanamaya kosha* of intellect and the *anandamaya kosha* of bliss; 3) The third of three *shariras*

Karma (to do + time) 1) The consequences of an individual's past conscious and unconscious actions in relation to other sentient beings echoing into the present life of that individual; 2) The Law of Cause & Effect; 4) Work; 5) Action; 6) Activity

Kirtan (pouring out + progression) A concert or other singing venue of *mantras* or devotional music in a call and repeat format

Klesha (affliction) 1) Obstacle; 2) The *kleshas* are five obstacles to yoga practice as identified in *The Yoga Sutras of Patanjali*: Ignorance, ego, attachment, aversion, and clinging to life (YSII.03)

Kosha (casing) Five successively more ethereal energetic "bodies" or sheaths that conceal the inner core of *Atman* as described in the *Taitomnitiriya Upanishad*, starting with the physical body—the *annamaya kosha* (the sheath made from food)—and ending with the *anandamaya kosha* (the casing made of bliss) the sheath closest to the transcendent Self

Kriya (action) 1) Action; 2) Activity; 3) A deliberate action to counteract *karma*; 4) A yogic technique to encourage liberation

Kriya shakti (action + power) The power of action

Kundalini (spring + hidden) The coiled spiritual power or *prana* that lies dormant until awakened at the base of the spine in the *Muladhara chakra*

Mahavatar (great + away + passing beyond) 1) Great avatar; 2) A divine being that has voluntarily reincarnated on earth to work on behalf of the souls trapped here

Manas (mind) That part of the mind that interprets information from the senses

Manomaya kosha (mind + spiritual form + casing) 1) The astral body; 2) The subtle body or *sukshma sharira*; 3) The casing made of mind; 4) The non-physical part of our selves created and maintained through the power of individual ego consciousness; 5) The vehicle of consciousness in dreams and out-of-body experiences; 6) The third of five increasingly subtle "bodies" or sheaths encasing the essential core of *Atman*

Maya (illusion) 1) The illusions of the physical world that masquerade as real for those without discernment; 2) Phenomenal reality; 3) The misperception of physical beings that they are separate from each other and from *Brahman*

Moksha (liberation) 1) Union with *Atman* and release from *karma* and physical incarnations; 2) Enlightenment; 3) Self-realization; 4) Liberation; 5) Illumination; 6) Transcendence; 7) *Kaivalya*; 8) *Nirvana*; 9) *Turiya*

Mudra (seal) Specific fixed hand and finger poses to encourage the reception of *prana* (though *mudras* may involve any of the rest of the body as well)

Mumukshutva (wanting freedom) 1) An intense desire to gain enlightenment; 2) The last of The Four Pillars of the Spiritual Aspirant (the *Sadhana Chatushtaya*)

Sanskrit Glossary

Namaste (hello) A formal greeting often accompanied by the palms pressed flat together in front of the chest with the fingers pointing straight up

Nirahamikara (without + I am + the doer) No belief in the control of the ego

Nirbija samadhi (without + seeds + deep absorption) The "seedless" eighth of nine levels of *samadhi* in which consciousness is absorbed into the *purusha*, sensory input from the physical world is absent, and the mind is no longer self-aware

Nirdvandvo (without + duality) Not subject to the dualities of the extremes of emotion or sensation

Nirmama (without + mine) Without claims to possessions or ownership of anything

Nirvana (without + desire) 1) Release from *karma* and physical incarnations and union with *Atman*; 2) Enlightenment; 3) Self-realization; 4) Liberation; 5) Illumination; 6) Transcendence; 7) *Kaivalya*; 8) *Turiya*; 9) *Moksha*

Nirvicara samadhi (without + thought + deep absorption) The seventh level of nine levels of *samadhi* in which intuitions from the Self reveal insights into the physical and spiritual worlds and the adept may render triggering *samskaras* harmless by manipulating *karma*

Nirvitarka samadhi (without + imagination + deep absorption) The sixth of nine levels of *samadhi* in which is experienced the complete absorption of the mind in the object of meditation, free from the fluctuations and distractions of consciousness

Niyama (law) 1) Observance; 2) Referring to the group of five Observances or *Niyamas* of *The Eight Limbs of Ashtanga* composed of *shaucha, santosha, tapas, svadhyaya*, and *Ishvara pranidhana*

Prajna (wisdom) 1) Discrimination; 2) The ability to see things without the filters of conditioning; 3) Wisdom; 4) Knowledge; 6) Awareness; 7) With a shift in pronunciation: The deep sleep state (represented by the third sound, "m," in *aum*), the third of four quarters of the aggregate of consciousness—mortal (intellect, mind, ego, and subconscious) and immortal (Self or *Atman*)

Prakriti (in front + creation) 1) Primordial matter which is composed of the three creative qualities (*Sattva*/intellect, *rajas*/activity, and *tamas*/inertia); 2) All *prakriti* and thus everything in physical reality is a blend of one or more of the *gunas*, defining consciousness and material objects

Prana (spirit vitality) 1) Life force; 2) Spiritual energy; 3) A source of vitality permeating the universe essential for living beings to create and maintain physical bodies and to support spiritual evolution

Pranamaya kosha (spirit vitality + spiritual form + sheath) The second of the five "bodies" or sheaths encasing the essential core of *Atman*, which animates the physical body with *prana* or *chi*, and manifests physically through the breath.

Pranayama (spirit vitality + control) 1) Breath control to acquire, direct, and enhance *prana*, speeding spiritual evolution; 2) The fourth of The Eight Limbs of *Ashtanga*

Pratyahara (withdrawal) 1) Contentment independent of sensual experience; 2) Fifth of the Eight Limbs of *Ashtanga*

Prayojakam chittam (similar + join + mind) (interior + mind) The internal organ of mortal consciousness composed of *buddhi* (intelligence or discriminating intellect), *manas* (mind), *ahamkāra* or *asmita* (the ego), and *avacetana* (the subconscious). See also *antahkaraṇa* and *chitta*.

Puja (honor) 1) Prayer; 2) Worship ceremony; 3) A ritual designed to strengthen the connection with the divine

Purusha (Supreme being) 1) The divine and immortal non-

Sanskrit Glossary

corporeal consciousness which animates all sentient beings, untouched by the *karma* of its incarnations or the *maya* of the physical, and beyond the capacity of mind or ego to describe; 2) Self; 3) Soul; 4) *Atman*; 5) Supreme lord; 6) *Vasudeva*; 7) *Ishvara*; 8) Cosmic Self, 9) Indwelling Self

Ragah (attachment) 1) Attachment; 2) Desire created by the recollection of pleasurable sensual experience

Rajas (emotion) 1) The essence of activity and movement; 2) One of the three creative qualities (*gunas*) of primordial matter (*prakriti*) that define, through their relative proportions, material reality and consciousness in the physical world

Sadhana (sit down + giving up) A habitual or daily spiritual practice designed to increase awareness

Sadhana Chatushtaya (sit down + giving up + four + pillars) 1) The Four Pillars of the Spiritual Aspirant; 2) Preparations for those seeking enlightenment

Sadhu (virtuous) 1) One who maintains a *sadhana* in order to advance spiritually; 2) A mystic; 3) An ascetic

Samācara (constant + proper conduct) Non-attachment

Samadhana (constant + meditation) 1) Focused and consistent meditation; 2) Maintaining *samadhi*; 3) The active maintenance of *samadhi* through mastery of *shraddha, titiksha, shama, dama,* and *uparati,* characterized by non-attachment and thoughtfulness, and devoid of sentimentality, gloating, mourning, hatred, desire, and extreme emotions; 3) Sixth of the *Shat Sanpatis* that form the third pillar of the *Sadhana Chatushtaya*

Samadhi (deep absorption) 1) A mental state in which the meditator attains union with the object of meditation and loses self-awareness (YS3.03); 2) Consciousness focused on one point (YS3.11 & 12); 3) A spectrum of mental states characterized by expanding awareness; 4) Linking the ego self with the spiritual

Self (Kriyananda); 5) The eighth and final limb of *The Eight Limbs of Ashtanga*

Samprajnata (constant + wisdom) 1) Having Self-awareness; 2) The grouping of the first four levels of *samadhi* (*vitarka, vicara, ananda,* and *asmita* stages) in which the experiencer maintains conscious awareness, yet is intensely focused on a single object

Samskara (mental impression) Behavioral Self-programming carried in the memory track of the causal body, and created by repetition over many lifetimes that leads to distinct and persistent traits of personality, attractions, aversions, tendencies, attitudes, and talents causing an unconscious pull towards like environments, life events, relationships, health, careers, etc., as experienced in past lifetimes

Samyama (together + observe) In which *dharana, dhyana,* and *samadhi* are practiced simultaneously, resulting in wisdom and, according to *The Yoga Sutras of Patanjali,* the potential of *yoga siddhis*

Sangatyagah (attach + sacrifice) Renunciation of attachment

Sangha (assembly) 1) Assembly; 2) A spiritually-themed group that meets regularly

Sannyasin (abandon + seeking) 1) An ascetic; 2) One who has renounced worldly affairs and possessions; 3) One who has taken the vows of renunciation

Santosha (possess + contentment) 1) Contentment; 2) Second of the five Observances or *Niyamas* of *The Eight Limbs of Ashtanga*

Sattva (spiritual essence) 1) The essence of intellect, illumination, and knowledge; 2) One of the three creative qualities (*gunas*) of primordial matter (*prakriti*) that define, through their relative proportions, material reality and consciousness in the physical world

Satya (true + go to) 1) Truthfulness; 2) Abstaining from deceit;

Sanskrit Glossary

3) The second of the five Abstentions or *Yamas* of *The Eight Limbs of Ashtanga*

Shala (school) An initiate into a discipline, order, or school

Shama (centered between extremes) 1) Mind control to maintain serenity; 2) Third of the *Shat Sanpatis* that form the third pillar of the *Sadhana Chatushtaya*

Shanti (inner peace) 1) Contentment; 2) Peace; 3) A respectful greeting

Sharira (body) Physical or energetic vehicles of various levels of consciousness

Shat Sanpatis (six + routes) Six personal qualities helpful in the quest for enlightenment that form the third pillar of the *Sadhana Chatushtaya*

Shaucha (cleanliness) 1) Cleanliness; 2) Purity; 3) First of the five Observances or *Niyamas* of *The Eight Limbs of Ashtanga*

Shraddha (faith) 1) Faith in the yogic journey as expressed by faith in one's self, in scripture, and in the *guru*; 2) First of the *Shat Sanpatis* that form the third pillar of the *Sadhana Chatushtaya*

S*iddhi* (extraordinary accomplishment) Various supernatural powers that may be attained by a yogi practicing *dharana*, *dhyana*, and *samadhi* simultaneously, according to *The Yoga Sutras of Patanjali*

Siddhim (making oneself invisible) Complete attainment within the Supreme Spirit

Sthula sharira (material + body) 1) The physical body, containing the *annamaya kosha* of flesh and the *pranamaya kosha* of *prana*; 2) The first of three *shariras*

Sukshma sharira (intangible + body) 1) The astral body; 2) The vehicle of consciousness in dreams and out-of-body experiences;

3) The mental or mind layer created and maintained by ego consciousness; 4) The *manomaya kosha* of the Hindus; 3) The second of three *shariras*

Sunyata (zero + gone to) 1) Non-existence; 2) The primal void

Svadhisthana chakra (one's own + dwelling + wheel) 1) The second subtle energy center or *chakra* associated with the reproductive organs; 2) The birthplace of the ego self; 3) Sacrum *chakra*. See also "*chakra*."

Svadhyaya (one's own + meditation on) 1) Self study; 2) Study of spiritual texts; 3) The fourth of the five Observances or *Niyamas* of *The Eight Limbs of Ashtanga*

Taijasa (made of light) Second of four quarters of the aggregate of consciousness—mortal (intellect, mind, ego, and subconscious) and immortal (Self or *Atman*)—dominant in the dream state and represented by the "u" sound in *aum*

Tamas (darkness + dwell in) 1) The essence of inertia, ignorance, and sloth; 2) One of the three creative qualities (*gunas*) of primordial matter (*prakriti*) that define, through their relative proportions, material reality and consciousness in the physical world

Tapas (heat + present) 1) Austerity; 2) Sense control: 3) Inner heat or light generated by a *sadhana* 4) Third of the five Observances or *Niyamas* of *The Eight Limbs of Ashtanga*

Tarka (reflection) A mental review of the day's events

Titiksha (Endurance) 1) Non-attachment to the good or the bad; 2) Forbearance; 3) Second of the *Shat Sanpatis* that form the third pillar of the *Sadhana Chatushtaya*

Turiya (fourth) 1) Union with *Atman* and release from *karma* and physical incarnations; 2) Enlightenment; 3) Self-realization; 4) Liberation; 5) Illumination; 6) Transcendence; 7) *Nirvana*; 8) *Kaivalya*; 9) *Moksha;* 10) Fourth of four quarters of the aggregate of consciousness—the Self that is both beyond and

Sanskrit Glossary

within the first three quarters, symbolized by the *amatrah*, the no-letter, no-sound that follows in the silence after intoning *aum*

Upanishad (bring near + sit down) 1) "Sitting at the feet of"; 2) Secret canon; 3) 108 to over 200 (depending on the authority) short Hindu scriptures up to 2,700 years old, that convey the spiritual wisdom and philosophy behind the more ritually-focused *Vedas*

Uparati (cessation) 1) Peaceful focus on actions of necessity or to further spiritual growth; 2) Fifth of the *Shat Sanpatis* that form the third pillar of the *Sadhana Chatushtaya*

Vairagya (break + attachment) 1) Non-attachment; 2) Non-attachment to sense objects

Vaishvanara (digestive fire) 1) Waking consciousness represented by the "a" sound in *aum*; 2) First of the four quarters of the aggregate of consciousness including both mortal (intellect, mind, ego, and subconscious) and immortal (Self or *Atman*)

Vanaprastha (forest + living in) 1) The secluded stage of meditative life in the forest; 2) The third of four traditional stages of life; 3) An anchorite

Vasana (desire) 1) Desire; 2) Attachment; 3) *Samskaras* that will remain dormant in this life but reemerge in future lives

Vasudeva (supreme soul + divine) 1) The divine and immortal non-corporeal consciousness which animates all sentient beings, untouched by the *karma* of its incarnations or the *maya* of the physical, and beyond the capacity of mind or ego to describe; 2) Self; 3) Soul; 4) *Atman*; 5) Supreme lord; 6) *Purusha*; 7) *Ishvara*; 8) Cosmic Self, 9) Indwelling Self; 10) Relating to Krishna

Vedas (knowledge) Dating from at least 1,500 B.C., these four collections of *Sanskrit* texts (the *Rig*, *Sama*, *Yajur*, and *Atharva Vedas*) are the oldest literature of India, with a focus on hymns and rituals as opposed to the associated *Upanishads*, with their focus on spiritual wisdom and philosophy

Vicara samadhi (thought + deep absorption) The second of nine levels of *samadhi* in which the meditator is absorbed in thought, melding with the deeper "subtle" reality of the object of that meditation

Vijnanamaya kosha (knowing + spiritual form + sheath) 1) Spiritual essence equivalent to the causal body, containing the higher intellect and discrimination, and part of the *karana sharira*; 2) The fourth of the five "bodies" or sheaths encasing the essential core of *Atman*

Virya (energy) Vigor

Vitarka samadhi (deliberation + reflection+ deep absorption) The first of nine levels of *samadhi* in which the meditator is absorbed in physical awareness

Viveka (wisdom) 1) Wisdom; 2) Discrimination; 3) Awareness of the genuine and enduring; 4) The spiritual world perceived as more tangible than the physical world

Yama (restraint) 1) Suppression; 2) Self-control; 3) The *Yamas* or five Abstentions are the first of the Eight Limbs of Ashtanga (*ahimsa, satya, asteya, brahmacharya,* and *aparigraha*); 4) God of death

Yativrata (sage + conduct) 1) The renunciate life of direct mystical experience and knowledge; 2) The fourth of four traditional stages of life

Yoga (union) 1) A discipline, technique, or practice designed for spiritual growth; 2) Merging the ego with the Self (Self-realization) leading to union with the immortal consciousness which animates all sentient beings; 3) Physical poses or *asanas*

Index

Abstentions, 41, 395-397, 405, 408
Acceptance, 333-336
Adhikara, 369, 395
Adhikara Darzana, 368, 369
After Death Communications, 229
After the Ecstasy, the Laundry: *How the Heart Grows Wise on the Spiritual Path*, 57
Ahamkāra, 145, 395-397, 402
Ahimsa, 41, 383, 395, 408
Ajna chakra, 161, 199, 341, 395
Alaska, 50-52, 77, 98, 104, 130-134, 139, 151, 224, 225, 257, 309, 310, 315, 329, 340
Anahata chakra, 161, 395
Ananda, 187-189, 196, 348, 360, 404
Ananda samadhi, 348, 395
Annamaya kosha, 235, 395, 399, 405
Antahkaraṇa, 145, 395, 397, 402
Antaranga, 396
Antaranga sadhana, 41, 51
Aparigraha, 42, 383, 396, 408
Arjuna, 27, 60, 183, 283-285, 387
Asamprajnata samadhi, 348, 396
Asana, 26, 29, 30, 35, 36, 49, 58, 63, 158, 191, 207, 348, 376, 382, 383, 385, 388, 396, 408
Ascendant, 392, 393
Ashtanga, 41, 49, 52, 376, 382, 395, 396, 397, 399, 401, 402, 404, 405, 406, 408
Asmita, 145, 395-397, 402, 404
Asmita samadhi, 348, 396
Asteya, 42, 383, 396, 408

Astral, 62, 182-184, 203, 220, 229, 234, 236, 238, 241, 242, 244-247, 253, 255, 256, 258, 261, 271, 284, 326, 350, 352, 353, 355, 358, 369, 391, 400, 405
Astrid, 257, 258, 261, 262
Astrological, 14, 276, 279, 331, 364, 392, 393, 394
Astrology, 28, 279, 364
Atman, 62, 108, 143, 144, 182, 236, 242, 395-403, 406-408
Attachment, 11, 25, 26, 30, 42, 54, 56, 60, 64, 65, 76-79, 82-85, 90, 91, 92, 94-100, 114, 116, 132, 143, 144, 172, 193, 194, 247, 248, 250, 252, 253, 266, 281, 282, 296, 297, 301, 304, 305, 324, 334, 340, 343, 349, 358, 360, 371, 385, 390, 398, 399, 403, 404, 407
Attraction, 29, 78, 79, 83, 89, 95, 126, 133, 134, 152, 154, 159, 161, 170, 180, 191, 193, 194, 255, 279, 281, 284, 311, 327, 340, 341, 358, 370-372, 395, 404
Aum, 3, 17, 63, 146, 197, 202, 211, 212, 254, 367, 377, 395, 396, 402, 406, 407
Autobiography of a Yogi, 8, 9, 94
Avacetana, 145, 396, 397, 402
Avatar, 9, 10, 41, 67, 397, 400
Awake
 The Life of Yogananda, 9, 151, 349
Awareness, 3, 6, 16, 22, 29, 37, 38, 42, 49, 54, 60, 84, 94, 104, 111, 113, 119, 142, 146, 153, 160, 161, 166, 167, 169, 170, 171-177, 181-183, 185, 191,

194, 199-203, 208, 209, 212, 213, 218-220, 226, 231, 244, 246, 249, 251-253, 261, 267, 276, 284, 285, 289, 290, 299, 302, 322, 324-326, 341, 345, 347-350, 352, 360, 362, 369, 370, 375, 377, 384, 396, 397, 402, 403, 404, 408

Babaji, 9-12, 14, 16, 25, 41, 42, 62, 67, 320, 344
Bahiranga sadhana, 41, 397
Bardo, 85, 182, 246
Beatles, 16
Beginner mind, 208
Bhagavad Gita, 27, 28, 48, 55, 60, 64, 77, 83, 89-91, 97, 99, 117, 128, 129, 146, 158-161, 171, 183, 187, 188, 192, 199, 200, 202, 207, 229, 235, 237, 240, 245, 246, 250, 254, 255, 266, 274, 281, 283, 284, 289, 295, 305, 328, 340, 345, 353, 357, 358, 360, 362, 372, 387, 388
Bhakti Yoga, 26, 382
Bible, 17, 27
Big Crow, Leatrice "Chick", 227, 289, 263, 264, 287-289, 294, 299, 302, 305-307
Black Elk, 107
Bliss, 3, 49, 52, 59, 92, 120, 121, 176, 187, 188, 191, 192, 193, 194, 195, 196, 209, 236, 240, 348, 359, 360, 395, 399
bodhi tree, 249
Boredom, 149, 373
Boys and Girls Club, 227, 263, 287, 297, 301, 302
Brahma Sutras, 28
Brahmacharya, 42, 53, 119, 121, 122, 137, 370, 383, 397, 408
Brahman, 28, 48, 182, 396, 397, 399, 400

Brihadaranyaka Upanishads, 182
Buddha, 43, 78, 95, 114, 125, 159, 189, 249, 310, 354, 355
Buddhi, 145, 146, 171, 395, 397, 402
Buddhism, 17, 170, 246
Buddhist, 57, 85, 119, 218, 354

Cause and Effect, 124, 259, 260, 261, 282, 284, 302, 328
Celibacy, 42, 121, 122, 132, 284, 397
Chabris, Christopher, 176
Chakra, 14, 138, 154, 161, 199, 207, 219, 264, 265, 284, 341, 350, 366, 369, 370, 395, 397, 400, 406
Chandogya Upanishad, 108, 361
Chicago, 5, 7, 13, 15, 26, 116, 233, 287
Children, 96, 104, 115, 122, 123, 127, 129, 131, 134, 137, 138, 139, 224, 226, 261, 266, 277, 278, 288, 294, 295, 296, 307, 312, 313, 333, 378
Chitta, 145, 396, 397, 402
Christ, 26, 194, 226
Christ consciousness, 194
Christian, 27, 365, 366
Clemens, Samuel, 16
Cloud of Virtue, 349, 398
Colorado, 20, 45, 104, 131, 151, 225, 320, 331
Compassion, 16, 30, 43, 68, 95, 101, 128, 138, 153, 161, 188, 212, 227, 228, 278, 282, 285, 288, 289, 290, 291, 292, 357
Concentration, 52, 59, 198, 199, 200, 201, 202, 208, 215, 253, 292, 367, 374, 384, 388, 397, 398
Conscious dreaming, 326, 391
Consciousness, 10, 31, 41, 39, 52, 54, 55, 57, 58, 60, 66, 84,

Index

85, 108, 142, 143, 144, 145, 146, 159, 160, 161, 166, 167, 169, 178, 182, 184, 193, 194, 196, 199, 200, 203, 208, 211, 216, 218, 219, 225, 228, 229, 233, 234, 235, 236, 237, 238, 239, 241, 242, 246, 248, 252, 253, 254, 255, 256, 260, 265, 271, 275, 288, 289, 297, 319, 323, 325, 326, 341, 344, 345, 347, 348, 349, 355, 359, 360, 361, 363, 365, 370, 372, 383, 395, 396, 397, 398, 400, 401, 402, 403, 404, 405, 406, 407, 408

Contentment, 15, 29, 30, 35, 48, 59, 98, 132, 153, 159, 160, 187, 188, 191, 192, 194, 196, 201, 210, 244, 247, 256, 280, 295, 304, 340, 357, 359, 383, 390, 402, 404, 405

Cosmic Self, 3, 143, 154, 396, 398, 403, 407

Coupeville, Washington, 140

CRAAPE, 159, 160

Crazy Horse, 39, 227, 228

Creation, 63, 96, 171, 203, 311, 319, 322, 325, 326, 328, 329, 331, 391, 402

Creator, 49

Dalai Lama, 230

Dama, 57, 58, 60, 384-386, 397, 403

Danapur, 12

Das, 17

Dass, 327

Death, 10, 33, 64, 72, 79, 85, 116, 117, 123, 142, 152, 161, 180-184, 201, 209, 210, 211, 223-225, 227, 229, 235, 239-241, 244, 245-249, 252-255, 257, 268, 274, 335, 336, 350, 358, 361, 369, 374, 408

Denali National Park, 72, 134, 315

Denver, Colorado, 7, 9, 13, 26, 61, 131, 134, 166, 181, 208, 312, 131, 367

Detachment, 82, 83, 114

Dharana, 51, 52, 198, 199, 201, 203, 208, 215, 292, 367, 383, 388, 396, 404, 405

Dharma, 15, 27, 28, 30, 58, 70, 90, 124, 132, 150, 173, 203, 227, 246, 250, 269, 285, 289, 295, 296, 310, 313, 318, 337, 353, 386, 390, 391, 397

Dharma-megha samadhi, 349, 398

Dhyana, 52, 198, 199, 201, 203, 292, 367, 383, 396, 398, 404, 405

Discernment, 70, 171, 189, 200, 266, 274, 349, 352, 354, 400

Disciple, 7, 9-12, 16, 62, 68-70, 72, 76, 77, 149, 150, 152, 166

Discipline, 41, 43, 57, 63, 68, 70, 158, 189, 218, 284, 319, 357, 367, 372, 373, 382, 384, 385, 388, 391, 405, 408

Do not disturb the dreams of others, 129, 389

Drongiri, 10

Dvesha, 79, 358, 371, 398

Earth life, 173, 190, 247, 303, 337, 344

Ego, 13, 25, 28-31, 49, 50 52, 53, 66, 79, 83, 84, 91, 95-97, 126, 138, 143, 145, 146, 150, 152-155, 158-161, 170, 179, 184, 190, 191, 199-201, 203, 209, 211, 218, 219, 225, 228, 229, 234-236, 239-242, 245, 246, 252, 253, 255, 258-261, 265, 270, 276, 277, 281, 283, 284, 289, 290, 296-298, 324, 330, 335-337, 340, 341, 343, 345,

349, 350, 354, 356-358, 360-362, 365, 370, 372, 389, 390, 395-403, 406-408
Enlightenment, 11, 15, 26, 27, 36, 37, 48, 49, 54, 55, 57, 60, 64, 70, 72, 79, 81, 91, 95, 98, 111, 138, 150, 161, 171, 172, 180, 182, 191, 199-201, 206, 236, 249, 266, 282, 288, 296, 297, 304, 324, 328, 329, 336, 338, 340, 345, 347, 350-361, 363-369, 371-374, 384, 392-394, 399-401, 403, 405, 406
Enthusiasm, 196, 373
Expanded consciousness, 10, 41, 49, 52, 54, 55, 57, 60, 85, 166, 253, 289, 347, 360

Fairbanks, Alaska, 139, 151, 315
Father, 103, 114, 115, 128, 138, 139, 182, 310, 312
Fear, 3, 42, 54, 60, 72, 78, 96, 104, 124, 146, 150, 152, 158, 159, 182, 185, 186, 194, 195, 200, 212, 243-245, 323, 327, 350, 364, 372, 387, 389
Fire Keeper, 19, 22, 43
First Nations, 19, 20, 35, 348
Forbearing, 389
Force = Intensity x Duration, 319, 326
Forgive, 290, 291, 350, 389
Fort Collins, Colorado, 45
Four Winds Prayer, 107, 108, 320

Gail, 133-135, 151, 152, 225, 251, 257, 258, 310, 315, 316, 339
Gayatri Mantra, 17
Govinda Hare, 17
Great Spirit, 20, 22, 49
Greed, 42, 43, 77, 78, 83, 124, 152, 248, 250, 364, 384
Grief, 90, 99, 116, 117, 171, 379

Gunnison, Colorado, 104, 181, 227, 293, 331
Gunnison Mike, 40, 44, 45
Guru, 9, 11, 13, 41, 50, 55, 56, 64, 67-72, 76, 77, 96, 111, 116, 155, 158, 283, 320, 363, 367, 398, 405

Hai Ram, 159, 322
Hamsa, 63, 398
Harrison, Jim 93
Hatha Yoga, 8, 26, 63, 382, 406, 407
Hawaii, 151, 223, 243
Hindu, 9, 14, 26, 53, 63, 70, 235, 236, 264, 295, 304, 366, 382, 406, 407
Hinduism, 27, 48, 67, 247
Householder, 11, 15, 122, 192, 203

Illusion, 54, 58, 78, 79, 99, 116, 129, 144, 146, 171, 260, 305, 326, 327, 330, 337, 338, 374, 400
Indriyas, 385, 398
Into the Wild, 51
Is That So?, 87-89, 114, 313, 314
Ishvara, 41, 48, 49, 143, 297, 345, 348, 367, 372, 383, 396, 398, 401, 403, 407
Iwa, 169-171, 212, 216, 399

Jhana Yoga, 27, 382

Kaivalya, 41, 150, 178, 191, 283, 337, 343, 347, 349-351, 354-359, 361, 363, 369-371, 375, 380, 398-401, 406
Karana sharira, 236, 399, 408
Karma, 4, 6, 27, 31, 36-38, 41, 56, 60, 64, 66, 69, 89, 90, 112, 113, 116, 124, 137, 138, 144, 146, 152, 154, 180, 194, 195, 202, 212, 226, 228, 230, 231,

Index

247, 250, 252, 253, 255, 257, 259-261, 264-266, 268-271, 274-279, 281-285, 296, 298, 299, 301, 302, 304, 305, 311, 319, 321, 327, 328, 335, 336, 338, 340, 341, 344, 349, 350, 352, 354, 361, 375, 382, 384, 388, 390, 396, 398-401, 403, 406, 407

Karma yoga, 27, 64, 298, 382, 388

Katha Upanishad, 144, 190, 235

Kellie, 133, 137, 139, 140, 309, 310, 312

Kentucky, 223, 224

Kirtan, 211, 368, 399

Kiza Park, 107

Klesha, 349, 367, 398, 399

Kornfield, Jack, 57

Kosha, 235, 236, 395, 399, 400, 402, 405, 406, 408

Krakauer, Jon, 51

Krishna, 9, 26, 27, 60, 183, 283, 284, 289, 297, 359, 365, 382, 387, 390, 397, 407

Krishnamurti, 357

Kriya, 31, 388, 399

Kriya shakti, 13, 400

Kriya Yoga, 5-7, 9-13, 15-17, 25, 26, 28-31, 34-38, 42, 48, 50, 55, 61, 63-65, 67, 68, 70, 83, 94-96, 112, 122, 123, 125, 131, 132, 134, 137, 138, 145, 146, 151, 152, 173, 182, 183, 188, 189, 192, 194, 198, 228, 233, 235, 236, 249, 255, 256, 264, 279, 281, 282, 299, 310, 311, 313, 327, 351, 353, 365, 369, 372, 376, 382, 388, 398

Kriya Yoga Center, 7, 9, 13, 26, 94, 173, 313, 376

Kriyaban, 13-15, 25, 26, 28-31, 36-38, 41, 42, 47, 49, 53, 63, 64, 129, 170, 171, 182, 183, 191, 196, 279, 289, 290, 295, 311, 319, 324, 327, 349, 366

Kriyananda, 7-9, 13-15, 19, 28, 42, 47-49, 54, 61, 62, 70-72, 98, 111, 112, 114, 116, 129, 138, 159, 166, 167, 171-174, 180, 182-184, 188-190, 193, 196, 202, 203, 209, 210, 215, 217, 224, 230, 233, 234, 237, 239, 243, 245, 253, 266, 275, 279, 284, 288, 290, 291, 295, 296, 299, 301-304, 317-319, 321-323, 329, 330, 335-337, 344, 349, 350, 352-361, 363, 373, 376, 404

Kriya-yoga:
The Science of Life Force, 29

Kundalini, 50, 63, 65, 120, 122, 207, 219, 236, 258, 368, 382, 400

Lakota, 19-22, 39-41, 45, 49-51, 104, 105, 107-109, 170, 206, 227, 263, 266, 284, 287, 288, 293, 294, 303, 307, 320, 366

Lakota oyate kin, 227, 266, 294

Law of Cause and Effect, 124, 259, 260, 282, 284, 302, 328

LeAnne, 119-121

Liberation, 11, 41, 55, 11, 124, 126, 150, 161, 203, 352, 356, 399-401, 406

Lipschutz, David, 6-8, 61, 206

Lodge Keeper, 20-22

Lokah Samasta, 17

Loving kindness, 287, 288, 291

Lower Forty-Eight, 132, 310

Mahabharata, 27

Mahasaya, Lahiri, 9-12, 16, 41, 42, 231

Mahatma Gandhi, 16

Mahavatar, 9, 67, 400

Maka Ina, 20, 108

Manas, 145, 146, 395, 397, 400, 402
Manderson, South Dakota, 107
Mandukya Upanishad, 146
Manifestation, 65, 187, 271, 310, 311, 317, 318, 320-326, 330, 331, 334, 391
Mantra, 3, 17, 28, 58, 62-64, 88, 96, 146, 158, 159, 176, 184, 191, 195, 202, 208, 210-212, 323, 330, 364, 368, 385, 386, 388, 391, 396, 399
Mataji, 9
Maya, 90, 116, 144, 146, 178, 179, 338, 396, 398, 400, 403, 407
Meditation, 3, 11, 14, 26-29, 31, 36, 41, 48, 49-54, 58-60, 62, 63, 65, 66, 77, 89, 96, 97, 114, 119, 120, 122, 126, 128, 145, 146, 149, 157-160, 164, 165, 173, 176, 184, 189, 191, 196, 197-213, 215-221, 223, 236, 237, 248-250, 253, 254, 265, 267, 273, 274, 278, 279, 291, 292, 295, 304, 323, 340, 344, 345, 347-350, 354, 360, 367-370, 373, 375, 376, 378, 382-388, 391, 395, 396, 398, 401, 403, 406-408
Metta Prayer, 352
Mikao Usui, 119
Mitakuye Oyasin, 19, 21, 22, 321
Miten, 17
Moksha, 41, 150, 288, 289, 399-401, 406
Mudra, 63, 174, 388, 400
Mumukshutva, 60, 172, 384, 400
Mysticism, 7, 13, 16, 23, 26, 36, 37, 40, 45, 49, 50, 54, 56, 57, 59, 63-66, 70, 82, 88, 92, 122, 125, 150, 154, 163, 165, 167, 170, 172, 173, 176, 178, 180, 182, 187, 192, 196, 199, 203, 211, 227, 228, 230, 231, 237,

244, 249, 253, 255, 259, 266, 270, 271, 284, 289, 301, 311, 327, 334, 344, 345, 355, 360, 365, 367, 372, 376, 378-380, 392-394, 403, 408

Namaste, 160, 170, 401
Narada Bhakti Sutras, 83
Near Death Experiences, 184, 244, 255
Nepal, 10
Neptune, 392, 393
New Age, 199, 253, 371
Nirahamikara, 91, 401
Nirbija samadhi, 349, 401
Nirmama, 91, 401
Nirvana, 150, 252, 352, 399-401, 406
Nirvicara samadhi, 349, 401
Nirvitarka samadhi, 349, 401
Nityananda, 26, 29, 50, 154, 352, 353, 376
Niyama, 47-49, 63, 92, 173, 216, 357, 363, 383, 388, 399, 401, 404-406
Non-attachment, 16, 26, 54, 56, 60, 82-85, 90, 92, 94, 95, 97-99, 113, 114, 132, 192, 210, 211, 250, 281, 291, 295, 337, 352, 384, 403, 406, 407

Observances, 47, 48, 399, 401, 404-406
Observer, 66, 160, 211, 252, 341
Oglala Housing Authority, 305
Om, See "Aum"
Om Nama Shivaya, 17
Osho, 17, 160, 213, 292, 334, 357

Passion, 60, 77, 95, 292, 318, 358, 371, 372, 387
Patanjali, 25, 26, 41, 48, 54, 64, 76, 121, 154, 202, 270, 289, 347, 388, 399, 404, 405

Index

Path Opens, 132, 311-313, 334, 353
Pema Chodron, 89, 334
Pig Life, 223, 240, 242, 248, 250
Pine Ridge, South Dakota, 40, 50, 104, 105, 227, 228, 248, 263, 264, 270, 287-289, 293, 294, 296, 297, 299, 301-303, 307
Porcupine District, 39
Prajna, 146, 401
Prakriti, 324, 325, 398, 402, 403, 404, 406
Pranamaya kosha, 235, 236, 402, 405
Pranayama, 35, 50, 63, 64, 158, 191, 216, 323, 367, 368, 370, 383, 385, 388, 391, 402
Pratyahara, 50, 383, 402
Prayojakam chittam, 145, 396, 397, 402
Premal, Deva, 17, 62
Prince William Sound, 329, 330
Puja, 41, 378, 402
Purusha, 143, 146, 325, 349, 396, 398, 401, 402, 403, 407

Ragah, 77, 78, 371, 403
Raja Yoga, 26, 382
Rajas, 324, 359, 391, 398, 402, 403
Ranikhet, 9, 10, 12
Reiki, 119-122
Reincarnation, 6, 27, 123, 228-231, 235, 239-241, 250, 259, 353
Relationships, 16, 38, 77, 84, 91, 95, 111-114, 123-127, 129, 130, 173, 190, 201, 203, 260, 276, 296, 358, 366, 375, 389, 392, 394, 404
Renunciation, 11, 26, 83, 91, 158, 160, 213, 283, 304, 370, 404

Resistance, 244, 310, 340, 356, 357
Roach, Michael, 365
Roads, Duncan, 215, 217
Roxanne, 5-8, 105, 108, 113, 223, 248, 251, 263, 270, 287, 288, 293, 336, 339, 340
Rumi, 17, 357, 366

Sadhana, 36, 41, 51, 370, 403, 408
Sadhana Chatushtaya, 54, 60, 171, 191, 384, 397, 400, 403, 405, 406, 407
Sage (person), 26, 202, 203, 236, 247, 253, 322, 357-359, 372
Sage (plant), 20, 39-41, 108, 109, 141, 142, 310, 312
Sai Baba, 319
Samācara, 83, 403
Samadhana, 59, 60, 384, 387, 403
Samadhi, 4, 11, 25, 27, 29, 41, 49, 51, 52, 59, 60, 98, 128, 176, 189, 194, 196, 198-201, 203, 209, 253, 292, 345, 347-350, 367, 370, 372, 373, 382, 383, 387, 395, 396, 398, 401, 403, 404, 405, 408
Samprajnata, 348, 404
Samskaras, 113, 154, 155, 161, 172, 191, 212, 229, 236, 239, 250, 252, 268-271, 277, 290, 301, 341, 349, 354, 356, 361, 399, 401, 404, 407
Samyama, 164, 202, 292, 404
Sangatyagah, 83, 404
Sangha, 13, 37, 303, 404
Sannyasins, 304, 404
Sanskrit, 17, 26, 27, 31, 42, 54, 55, 59, 68, 83, 91, 121, 122, 171, 187, 211, 216, 395, 407
Santosha, 48, 187, 357, 383, 401, 404

Satsang, 8, 13, 14, 16, 17, 61, 71, 218, 269, 367
Sattva, 324, 359, 391, 395, 398, 402, 404
Saturn delay, 330, 331
Satya, 42, 383, 404, 408
Schweig, Graham M., 91, 200, 360
Seattle, Washington, 103, 115, 128, 223, 224
Seeker, 11, 28, 34, 47, 52, 54, 58, 60, 71, 161, 246, 359, 363, 366, 379
Self, 3, 13, 21, 25, 29, 31, 50, 54, 77, 108, 143, 144, 148, 150, 154, 160, 173, 182, 192, 194, 199, 201, 206, 209, 216, 226, 236, 241, 242, 245, 253-255, 261, 281, 283, 284, 312, 345, 348-350, 354, 358-360, 363, 365, 367, 396, 398, 399, 401-404, 406-408
Self-awareness, 15, 26, 35, 117, 2489, 252, 253, 254, 289, 301, 347, 401, 403, 404
Self-discipline, 16, 25, 26, 37, 48, 189, 322, 353, 383
Self-examination, 35, 69, 153, 154, 172-174, 389
Self-knowledge, 92, 146, 173, 174, 318, 322, 329, 330, 384
Self-realization, 28, 29, 111, 146, 151, 154, 166, 170, 194, 196, 253, 254, 266, 322, 347, 350, 352-354, 357, 358, 360, 361, 367, 371, 399-401
Self-study, 29, 48, 92, 172, 363, 383, 406
Sergeant Pepper, 16
Sermon on the Mount, 226
Service, 6, 16, 26, 27, 64, 71, 104, 107, 158, 188, 190, 227, 282, 283, 288-290, 294-299, 301-303, 305, 307, 382, 388

Sex, 35, 42, 43, 58, 94, 120-122, 124, 188, 315, 317, 324, 333, 334, 366, 397
Shala, 68, 69, 72, 405
Shama, 57, 58, 60, 191, 384, 385, 403, 405
Shaman, 51, 119, 141-143, 145, 158, 181, 185, 320, 344, 348
Shanti, 17, 405
Shariras, 235, 399, 405, 406
Shat Sanpatis, 55, 56, 59, 319, 384, 397, 403, 405, 407
Shaucha, 47, 383, 401, 405
Shraddha, 55, 60, 384, 403, 405
Shvetashvatara Upanishad, 48
Siddhim, 358, 405
Siddhis, 62, 64, 65, 78, 180, 202, 219, 338, 405
Simons, Daniel, 176
Simplicity, 84, 132, 173, 205
Simplify, 318, 391
Sioux Nation, 287, 306
Skinny Dick's Halfway Inn, 139
Soul, 27-29, 35, 42, 47, 54, 56, 59, 65, 67, 78, 85, 94, 99, 101, 127, 137, 138, 143-146, 150, 160, 171-173, 177, 182-184, 187, 193, 196, 201, 203, 213, 219, 228-230, 235-238, 241, 242, 245, 247, 252, 254, 255, 258-261, 266, 269, 289, 328, 334-336, 340, 348, 349, 351, 354, 360, 361, 369, 372-374, 379, 396, 398-400, 403, 407
South Dakota, 8, 43, 104, 227, 293, 294, 312
Spirit, 38, 43, 49, 63, 85, 99, 108, 116, 140, 11, 160, 166, 170, 171, 175, 176, 179, 184, 231, 234-237, 245, 252, 255, 258-261, 320, 339, 348, 353, 358, 360, 380, 402, 405
Stampede Road, 51, 139
Start Where You Are, 334
Stephenson, Ian, 226

Index

Sthula sharira, 235, 405
Subconscious, 145, 146, 188, 202, 203, 298, 315, 317, 321, 323, 324, 329, 391, 396, 397, 402, 406, 407
Sukshma sharira, 236, 400, 405
Sunyata, 345, 406
Surrender, 29, 30, 37, 49, 51, 98, 200, 207, 283, 331, 334, 341, 343-345
Svadhisthana chakra, 406
Svadhyaya, 48, 92, 383, 401, 406
Swallow the Teachings, 176, 340, 351, 376

Tamas, 325, 359, 391, 398, 402, 406
Tao te Ching, 98
Tapas, 48, 383, 401, 406
Tarka, 63, 173, 212, 406
Tawapaha Olowan, 107, 109
Teaching from a *Guru*, 368
Temple of Kriya Yoga, 7, 26
Tenzin Wangyal Rinpoche, 85
Teyata mantra, 17
The Diamond Cutter, 365
The Eight Limbs, 41, 47, 49, 50, 52, 63, 122, 173, 198, 352, 363, 366, 376, 388, 395-397, 399, 401, 402, 404-406, 408
The Farmer's Son, 338
The Four Pillars, 53-63, 171, 172, 191, 384, 400, 403
The Four Pillars of Meditation, 205-213
The General & the Monk, 273, 274
The Lakota Partnership for Housing, 293
The Pond and the Jewel, 163-166
The Rabbit & the Cobra, 157, 158, 161
The Spiritual Science of Kriya Yoga, 28

The Thornapple Tree, 75, 76, 97, 163, 193
The Tibetan Yogas of Dream and Sleep, 85
The unconscious, 173
The Woman at the River, 81-83
The Yoga Sutras of Patanjali, 25-28, 41, 43, 48, 50, 52, 54, 64, 76, 83, 97, 111, 121, 128, 143, 144, 154, 171, 199, 202, 208, 270, 289, 325, 345, 347, 348, 352, 360, 361, 367, 388, 399, 404, 405
Thought, word, and deed, 31, 43, 260, 310, 363, 366, 375
Titiksha, 56, 57, 60, 319, 384, 403, 406
Transcendental, 25, 29, 295, 354
Transcendental meditation, 295
Trimmer, Shelley (Shelliji), 9, 42, 49, 70, 166, 200, 203, 204, 217, 230, 252, 254, 358, 375, 376
True North, 93
Tunkashila, 40, 107
Turiya, 146, 150, 354, 399-401, 406

Unitarian Universalist, 107, 305, 306
Upanishads, 28, 64, 108, 144, 218, 388, 408
Uparati, 59, 60, 384, 403, 407
Uttarakand, 9

Vairagya, 54, 60, 384, 407
Vaishvanara, 146, 407
Vasana, 407
Vasudeva, 63, 143, 396, 398, 403, 407
Vedas, 122, 397, 407
Vicara samadhi, 348, 404, 408
Vijnanamaya kosha, 236, 399, 408

Virya, 29, 408
Vitarka samadhi, 348, 404, 408
Viveka, 54, 171, 384, 408

Wakan, 40
Wakan Tanka, 22, 41, 51
Watson, Erica, 93
We Are One, 153, 178, 289, 297, 345, 361
Wellness Center, 119
Whidbey Island, Washington, 139
White Clay, South Dakota, 104, 105
Wichasha wakan, 107
Woodstock, Illinois, 61, 233
Wounded Knee, 294

Yama, 41-43, 47, 49, 63, 216, 383, 388, 395, 397, 405, 408
Yativrata, 53, 408

Yoga, 41, 49, 59, 78, 83, 90, 94, 122, 128, 161, 170, 254, 266, 274, 283, 284, 290, 305, 325, 345, 347, 359, 360, 367, 382, 383, 390, 399, 408
Yogananda, 7-9, 16, 29, 71, 94, 146, 147, 151, 152, 196, 220, 253, 323, 349, 354, 356, 358, 370
Yogi, 8, 11, 16, 27, 48-50, 54-56, 62, 64, 66, 75, 76, 78, 83, 90, 91, 114, 117, 125-128, 132, 137, 138, 146, 151, 158, 163-165, 170, 182, 183, 188, 190, 192, 194, 230, 235-237, 240, 244, 253, 255, 256, 260, 267, 268, 272, 281, 285, 295, 311, 315, 317, 326, 337, 349, 352, 354, 355, 371, 388, 398, 405
Yukteswar, 9, 16, 71, 354

Zen, 17, 170, 218

www.ingramcontent.com/pod-product-compliance
Lightning Source LLC
Chambersburg PA
CBHW021427080526
44588CB00009B/450